The Industry Guide to Musical Theatre Auditions

Also by Shaun Aquilina:

Musical Theatre for the Female Voice: The Sensation, Sound, and Science, of Singing

The Industry Guide to Musical Theatre Auditions

Interviews with West End Creatives on How to Get the Part

Shaun Aquilina

methuen | drama

LONDON · NEW YORK · OXFORD · NEW DELHI · SYDNEY

METHUEN DRAMA
Bloomsbury Publishing Plc, 50 Bedford Square, London, WC1B 3DP, UK
Bloomsbury Publishing Inc, 1359 Broadway, New York, NY 10018, USA
Bloomsbury Publishing Ireland, 29 Earlsfort Terrace, Dublin 2, D02 AY28, Ireland

BLOOMSBURY, METHUEN DRAMA and the Methuen Drama logo are
trademarks of Bloomsbury Publishing Plc

First published in Great Britain 2026

Design by Lara Himpelmann
Cover image - Wicked, The Musical by Suhaimi Abdullah via Getty Images

A catalogue record for this book is available from the British Library.

A catalog record for this book is available from the Library of Congress.

ISBN: HB: 978-1-3505-7350-5
PB: 978-1-3505-7349-9
ePDF: 978-1-3505-7351-2
eBook: 978-1-3505-7352-9

Typeset by Jones Ltd, London
Printed and bound in Great Britain

For product safety related questions contact productsafety@bloomsbury.com.

To find out more about our authors and books visit www.bloomsbury.com and
sign up for our newsletters.

To Sarah

Contents

Acknowledgements ix

Introduction 1

1 Casting directors 3
Introduction 3
Preliminary stages: Submissions, CVs, headshots and reels 4
In the room: Singing, dancing and acting 13
In the room: The professional personality 20
Casting decisions 30
New shows, new productions and re-casting 33
Great auditions 41
Conclusion 44

2 Choreographers 47
Introduction 48
Getting the casting right 48
Technique 50
Storytelling 53
Physicality 55
Individuality, uniformity and character 57
Other attributes of the performer 59
Principal values 61
Background checks and references 63
Entering the room 65
Casting a new show and re-casting an ongoing show 74
After the auditions 76
The choreographer's discipline 79
Creatives in the rehearsal room 81
West End versus Broadway 83
Great auditions 85
Conclusion 87

3 Musical directors 89
Introduction 90
Vocal technique 90

Storytelling: Narrative and character 97
Musicality 102
Song choice 103
Preparation 107
Taking direction 110
Company personality 113
Nerves 114
Workshops 116
New shows and re-casts 118
Collaborating with the rest of the panel 119
Deciding on the cast 123
Great auditions 131
Sean Green on the UK Musical Theatre industry for Black performers
        and creatives 132
Conclusion 136

4   Directors 137
Introduction 138
Early process 138
First rounds 141
Professionalism and personality 154
Recalls and finals 156
Taking direction 160
Making decisions 163
Most valued qualities in a performer 168
Be yourself 172
Broadway 174
Great auditions 176
Conclusion 179

Conclusion 181
Context 181
Panel 182
Auditionee 182
Task 183
Panel and auditionee 183
Auditions 184

Bibliography 185
Index 187

Acknowledgements

My thanks go to Neil Rutherford, for an early discussion on this project and for putting me in touch with many of the interviewees; to all at Methuen Drama, especially Dom O'Hanlon for such enthusiasm and professionalism; to Jonathan Stirland for reading an early draft of Chapter 1 and suggesting further areas to explore; to Anna Rantou for aiding me with transcriptions; and to Sarah, whose continued support as well as confidence has been a gift.

I am indebted to all the interviewees in this book, who were so generous with their time and experience, and have provided such insight, with warmth and kindness.

Introduction

One summer, I was in central London to audition for the West End production of *The Phantom of the Opera*. I was rehearsing another show at the time and the company had given me the morning off. I went to the venue on Shaftesbury Avenue and in the audition room were the pianist and a panel of eight creatives – two directors, two musical directors, the choreographer and three from casting. I sang, someone in the centre of the panel complimented me, and I left. I never heard anything back.

When I thought about why I didn't get the job, I thought about many things. Didn't I sing well enough? Had I chosen the wrong song? Did I have the wrong look? Didn't I connect with the panel? Was I just not what they were looking for? Years later, I turned those questions around, trying to understand not only my own experience but what makes any audition a successful audition. What does it mean to 'sing well'? What is the 'right song' to choose? What does it mean to 'move well' and 'act well'? How do you suggest the right look? How do you connect with a panel? To get the answers, I needed to ask the people who know: the creatives sitting on the audition panel.

I spent more than a year connecting with creatives who audition shows across the West End, Broadway and internationally. I held one-to-one interviews with sixteen of our most experienced and recognised: four directors, four musical directors, four choreographers and four casting directors. We discussed everything we could about auditioning for musical theatre: getting an audition, first rounds, recalls and finals; the requirements of the show and the role; auditioning for a new show, or a new production, or an ongoing production; what makes good singing, acting, dancing and movement; taking direction from creatives; professionalism and building a company of nice people; finding covers; celebrity casting (often called commercial casting); differences between the West End and Broadway; and their favourite audition memories. I transcribed the interviews and arranged what the creatives had told me into the four chapters of this book.

Their insights are profound, and what you will read is both their understanding of the practical needs of a production and their deeper understanding of artistry, performance and how to create great musical theatre. Sharing that understanding and embodying it in your performances and professionalism could make the audition process easier, happier and, with luck, more successful.

1 Casting directors

Pippa Ailion has cast over 200 theatre productions. Her West End shows include Moulin Rouge! The Musical *(Piccadilly Theatre),* The Book of Mormon *(Prince of Wales Theatre) and* The Lion King *(Lyceum Theatre). Pippa Ailion won the 2020 Casting Directors' Guild (CDG) Award for Best Casting in Musical Theatre for* Come From Away *and the 2023 What's On Stage Award for Best Casting for* Spring Awakening. *She was awarded an MBE in 2018 for Services to Theatre and Diversity in the Arts, and a special recognition Olivier Award in 2023.*

Jim Arnold has cast numerous shows for West End and regional theatres, and for UK and international tours, including Wicked *(Apollo Victoria and UK & Ireland tour),* Pretty Woman *(Savoy and UK & Ireland tour),* Shrek *(Eventim Apollo and UK tour),* The Prince of Egypt *(Dominion Theatre),* Spend Spend Spend *(Royal Exchange Theatre),* Charlie and the Chocolate Factory *(Leeds Playhouse and UK & Ireland tour),* The Great British Bake Off Musical *(Noel Coward and Everyman Cheltenham) and* Bonnie & Clyde *(Garrick and UK tour).*

Stuart Burt has several shows running in the West End, including Cabaret *(Kit Kat Club at the Playhouse),* Sister Act *(Dominion Theatre),* Standing at the Sky's Edge *(The National and Gillian Lynne Theatre) and* Mrs Doubtfire *(Shaftesbury Theatre). He has won four CDG Awards for West End Musical Theatre productions and UK regional productions. Stuart Burt was head of casting for the Ambassador's Theatre Group and has twice been included in The Stage 100 list of the most influential people in British theatre.*

David Grindrod has held a long association with Andrew Lloyd Webber, casting musicals such as Joseph and the Amazing Technicolor Dreamcoat, Jesus Christ Superstar, Evita, *and* The Phantom of the Opera. *He has also cast worldwide productions of* Mamma Mia, *and further West End credits include* Back to the Future *(Adelphi Theatre) and* Chicago *(Adelphi, Cambridge, and Garrick Theatres). David is also behind musical theatre TV casting shows such as* Mamma Mia! I Have a Dream, Superstar, Over the Rainbow, Any Dream Will Do *and* How Do You Solve a Problem Like Maria?

Introduction

Casting directors are experts at understanding the needs of the production and then finding and presenting auditionees who could meet those needs. They don't claim to be disciplinary experts in dancing, singing or acting (though some have trained in those disciplines) but a lifetime in theatre, working alongside high-level creatives, means they recognise quality performances. They also spend more time in auditions than any of our other creatives.

In this chapter, we'll see how they begin the casting process by putting together a breakdown of what the production is looking for. This leads to thousands and thousands of submissions from potential auditionees. There are far more than can be auditioned in person, so we'll see how our casting directors begin to filter through and select the performers they want to meet. They'll give advice on what makes an effective CV, headshot and showreel.

Once casting directors are in the room with their auditionees, there's a lot to assess. Of course, they're looking at performance ability across the three disciplines of musical theatre, but there's also a holistic view of the performer as artist, one who brings skill, confidence and creativity to their work. Auditionees also have to be assessed on personality and what they would bring to the workings of a theatrical company through the rehearsal period and into production.

There are a couple of trends in musical theatre that our casting directors are well placed to discuss: commercial casting and TV casting shows. We'll look at both of those and what effect they have on the industry.

Finally, we'll hear our casting directors' great audition memories, including the moments some of today's stars first arrived in their audition rooms.

Preliminary stages: Submissions, CVs, headshots and reels

The casting process begins long before any performer is seen for an audition. Pippa Ailion says it often starts when she is contacted by a member of the production team or the creative team:

Pippa Ailion: It's usually a conversation with the producer or the director. Because of working for years, I have a lot of contacts and have worked with many wonderful inspiring creatives. So we're very fortunate that we have a great relationship with management, producers, both here and in New York, directors, musical directors/supervisors and choreographers. So usually I get contacted by the producer. I'm just about to go into some *Hello, Dolly!* [London Palladium, summer 2024] auditions and I'm working again with [director] Dominic Cooke. I get an email from Dominic saying, "it's on again." We cast it prior to Covid but obviously that was all cancelled, but now it's on again. So I get contacted by Dominic, and then I get contacted by the producer to do a deal. So that's how it works. And if it's a project we can't do because of schedules, which happens frequently, there's a moment of regret but you move on very quickly because you can't fit it all in. We just physically can't fit it all in.

As those conversations progress, casting directors are able to put together a breakdown of the performers they're looking for and the roles they need to fill. Once this breakdown is released, they receive thousands of submissions:

Stuart Burt: If it's a West End musical, it's going to be a cast of roughly between twenty-two and twenty-eight. I don't limit who I send it out to. I use Spotlight as a tool, as my primary casting tool, but I send it to all agents, personal managers and dance agents, so I'm likely to get 3,000–3,500 submissions for that show.

Pippa Ailion expects to receive nearly double that for some of her projects. And as well as the response to the casting breakdown, her team will actively seek out auditionees they want to see:

Pippa Ailion: When we put out a breakdown on Spotlight, for a musical, it's not unusual to get 5,000 or 6,000 submissions. Per show. And then of course, we do our own lists. I always say to my team, I want to see your lists of who you think are right for these roles. So we have our own lists that we check, then we go through all these thousands of submissions, and you can only see so many so you have to be extremely selective. You have to know the demands of the show to be selective. Sometimes there are height restrictions, specific physical qualities or vocal requirements that the musical director will be looking for. During the process the candidates have to be able to sing the songs of that role. They have to fit the brief.

But the biggest response to a casting breakdown that I heard about in this process was for the West End re-cast of *Wicked*. The show's casting director, Jim Arnold, says they received close to 9,000 submissions:

Jim Arnold: It was quite a big cast change this year; we were looking to replace two thirds of the performers in a cast of thirty-eight, which is still more than the full cast of some West End shows. We had nearly 9,000 submissions and a third of them were dancers, a third of them were singing ensemble and a third of them were principals and standbys. So it was a lot of people. And I believe firmly that if you're paying your entry fee to Spotlight, you should have the same opportunity to see the jobs that are going out there, so I would send it to all agents and all performers, so that everyone can see that we're looking. I also think it's quite important to strive for diversity in every respect, to be able to send out the breakdown and say to everyone, "This is what we're looking for; if you think you're right for it, please apply." I think that's really important for me to do for any production, but that does mean then you get a higher number of submissions and I do spend a long time, sometimes weeks, going through CVs to decide who to bring in.

The numbers are vast and there's no way a production has the time, or money, to see everyone, so it's the casting director's job to select which performers get to audition. They do that in stages, and the first stage is often based on CVs and headshots:

Stuart Burt: It starts like a filtration system. So basically, I go through various passes through the submissions, initially making very quick judgments on what is presented to me. And taking a first pass, I'll go from 3,500 to maybe 2,500. I just have a very quick system where I know what I'm looking for and I have to make a very, very instinctive, quick judgment on that first pass. I know quite a lot of people, so I can make those judgments really quickly. And then I have to obviously think about what time I have with the creatives, how long they want the process to be, how many people we can actually see and try and whittle that down to that number, while having a bank of people who would go into the process should those people not want to come in for any reason. So I've got always got a backup list as well.

Shaun Aquilina: So that initial pass when you're taking out a thousand people just on CVs and headshots, what is it that tells you "I want to see that performer but not that performer"?

Stuart Burt: Shaun, we've got to be really, really honest with ourselves that not all agent submissions are good or correct, or they've actually read the brief. Certain agencies will just submit all of their clients, regardless of what their skillset is, regardless of their suitability, and quite often it's very apparent they haven't actually really looked at the brief. So that is a very easy pass. So what I'm saying is, I'm making a quick judgment on how do they fit, really roughly fit, the brief. And some of those submissions are just silly submissions, like they don't even count singing as one of their core skills, or it's a dance show and this person doesn't even have any dance as highly skilled, or has done no formal training. So, in the kindest way, it's getting rid of the nonsense suggestions. Then we're left with what we actually need to deal with, and that's when I spend more time with them.

Jim Arnold has been casting *Wicked* for many years and knows what he needs from performers. Going through their CVs and headshots tells him whether they have a suitable look and can sing the required notes for the roles:

Jim Arnold: The first thing I will look at is vocal range and photos. Do they look like they could play Elphaba or Fiyero? Are they in the right playing age range? Do they have the required vocal range? Does it say on their CV that they can belt a top F5, which is what they have to reach in "Defying Gravity"? If they say they can only belt to a D, then they probably won't be able to play or cover Elphaba. For the Singing Ensemble, anyone who wants to be considered for a female identifying track, they need to be a Soprano 1 or a Soprano 2, but some also have to be able to belt to E5. Similarly, if they're up for a male identifying track in the singing ensemble, most of the actors need to be able to sing up to at least G4 or A4, and we need a few to be able to hit a top B4. So once you've been doing the show long enough, you can scan someone's CV and decide fairly quickly if they have the required vocal range and if they could be considered for the show. And then if they say that they have that vocal range, and they look a certain way, then you might start looking at their training and experience, so there's lots of different things that can add up to them being capable of doing eight shows a week in a West End show with the rigours that are required.

Dance skills can also be assessed on paper, in the early stages. Jim Arnold says it's about drawing out an idea of who that performer is and whether they might fit the production:

Jim Arnold: Movement skills in *Wicked*, anybody in the ensemble, whether they're a dance ensemble as a full-on dancer, or whether they are in the singing ensemble, they also have to be able to move and count: so have they been in a show that's a dance show, or have they taken dance classes, what training have they had, have they had any movement training? It's all the things like that, that add up to a picture of who that performer is, and what they might be able to do. And then I might listen to the vocal reel, and so on, and it just builds that picture up even more. And then, if there's enough there for me to think they might be capable of this, then I'll click on "Yes." And then I find that I have probably 400 more people than I need so then I have to go through them again, and filter them down even more, and try and pick out the people I think are more likely or the most appropriate for that ensemble.

Submissions come in from a mix of performers, some of whom are known to the casting directors and some unknown. Stuart Burt can be casting eight to twelve productions a year, and that means he knows the talent pool extremely well:

Stuart Burt: I think it's actually massively beneficial to all the projects that I work on because sometimes we're working on multiple projects at the same time, but then there's a really fantastic cross pollination. If I'm in the room, continually meeting people – new people, people who are known to me – I feel like my breadth of knowledge of the actor fraternity is strong because I'm so busy. And also I've got two really fantastic team members who work with me and then they have their own contribution, as well.

Jim Arnold also makes it a priority to know the available performers and the emerging talent. His casting process is active and anticipatory:

Jim Arnold: Part of my job throughout the year is, I'm going to see school shows, I'm going to see showcases, I'm going to see other productions, so that I can try and find people that I think are really right for other shows that I work on, not just *Wicked*. It's to expand my vocabulary of actors and my knowledge of actors, so that I go, "ok, well, I saw that person, they'd be really right for an Elphaba cover, or they'd be really right for that role in *Spend Spend Spend*." Or even just in general, for other shows that are coming up in the future, I'll go through the Rolodex in my head of people that I know and go through lists of previous shows that I've worked on. And I've worked on so much now that usually there's very few things that come up where I can't go, ok, well, they're looking for a woman in their sixties to seventies: right, I've cast that, I've cast that, I've cast that, let's go back and look at those, also send a breakdown out, also think about all the shows I've seen recently over the last few years – and come up with lists of ideas through that. I think a really important part of my job is to try and find the people that are right for those shows and think, what am I working on that that person could be in?

By the time they get into the audition room, Pippa Ailion is well prepared for the new and the familiar auditionees:

Pippa Ailion: I always make sure I have their CV in front of me, and the director has a CV, as well as the producers having a CV, so that if I'm asked a question, I can immediately input the knowledge that we have of that actor. And I love finding new talent. Sometimes you don't have the history, you don't know what they've done. Whereas we know so many actors, because we've done so many shows over so many years, we know them intimately, and we've cast them many times, and we can input a great deal of information if required.

CVs also tell a panel about an auditionee's training. For young performers considering a degree in musical theatre, there's often a choice between drama schools/ conservatoires and universities. Stuart Burt says he doesn't discriminate between those two types of training but admits to having a more established relationship with one of them:

Stuart Burt: I think the truth is, I have more knowledge of what the traditional drama schools are, I have a better relationship with them, so I know exactly what the training is. And I'm developing my relationship with those which are university based but I know them less because I just don't have as much access to them.

Jim Arnold weighs training against experience. Sometimes, it doesn't matter if an auditionee hasn't trained at all, if they've proved themselves in previous shows:

Jim Arnold: Experience can balance out training. So if it's someone's just graduated versus someone who didn't train but has done five big West End shows covering lead roles, well, that doesn't matter whether they've trained or not. I was recently speaking to a friend who's a performer, who didn't train at all, and has now got a lead role in a big tour of a West End show, never trained and went straight into the industry at the age of eighteen. So training doesn't necessarily equal ability, and it also doesn't necessarily equal that you're right for this particular show. It's just another thing that helps build up a picture of what that performer can do. So if you've had a certain level of training at a certain school that might give me an idea that ok, yes, maybe you have the ability or the knowledge of how to look after your voice over eight shows a week, belting your head off. *Wicked*, for instance, or *Pretty Woman*, which I cast, they are big sings! So to have the ability and the knowledge to be able to look after your voice, and have had a certain level of vocal training to know that you can do it eight shows a week, that's useful.

This last point, about training as an indication that a performer knows their craft, is echoed by David Grindrod. The performance demands in musical theatre are high, and he wants to be sure that the production is making a sound investment in its cast:

David Grindrod: They have to do eight performances a week. That's what it is, and it's tough. And they've got to understudy, they've got to do their roles, they've got to do this, they've got to do that, so it's a tough, tough business. And because we're spending so much effort and time, and the money, we have to have some assurance that their skills, that are coming to us, have had some sort of formal training or foundation.

The next stage of filtering submissions moves beyond CVs and headshots. As Jim Arnold mentioned earlier, the vocal reel is often looked at next. Stuart Burt says this is especially useful for submissions from less familiar performers, and when the time pressure on the director, MD and choreographer makes audition slots precious:

Stuart Burt: So the second pass, if they're new to me, that's when I'll start spending more time with them, looking at their showreels, their vocal reels, dance reels. Because if I don't know them, or I haven't seen them in a show, or I don't recognise any of their credits or their training, then I have to make sure that I know who's coming into the room because positions are sacred. And also I try to do a boutique casting process where I know every single person that's coming in, and I can say to the team, "Oh, they've just finished on this", or "They're just graduating from there." I know every single person and so the hit rate's going to be high. I don't really believe in a numbers game. Because one of the challenges we have in casting at the moment is that our creative teams have very, very limited availability to cast and very, very limited shared availability is more the thing. So I want to make sure that every single meeting counts.

Pippa Ailion echoed this point about shared availability. When the creative team is together, it makes the process much smoother:

Pippa Ailion: You have to be extremely flexible when casting. Sometimes you can get the whole team, like with *Hello, Dolly*! next week I've got the whole team. I've got the director, Dominic Cooke, I've got the musical supervisor Nick Skilbeck, and I've got the choreographer Bill Deamer [see Chapter 2] all week. It's bliss, because you know that you will get things done. But when you don't have a musical director, or a choreographer, you have to be hugely flexible about your process. But my ultimate aim is to get a group of the most suitable actors for each role to the end of the process, which encompasses the singing, the scene work, and the dance or movement work, and then to be able to put them in front of the final creative team in the allotted time we have.

So how a performer comes across on paper, in their CV and headshots, and on screen, in their vocal and dance reels, significantly influences whether they'll get to perform in person. I asked Jim Arnold how a performer can maximise their chances of getting into the room:

Jim Arnold: I think the most important thing any actor or performer can have is perseverance. That's the most important thing. But there are other things that they can do: make sure their headshots are up to date; it's very useful to have a voice reel, particularly for musical theatre, so that I can hear the quality and tone of their voice, and hear whether it's the right quality that we need for that particular show; a dance reel is quite useful if I'm looking for dancers, and a showreel can be useful to see what someone's presence and acting ability is like; and make sure that everything is up to date on their CV, that their skills are correct and that it's not overwhelmingly long. We get thousands of submissions for certain projects, and then looking through all those CVs, I don't have a huge amount of time to consider every single person. I try and look at every single one, but I don't find it particularly useful to see that someone's put "experienced barista" on their CV. So having a concise CV with all your skills, all the experiences that you've done, put there in the correct order, split into tabs so you can see at a glance all the musicals you've been in, versus other stage shows, versus the corporate videos that aren't necessarily as useful to me in my line of work.

When it comes to headshots, the fundamental thing to get right is an accurate likeness:

Jim Arnold: A headshot that looks like them! A headshot that isn't going to surprise us when they walk through the door! Face on. I would suggest for anybody with long hair, just make sure it's brushed out of your face. You can have lots of arty shots, and that's fine, but a shot over your shoulder, smoking a cigarette, not necessarily useful to me. You can have any kind of photos you want but I think your main headshot needs to look like you and be facing the camera, and be a good representation of yourself. The thing about Spotlight and other casting breakdown services is that you can have a portfolio of photos. So you can have photos of yourself in action, you can have videos of yourself in action, you can have videos of yourself in different costumes, or being arty, or whatever you want. But I think your main headshot just needs to look like you.

Vocal reels also need to cover some basics that can be accessed quickly by casting directors. Displays of vocal range, vocal quality and an ability to sing in different styles should all be present. Stuart Burt says vocal reels, showreels and self-tapes are an increasingly important part of casting:

Stuart Burt: Showreels for theatre are still quite a new thing, and I think that although they existed pre-pandemic, I think post-pandemic they've just become really quite vital, because I think that, sadly, post Covid, people realised that they could do a lot on self-tape. And so actually, that means that our time in the room, face to face, is less. So basically, a good vocal reel for me, I'd like it to be visual, not necessarily just the vocal line. And what I realised I respond to is a single reel, cut together, with maybe three different styles of song. And so it would be, for example: "The Wizard and I" / "If I loved you" / "Since you've been gone". So you've got "contemporary"/ "straight up, legit musical theatre"/ "pop-rock". And that allows me to very quickly go to those moments and go, ok, I have a semblance of where you are vocally and what style suits you best. And the best choices are actually probably quite well known songs, because if they're quite well known within the musical theatre canon or in the pop-rock canon, I know what the most challenging vocal bits are, so I can even fast forward and go, "Right, ok, I know I need a B flat because I'm casting Tony in *West Side Story*

so I'm gonna go to that bit because I know that's what I need to find out." So I
always feel like, actually, choose songs which are quite well known rather than
stuff which is quite obscure.

Performers have to choose what type of footage to include. Stuart Burt would rather
see footage shot specifically for a vocal reel than show footage, as that allows the
performer to pitch their performance appropriately:

Stuart Burt: I think show footage is, for me, a bit of a no-no, because it exists
theatrically within itself for another reason. Whereas I think all I want to do is get
to know you as an artist. Now I truly believe that theatre cannot live in this box,
the way that we are framing ourselves, now, on a video call. I don't believe that
musical theatre can exist in that space. So I prefer shots which are maybe waist
up so it gives you a little bit more literal space to physicalise your performance.
Also, what we do in musical theatre is heightened, it's a magnified reality, so I
think that just having that wider shot is great. One thing I found that I really like,
which is just a bit of a cheat to be honest, is people singing with a microphone
just in front of them, as if they're in a recording studio. Doesn't even matter
whether it's a real microphone or not. It allows you to make acting choices but in
a way that you get an impression of you delivering something. And so I think it's a
really clever way of going, "This is a snapshot or a flavour of me" rather than "I'm
standing, and I'm giving the full 'Empty Chairs at Empty Tables' like I'm on stage."
It gives you licence to make softer choices, I think.

Self-tapes are also increasingly used in casting, especially since Covid. Jim Arnold
says they're useful when the availability of the creatives or auditionee makes it difficult
to meet in person:

Jim Arnold: I spend a lot of time looking through self-tapes for shows where
the director or the producers aren't necessarily in the country or around. So,
I'm currently casting for a few roles for a production of *Miss Saigon* that's at the
Gothenburg Opera, in Sweden. It was an acclaimed new production from Oslo,
[staged at the Folketeateret], and Gothenburg Opera wanted to bring the show
in next year for a run there. So I've been asked to look for people for a few roles
in the UK and we're looking at a day of recalls in London but right now the first
rounds are just looking for people via self-tape. So yeah, some shows could do
a lot with self-tapes, for the first round, certainly. For other shows, sometimes if
there's someone I know could be really good but they can't attend the first few
rounds, I might get them to send in a tape to sing, and then I can show that to
the musical directors and say, "What do you think?" Or if someone has attended
a first round, but can't come to the recall, I get them to tape the recall material,
and then I can show that to the director and the musical director, and say, "What
do you think?" And then they go, "Ok, we'll get them back in again to do more
work on it." So yes, a lot of self-tapes, but certainly more since the pandemic.

The final element that helps get a performer into a face-to-face audition is timing. Jim
Arnold says it needs to be the right time for the production but also the right time for

the performer, who must be maintaining their skills and abilities in readiness for an audition:

> **Jim Arnold**: Applying for productions at the right time, having your agent suggest you. I don't love being inundated with pushes, but if your agent or you feel that you're really right for something, then absolutely feel free to write in. But make sure that when you do apply that you're absolutely match fit. Take classes. Dancers take classes all the time but it's not quite the same with actors and musical theatre performers, they don't necessarily go and take class all the time. But I would say make sure that you're honing your skills constantly so that when you get to the point of applying for something, you know you're ready to go in for it. I get a lot of submissions from people that, looking at their CV, looking at their experience, looking at their showreel, looking at their voice reel and everything else, perhaps aren't quite ready to be in a show of the scale that *Wicked* is, or *Phantom of the Opera* or *Les Mis*. So just making sure you're absolutely ready when you're applying, but it's very difficult, because there's a huge amount of people. And I find a lot of my job is trying to filter and find reasons to bring people in. But it's tough. It's really tough.

The first face-to-face auditions can be for the casting director only. Pippa Ailion runs pre-screens, where she auditions performers before bringing them back for the show's creative team:

> **Pippa Ailion**: The process is usually that we do pre-screens on our own, without the musical director, without the choreographer, without the director, so that we gather a group of actors that we think should be taken through a process. We usually do a week of pre-screens, probably seeing fifty to sixty a day, in person. And that's me, and a very good pianist who we work with a lot, who can actually input because you don't have a musical director there. And it would be quick. They would come in and sing their own song, and sometimes we skip that preliminary session and send the required call-back music out. It depends how long our process is. If it's a big musical, the process is usually from start to finish six to eight weeks. So overall, when we do auditions for a show, and this is including the dance calls, because you have quite a large cohort in the dance calls, we probably see a thousand performers plus. Per show. Probably more. For twenty to thirty roles. And from that thousand, we would probably present about 120 or more to the creative team. That includes the dancers.

Jim Arnold also does pre-screens for *Wicked*, seeing similar numbers of performers:

> **Jim Arnold**: Because we have the luxury of time, because we want to spread the net wide, find more people, try more people, we would usually do about five days of pre-screens for singing ensemble where we can see approximately 70 people sing per day, so about 350 people in total. For the dance ensemble, we can see about 50 to 60 dancers per dance call and we hold eight dance calls so I usually pick out about 450 dancers to see for those; and then for principal roles, again, it depends on the number we're looking for, but if it's a full recast, I

would want to see perhaps twelve, thirteen, fourteen people per role. And then we will recall people and then filter them down until we find the people we want to take forward to finals. So I would say, usually we can see approximately a thousand people for *Wicked*. Some shows can be a tenth of that, if not less, it depends on the show and on the availability of the director and the creative team. Some shows only have a week to hold auditions, so we can see maybe a hundred people for all roles and ensemble. And there are some people that might be really right for it, or are very talented, that we just don't have the time or opportunity to see. But unfortunately, if we saw everyone that applied, then I think I'd probably be auditioning all year, and the shows don't have the resources to do that.

In the room: Singing, dancing and acting

Once the process is into face-to-face auditions, the first round can often be a quick performance of a song, chosen by the auditionee. David Grindrod says it's vital that auditionees pick material that aligns with what the production needs:

David Grindrod: It's whether they've hit the brief. So if I need a tenor, don't come in and sing the baritone stuff. If I need a top sop, don't come in without that material. So it's up to the actor to actually come in knowing what the brief is and give us what we want. And certainly for that first round you're looking for top sops, you're looking for tenors, (which are rare as hen's teeth), and a character, and that's what you start with. I call it a sweet shop, really, I bring in all sorts and, hopefully, something will start to work with the creative teams.

As well as hitting the brief, David Grindrod assesses the level of an auditionee's vocal technique. There are times when performing in other shows has taken its toll on their voice:

David Grindrod: Oh, yeah! Yeah, you can tell who's been trained, who hasn't been trained, who knows how to look after their voice. And some kids who have been in shows, all of a sudden they've belted too much and they've lost the mid-range. You start to work that out, what shows they've been in, whether you feel there's vocal stamina there. There's lots that goes on in those five to ten minutes with that.

And there's acting through song. David Grindrod says this is a hugely important aspect of an auditionee's performance, but some take it too far:

David Grindrod: That's what it's about, really, but some connect too much. I was doing classes last night and my main word of the evening was simple, simple, simple. People just over complicate it and as long as they've got the essence of what we require, we don't need all the arms and everything else that's going on with it. And that's due to nerves as well, nerves take over, and suddenly everybody "BELTS IT LIKE THAT!" And so you just go, "Whoa! Just calm down a minute." And so it's how we and the actors deal with that.

Pippa Ailion has a background in classical theatre, and so she assesses the acting side of the song, wanting to see the auditionee's use of space, presentation and narrative:

Pippa Ailion: The first round is usually "come in and sing your own song" and that choice of song is very revealing: it is very informative about the way they tell the story, how they reveal their personality. I always say, don't ever choose anything too difficult. Don't give yourself a huge challenge in your first audition. All we want to see is how you can tell a story. And how you focus in a space. A lot of auditionees come in and they're wobbling around and they face the wrong way to start with! I've had people start an audition with their back to you, or start an audition in profile: why, why? So it's how they present themselves, how they stand, how they root themselves, how they focus, how they engage, how they tell the story through their chosen song.

Pippa Ailion is also assessing singing technique. She says it may be that a singer from another discipline needs extra support or an actor develops vocal strength through the rehearsal process. Whatever the case, she's listening out for technique:

Pippa Ailion: There are a lot of people who need that support, who really need that support. Especially in the past few years, there's been a lot of imports from the pop world – well, they sometimes haven't got the muscle to support eight shows a week. So, if they are cast, they need support. I have seen straight actors who have been cast in a role that demands singing. They sing a little but I have seen them grow fantastically, and by the end of the rehearsal process the development in their voice has been substantial. And that's just by singing every day and using the exercises that the musical director or the vocal coach gives to support them. It is quite remarkable the improvement that regular singing makes.

Stuart Burt says auditionees need to do the basics in their first round and perform a song that shows their voice. More detailed assessments will be made in the recalls:

Stuart Burt: I think a lot of people forget that it's a singing call: I want to hear you sing! I know it sounds really obvious but your song choice is everything! I don't want "Franklin Shepherd, Inc.", I need to hear you full voice and that song's not useful to me. And obviously we need to see acting through song but don't forget we're there just to give you a quick tick, going "vocally, they are right for the show" and then we'll bring you back on show material, and we'll explore more stuff with you. I think people truly forget that they are to sing.

When it comes to technique, Stuart Burt wants to see auditionees who understand their voice and know how to use it:

Stuart Burt: Musical theatre has been my thing since I was eleven years old. I've listened to it, I've loved it, I've watched it, I've performed in it, so I have quite a good understanding of the voice. And I've cast quite a lot and I've spent a lot of time with really fantastic musical supervisors, directors, accompanists, and so I know what it is. I think technique is always paramount. We would talk about eight shows a week for a twelve-month period. So, I don't want to see your technique but I want to know that you've got it. And it's actually about an artist who knows their voice and how to use it. And again, it goes back to song choice. There are some people who make bad decisions because they're not in full command or they don't fully understand their voice. You might have someone who comes in and they sing "Giants in the Sky" and they can sing it perfectly after lunch, because they've had all day to warm up, but they think they can sing it at 10:30 am, and they just go for it, and it's not there. And it's those red flags, when you kind of go: they don't know their voice, they haven't yet got to grips with that. So there's the technique stuff, and we'll check ranges, and we might do some scales towards the end of the singing call, but I think it's more to do with people who understand what they're doing with it.

I suggested that Stuart Burt is looking for auditionees who are vocally secure and can demonstrate that, giving the panel confidence that they can perform as required. He agreed and added that part of that is picking songs that suit where the auditionee's voice is during the part of the day when they audition. He called these 'morning songs and afternoon songs':

Stuart Burt: Yeah 100 per cent, that's exactly it. I want to be like, "They know what they're doing. They know their voice, they know their limitations, and they know their strengths." And I'm a big advocate of morning songs and afternoon songs, 100 per cent. I think every single person in their rep should have a couple of songs that they're like, "I can bang this out perfectly at half nine", and then I've got this collection of songs which I need to be on top form for. I'm a big advocate of morning songs and afternoon songs.

I wanted to question what 'good singing' is for musical theatre. The immediate answer was that it depends on the demands of the show and the demands of the role. Stuart Burt has cast many contrasting performers:

Stuart Burt: What makes a good singer really depends what we're looking for. The performers I cast in *Standing at the Sky's Edge* have completely different voices to the performers I cast in *& Juliet*. And there's some people that I cast in *Standing at the Sky's Edge* who have never done a musical before but their singing is exactly what the piece needs. So "what is a good singer" depends on what the material is.

Jim Arnold agrees, but adds there are also fundamentals that always need to be present:

Jim Arnold: It varies show to show. But first of all, are they able to sing it? Are they able to sing in tune? Are they able to pitch? Are they able to sing it in the way that the composer, or the musical supervisor and director, and the director, would like them to sing it? Do they have the right vocal quality? Is it a nice sound? Simple things like that; well, maybe not so simple. And also from my point of view, can they act through song? Can they tell that story, even in a standalone song? Can they make us feel something? Do we believe them? Even with just a first sing, we're looking for vocal ability, vocal range, vocal quality, acting through song.

Shaun Aquilina: Do you prioritise one over the other, the technical singing versus the story-telling?

Jim Arnold: Again, depends on the show. Hopefully, you can marry the two. Hopefully, you can find someone who can do all of it. That's ideally what we're looking for. But sometimes there might be a compromise on one side or another depending on the sensibilities of the creative team and the show you're working on. So, it might be that the singing isn't necessarily the thing that's the most important thing for the director. For instance, an actor may not have a vibrato, but a vibrato is another tool in a singer's toolbox, it's not necessarily the be-all and end-all. If you don't have a vibrato, you can still be a singer and be a great singer and be a really fantastic actor. We all know those great actors who have done musicals who aren't necessarily the strongest singers technically, however, are amazing storytellers, and it's an amazing experience watching them. So it just depends on, again, the requirements of the show. But for me, if you can marry it all, and then find someone who's also really good at taking notes and able to adapt and listen to the other actors, and knows how to create that character, then that's the ideal. That's what we're really looking for, someone who can do all of it. But sometimes, compromises can and do need to be made.

What 'good singing' is might also change depending on the panel. David Grindrod believes there's a lot of subjectivity:

David Grindrod: It's all to do with taste, I guarantee. And I've been in these situations where I'm working with three MDs, on three separate shows, and I'll bring in the same actor for those three things, because he or she's got a really good voice, and then one of those MDs will go, "Well they can't sing." It's definitely taste and style. But it does make me laugh when you've brought somebody in and then you get this flippant remark, "Well, they can't sing." You just go, whoa, hold on a minute, how does that work out? But it's a taste thing, as well, some come from a classical background, some come from a pop background.

When assessing dance calls, our casting directors suggested they were more likely to defer to the choreography team. General audition experience gives them a feel for good dancers, but they still leave it to the experts. David Grindrod says this is how he works, but also provided an interesting analysis of choreography styles in musical theatre:

David Grindrod: I'm not a dancer, believe me this body does not dance, so I do go towards the choreographer or the dance captain. But I have seen enough dancers, and I've been in enough auditions to go, "Isn't that one quite good?"

Or "That one seems to be giving you what you want?" And so it's more of a collaboration. And also, the more I work at it, the more I think, for choreographers, some are earth-bound, and some are more air-bound. That's what I always call it. So certain choreographers, like Arlene Phillips, they want quite small, chunky earth-bound kids, who will do that kind of choreography, whereas if you do something like a Stephen Mear [see Chapter 2] number, they're a bit more, quote "old fashioned", it's a more old fashioned style with a tap and something else that those other kids couldn't do. So it's a bit of a mix and match with who you're working with, as well.

We'll see what our choreographers make of this distinction in the next chapter.

I also wanted to know if choreographers display the same subjectivity of taste, referred to earlier in MDs. David Grindrod says they do:

David Grindrod: Oh yeah, yeah, yeah, absolutely. It's even worse. It's hysterical.

Shaun Aquilina: How does a performer deal with that?

David Grindrod: You just have to keep coming through. I was talking to students last night and I always say that once you get through to a final, whatever show it is, the people that are in the room can all do it. So there's not a problem there, you can all do it. In the end, it comes back to height, shortness, tallness, bigness, can you fit into that costume, have you got the right hair colour, can you wear that wig? And that's in the end, unfortunately, what it comes down to, and it's tough for the artist to accept that.

Jim Arnold agrees that there is a subjectivity to dance auditions, with some choreographers looking for technique and others emphasising movement and narrative:

Jim Arnold: Again, it's down to the sensibility of the choreographer and the director. Strong technique for a dancer is really, really important, depending on what it is that they're doing, but there are some choreographers that are more movement based who come to it through text and storytelling; there are other choreographers that like more clean lines, that are really, really technical, and like having everybody lined up doing exactly the same thing. Sometimes it's about the sensuality of the dancer and what story they're being able to tell through their movement and it doesn't necessarily matter about the steps so much. I've been in dance calls where they've asked people to improvise through dance. They're given a nugget of information about the show, or about the characters that they're supposed to be, and then asked to improvise a whole dance, around the dance studio. And that's because that choreographer's way of working is to collaborate and they come to create stuff, working with dancers in a workshop setting, in the rehearsal. So it just depends on what they're looking for. And my job is trying to filter and bring in those people that have the necessary skillset that we're looking for. So if they're more of that kind of collaborative, improvisational way of working, then I might look for people who have a background or training in contemporary dance. Whereas if it's a big tap show and it's going to be about the kick line with twenty dancers in a row kicking their legs up and tapping, then I might look for people who have strong tap dance, and have been in four different tap shows. So it depends but technique, experience, ability to tell a story and then a musical ability to sing, too, is always helpful.

Stuart Burt has also gained experience in assessing dance calls through years of auditions. As with his assessments of vocal ability, he's looking to see that an auditionee knows their ability and how to utilise it:

Stuart Burt: I'm not a trained dancer but I've been around really fantastic professional practitioners. And again, you can tell people who don't quite know their skill level. Like knowing how to pace themselves through a dance call: there's some people who go full out quite a lot, and by the end, by the time you take it down to fours, they're absolutely knackered. But you've got other people who have paced themselves really brilliantly. Also, it's interesting at what point people start to add in the character element or the reason why we're dancing. A lot of people leave that towards the end whereas some people bring in the performance element as they're being taught it, which is, I think, more beneficial. So I look for stuff like that. It's the same thing, it's about self-awareness.

However, Stuart Burt says that dancing is more clear-cut than singing, and we'll see this echoed by other creatives in later chapters:

Stuart Burt: The thing is with dance; it's more like, there is a right, there is a wrong. Whereas there's more space for interpretation when it comes to musicality.

Acting is integral to the performance of singing and dance, in musical theatre, as well as being its own discipline. Acting is what Pippa Ailion prizes most of all in an auditionee:

Pippa Ailion: Because I come from a teaching background and have worked with extremely talented and creative directors, whom I've learnt a lot from, I always say I'm looking for the actor in the musical theatre performer. I mean, I'm in huge admiration of dancers. The way that they can just pick it up like that is fantastic. But you can't just dance, you need to be an actor the whole time. You've got to be able to tell the story and you have to be able to communicate and to interpret.

I wanted to know what 'good acting' is in musical theatre. For Pippa Ailion, it's about presence, craft and engaging with other characters on stage:

Pippa Ailion: A good actor in musical theatre is someone who can handle dialogue and who can listen, react in the moment, access emotions, stand still. A lot of musical theatre performers have not been taught, or have not learned, to be able to focus on the person they are communicating with. They don't treat it like a conversation, they're all over the place. So I'm looking for someone who has that facility, who could handle the dialogue, make it real, make it honest and engage with the person they are speaking to.

In later stages, there's also the question of chemistry. Finding actors who create excitement when playing opposite each other brings vitality to the production. Pippa Ailion says chemistry is so important that it gets its own section in the audition process:

> **Pippa Ailion**: When you are casting a show, you are balancing a cast. Actor A may be the most brilliant singer, with wonderful scene work, but when they've got to engage in scene work opposite Actor B, the spark may not ignite. It's chemistry. We do a lot of what they call "chemistry reads." If you've got two leading players who've got to spend most of the production together, there has to be a connection. And that has to shine out. And it's very apparent when it doesn't, on stage and in an audition.

> **Shaun Aquilina**: And do you think that is in a performer's control? Can they create chemistry with another performer?

> **Pippa Ailion**: I think an actor's job is to transform so I would say that they should be able to. But chemistry is a very strange thing, isn't it? It's very personal, so some people just can't access it when they need to.

In Chapter 4, we'll hear a different view on the actor and transformation from director Rupert Goold, who believes a key part of musical theatre is not transformation but self-revelation.

David Grindrod agrees that quality in acting comes out in dialogue and playing against others in the scene. He also wants to see an active mind and a drive to be part of the production:

> **David Grindrod**: It just depends how they read it, how they play off a reader as well, if they have fun with it, don't ask too many questions but just get on with it. Sometimes they can over analyse and you can tell that, and it all goes pear shaped. But sometimes, you can spark off something, and then the panel knows that the auditionee's brain is ticking away. And you want to see that the auditionee wants to be part of the show, as well, that they've got that enthusiasm and the passion for it.

Jim Arnold wants to see intelligence and personality. He says making a performance choice is vital:

> **Jim Arnold**: It's really important that an actor has a point of view, and that they have an opinion about the role they're coming in for, or that they're coming in to understudy, and that they have something to bring to the table, and they have something to say.

On the production side, the acting ability of musical theatre performers can be underestimated. David Grindrod says he's battled against that kind of opinion:

> **David Grindrod**: The meetings I've had with the great and the good who say, "Now the thing is, we don't want musical theatre people." Oh, really? You're doing a musical. "No, we need actors." Well, actors aren't trained to sing. So I

have to do this balancing act and woo these creative teams around until they say, "Oh, yes, they can do it, can't they." So it is funny, I have to say, it does make me laugh.

We'll hear a lot more about what makes an auditionee successful in their acting, and in their singing and dance, through the rest of the book. What all our casting directors agree on, though, is that what's needed from an auditionee is determined by the requirements of the show:

> **Jim Arnold**: The place that I always start at is: what are the requirements of that show? Vocally, what do they need to be able to do? Acting wise, what do they need to be able to do? Dance wise, choreographically? What other criteria are there? I've just cast *Spend Spend Spend* at the Manchester Royal Exchange, and there were certain criteria there that we were looking for. It's a show that's about someone from Yorkshire, it's very much set in the heart of Yorkshire, so we were looking to explore people that were from Yorkshire, but also to explore actors that are from Manchester as well, because of the theatre it's at. So there are other things at play and you go, "Ok, well, that person's been in five shows in the West End but isn't from Yorkshire and isn't from Manchester; and that person has been in two shows, has trained at this place and is from Yorkshire." So I might try the Yorkshire person with two shows over the non-Yorkshire with five shows, and it's just about balancing who I think is going to be capable of doing it, who's the most appropriate for it, who is most suited to what we're being asked to find.

Pippa Ailion agrees and says that roles are often weighted towards particular elements, like singing or acting. But she adds that auditionees need to be skilled all round:

> **Pippa Ailion**: It depends on the demands of the role. Sometimes, really good actors who are not great singers are cast, and sometimes performers who sing fantastically but are not good actors, but they are not of my choosing. I think you have to marry it all. Actors need to offer all the skills because the competition out there is vast. And that's why you also need to be good at sight reading, because you could be suddenly given a page of script and you have to be able to interpret and communicate that in the room with no preparation. And you have to be able to dance. You have to be able to do it all if you're going to succeed in musical theatre.

In the room: The professional personality

Auditionees in the room also need to show their professional personality. This includes their creativity, receptivity and preparation. A major element is how they work in rehearsals. We'll see throughout this book that the rehearsal process is vital and always in the minds of the audition panel, and there are rehearsal qualities an auditionee needs to demonstrate, one of the most important being their ability to take direction:

David Grindrod: Oh, they have to! You can't not be open to all that, and open to talking about the character, the essence of it, and take direction, really. There's nothing more frustrating.

Pippa Ailion says it comes down to listening, and auditionees need to be able to react in the moment in response to a direction:

Pippa Ailion: So many people don't listen, especially in auditions. They don't. They don't listen when the director gives them some direction to just see how they can shift and adjust. And that is hugely telling. And it is something directors pick up on immediately. I know it's very hard in an audition situation, because your nerves are bubbling away, your lines are jangling in your head and you've rehearsed at home one way, and now every auditionee memorises the script – well, nearly every auditionee – that has become the norm. And so you've got all these things going on inside you, and the director is giving you an instruction, and if you don't listen and actually take on board and deliver what is being asked of you, that doesn't make for a successful audition.

Jim Arnold says creatives give direction to shape the story and vision of the production, but it's only effective when enacted by the performers. That means taking direction in an audition is about testing the potential for a creative relationship:

Jim Arnold: From a director's point of view, certainly, they want to know if they can work with that person. Ultimately, the director is the director because they want to create a story. They want to create a production that is telling the audience something and they're trying to create that with the actors. And if the actor is intransigent and isn't able to take on board anybody else's point of view, such as the director's, and isn't able to take a note and go with it, then why would the director want to work with that person? It's not about going, "You have to do it like this and if you don't, you're out," it's about having that collaboration and the director finding out, "Could I collaborate with this person? Would they be able to listen to my point of view, and take on that direction and give it a go and play?" Play is the most important thing about acting, I think. They have to be able to adapt and listen and play, whilst also bringing their own point of view to it. But if they're so stuck in their own way of doing it, and they can't make an adjustment even with the slightest bit of direction in an audition, then a director is going to be quite reluctant to work with that person. So I think for an auditionee, the most important thing is being open and able to listen to what's being asked of them. Even if they don't necessarily agree with it, that's then for rehearsals. In the audition process, it's about listening to what you're being asked, what the director would like, and trying to make that adjustment and trying to grapple with that intellectually and say, "Ok, so how do I, as me as the actor, with my opinion, how do I make that work? And how do I reconcile that?" But playing really is the key to it. It's like, "How can I play with this, and how can I adjust?"

I wanted to know more about this idea. I asked Jim Arnold how he finds out if an auditionee has the ability to play:

Jim Arnold: The recalls would be the time at which we find out. Recalls will be the first time we see them with any kind of show material – script or song – and often the director will just give them a brief note to say, "Could you try it like this?" or "How about if you can adjust the way that you're singing that because this is what I believe the motivation of that character to be?" And then they ask them to do it again and if they can make that adjustment, or you can see that they're trying to make that adjustment, then they might want to take it forward and bring them back and do a work session. Or sometimes the director feels that they've seen enough and they go, "Yes, I think they made enough of an adjustment. They're great. I really like their personality. I really like the way they're doing this, what they brought to it, their voice is fantastic, and we'll just offer it to them after the one recall." And sometimes it takes a few more work sessions, or a few more recalls before they're confident to do that. But that's down to the sensibility of the director as well, and the musical director, and how they feel about things. But usually it's from recall stage when they start delving a bit more into it. Whereas for principals, for instance, we usually bring people in with material from the show straight away from the first round, and the director might give the odd bit of direction then, and they might go, "Well, they didn't quite make an adjustment but there's also some really good stuff so let's get them back and try working with them again." It's very rare that people meet once and then are just offered the role. I think a director likes to be confident that that person can not only achieve what they need to be able to achieve but also can play and be the person they want to work with and collaborate with.

Stuart Burt says the panel is always aware that an immovable auditionee is likely to give the same performance on opening night that they gave in the audition, with little development in rehearsal. That makes for an unrewarding process in the creation of the piece:

Stuart Burt: Oh yeah, if you just try to move them into a different position, into a different headspace, a different point of view, and they can't be moved, then it doesn't matter how extraordinary they are at the thing they do, we can often say to one another, what we get in the audition is what we're going to end up with in the final show. You can already see it and that is not interesting, that's not fun, because there's nothing to be shared or explored or discovered. So, if we find people who are immovable, we're less likely to go with you. Again, it's about being comfortable and having an access to creativity, about you being in command of yourself, which allows you that space to move.

There can be exceptions to this, but they are specific and tend to be around technical feats, as Stuart Burt explains. He also says that, ultimately, auditionees need to be artists, and he gives a definition that can guide our thinking about artistry:

Stuart Burt: Going back to super-duper technical dancers, you're like, if that's what they finally deliver in the show, because we need it to end with twelve fouettés and a split leap: great! If that's what their skill set is, fantastic! But I think every creative I work with at the moment wants people to contribute in the room. They want to work with artists. And I use the word artist all the time – I don't say performer, I don't say actor, I don't say dancer, I say artist – because I think that is an empowering way to look at yourself. And the creators I work with, that's what they want.

Shaun Aquilina: What do you think is good artistry? Is it possible to articulate that?

Stuart Burt: Honestly, artistry is when you're fully in command of who you are as a performer, and who you are as a human being. It's the confidence of self-expression. That's artistry.

Artistry doesn't only apply to auditionees. Stuart Burt says it's part of his work, too, and this emphasises the creative and instinctive approach he takes to casting, which has been so successful:

Stuart Burt: I consider myself an artist. I consider myself to be a theatre artist. Casting to me is not an administrative task, I find it wholly creative. There's a lot of organisation that goes into it and there's a lot of diplomacy and politics involved, but I see it as a creative thing. And it's the same with an actor: it's all about instinct. And that's something that you develop over the years, I think. And again, it's about point of view. I've always felt really strongly about theatre, specifically, I've been living it and breathing it since I was eleven, and it's the one thing that picked me up and has never let me go. There's nothing else that's had an effect on me, and I'm very lucky that I get to carry on, and I can make a living from it. And I'm still doing it at forty-four, I mean, lucky me! Because it's really, really difficult. But yeah, it's instinct. And it's about . . . knowing that I'm right all the time!

Stuart Burt laughed playfully at this final comment.

Professionalism is another important quality in an auditionee. We'll look at a lot of definitions of professionalism throughout this book, which will often include preparation, commitment and a particular attitude to the audition. Pippa Ailion explained professionalism by starting with what is unprofessional:

Pippa Ailion: There are some actors that I call passing through actors. They enter an audition and they're on the way to somewhere else already. It's like, "Aren't you lucky I'm here, and I want to get out as quickly as possible." So that's not helpful or productive! That's not professional. You've got to have someone that you feel, first of all, wants a job, and has prepared well, and we want to know that you're going to be a good company member. We want to be able to like you. We want to give you the job. And it is a job. It is a job, and for musical theatre, usually it's a year's work. And you have to treat it like if you were going for an interview for a bank or any other job, you would look good, and you would prepare, and I would expect that from people who come in to audition. And if they are not prepared, or they pass through, or sometimes they're a bit prickly, or they talk too much – that's a constant thing, talking too much! Every audition is allotted anything from five minutes to fifteen, and if you're on a short audition schedule, you can't have someone that's chat, chat, chat, chat, chat. Come in, do what you've got to do and get out. That's what I say.

Professionalism is also about preparation. Pippa Ailion wants to see auditionees who have prepared their material and warns that the spoken part of an audition is often ignored by MT performers in favour of a song:

Pippa Ailion: Knowing their material, knowing the audition material. That's what they're coming in to do. I don't mind if people hold the script, though it's become the norm to learn it. However, sometimes, you know that they're not free to perform because they're desperately trying to remember the words. It's funny, musical theatre performers know every word of their songs, that's not an issue – it's the script they don't know. Because they obviously concentrate on the song, and they pick up the script on the way to the audition and they are not familiar with it. There has been no investigation or real thought about it. But it's a two-part component; one is as important as the other.

David Grindrod echoes Pippa Ailion's earlier comment about taking a practical perspective on auditions. He wants to meet auditionees who are smartly dressed and pleasant to talk to:

David Grindrod: It's a job. I always say to students, yes, it's an audition, but it's not, it's a job. You're going to pay your rent, pay your mortgage, pay your bills, it's a job. And yes, it's wonderful that it's a job where you give yourself, you can do artistic things, that's a bonus, but in the end it's a job. So come in for a job interview: look smart, not great, but look smart, look like you're ready to work, you're affable, when we speak, we actually have a chat and you're a nice person. It sounds really simplistic but in the end that's what it is. And then on top of that, you can sing a top B flat or you can do a pas de deux or something, and that's a bonus.

For Stuart Burt, professionalism comes back to the auditionee's relationship with themselves. It's about self-control and purpose:

Stuart Burt: Professionalism is knowing why you're there and what you're going to do there. Simple. What you don't want to be is cold. Sometimes professionalism can be seen as too precise or robotic, like, "I'm walking straight to the piano, and I know exactly what it is, and we cut here and we go here." I think that professionalism is someone who is fully in command of themselves. Knowing why they're there, knowing they should be there and wanting to be there: that's professionalism to me.

Nerves can make self-command difficult in auditions. The topic of nerves will come up again and again from our creatives, but David Grindrod says auditionees have to be ready for them:

David Grindrod: Auditionees are very nervous. But then going back a step, that's why I go into colleges and do work with students to warn them that that could happen. And they will get very nervous, and, for example, the left leg will start to do things it hasn't done before, and that will throw them completely. So that's when you need to get the actor into the right frame of mind prior to going into the room. And yes, as a panel, there is a moment where you see them and go, "Oh, this looks interesting," or "This doesn't look interesting," but then it's what they come up with, certainly for the musicals, when they start to sing.

Jim Arnold has great sympathy for auditionees. He believes the casting director should be trying to make their time as positive as possible:

Jim Arnold: Another really important part of my job is making sure that the actors and the dancers and performers feel like they're having a good experience. I have someone in the waiting room as a runner, assisting me, who will chat to them, make sure they're ok, that they're looked after. If they're running late, that they calm down, they give them some time to gather themselves. And then, when they come into the room, to greet them at the door and say, "Welcome to the room and thank you so much for coming in, and thank you for doing all of that work." Auditioning is really difficult. It's terrifying. Some people are really good at it, and other people just fall apart. And I can't be everyone's counsellor but what I can do is hopefully make people feel like they're being respected when they come into the room. And I think that's a really important part of my job because it's a really difficult thing. And we can't do our jobs without people wanting to come in for our shows.

There are other qualities in an auditionee that our casting directors are looking for. We'll hear different views on intelligence in an actor, but for Stuart Burt, that's not precisely the quality he's looking for:

Stuart Burt: I think it's more about instinct than intelligence. I have met some really incredible actors who leave and the room and we're like, "Wow!" And me and the director go: "They don't know, they couldn't articulate, what they've just done." There were just people I've met who probably wouldn't be considered massively intelligent in a traditional sense, in an academic sense, but their understanding of themselves and instinct about the human condition allows them to act magnificently. I think as long as you can do it, you don't need to talk it.

Shaun Aquilina: So it's an emotional intelligence?

Stuart Burt: Yeah, that's what I believe, yeah.

David Grindrod is looking for individuality and bravery:

David Grindrod: It's guts. Yeah, it's guts. And I've done it for such a long time and there's a certain type of person I really enjoy watching: they're quirky; they're a bit odd; they're this; they're that; there's something that I engage with personally. And then on top of that, you've got the acting and the singing. But there's just something there that you go, "Ooh they're interesting," or "Let's go with a bit of that."

The final quality that's as important as professionalism and preparation is being a nice person. Nearly all our creatives hold this as an important value. It partly comes back to considering the rehearsal room and the desire to be surrounded by positive people, and it helps the run of performances. David Grindrod says it shouldn't be underestimated:

> **David Grindrod**: If they come in the room, and they're nice people, they're affable, I know that sounds really stupid, but if they're a nice person and do what we want them to do, we go, "Oh, I think they'd be nice to work with." And they don't give us any "me, me, me, me, me." That's a major thing now, that we look for people who are just nice and just do the job and just get on with it. Yes, we do look and go, "Ooh I don't know if that's going to last eight performances a week," or "I'm a bit concerned about that," but if there is a concern, but we do like them, we bring them in for a separate session with a vocal coach. And the vocal coach, then, can have an objective view and tell us the facts.

Stuart Burt looks for an attitude of 'shared generosity' in his auditionees. He gave an example of seeing it in the audition room:

> **Stuart Burt**: Talking about dance calls, again, I really like to keep an eye out for people who help one another. I think that's really interesting. That's something I really pick up on in a space. If someone joins late and someone else will go, "Oh, you missed the first three counts and it's this, this, this," then I'm like, "Oh, that's smart." Or people who ask each other. Because at that point anybody could get the job and I think there could be shared generosity in a space, which I pick up on.

Casting directors check up on auditionees before offering them a contract. David Grindrod says it's part of their responsibility to the producers to know about the people they are employing:

> **David Grindrod**: We talk to other casting directors, asking, "We're just about to employ this person, are they a nice person?" I don't think the actors realise that we all talk to each other, as well. But I think that's important, and it's important to the producers. They're putting a lot of time and effort and money into the show and it's our responsibility to come through with a company that's going to work.

Pippa Ailion agrees. But she's also willing to give actors the benefit of the doubt and will push for them to get the job:

> **Pippa Ailion**: Today, before any contract is offered, checks are done. Everybody is checked up on today. And there are many times when a bad report has come back, from a show they did six or seven years ago. So you have to say to the creative team and producers, "Look, people grow up, people change and to give them a black mark and not offer a job on someone's opinion seven years ago is

not on." And I always fight for performers completely. I've seen a lot of performers get bad reports and I fight for them with my life and say you've got to give them a chance. You must allow an actor to grow, develop and change.

I asked Pippa Ailion whether it's possible to get a reliable read on someone's personality in an audition. She admits it can be difficult but that the subsequent rehearsal and production process are also a significant influence on how performers behave:

Pippa Ailion: You hope you'll be working with a lovely group of people but you just don't know that. You start with a nice group, but actors, especially young actors, do get a bit bolshie sometimes, a little negative. They start with all the right intentions, but they end up somewhere else. I think the way they are handled during a production by the in-house team and the management counts a lot for the way a cast behaves. If a cast is handled well, if they are respected, then I think actors do a brilliant job. I have huge respect for actors and I can't bear it that they sometimes get paid poorly and not respected.

If an auditionee does present as potentially difficult, David Grindrod says they can still win through with the panel:

David Grindrod: It's not a big red flag but it's something to be aware of. And some choreographers or directors can go "That is the person that I want." and you just go, "Ok, that's fine." And I'm not going to argue with that, because they're the captain of the ship, but I think we just then have to be aware of that person or say some something to them.

The preference for nice people to work with is so important that I discussed it in depth with Jim Arnold. He says it can be very difficult to judge, but there are several indicators to watch for:

Jim Arnold: We make snap judgements about people when they come into auditions because you have to, you don't have a huge amount of time to spend with people. But you can get a sense of who they are as a person and what they're going to be like as a company member by their energy and how they react to people, whether they are willing to listen and take on direction, how they treat the pianist, how they speak to them, how they speak to the reader, whether they say thank you to the reader or the pianist afterwards, and how friendly they are when they come into the room. Sometimes they can be really chatty, and some people will really take to that. But this is the thing that is difficult about when people come into the room: again, it's the sensibility of the creative team, how they react to people, and you can't control that. So someone might come in who I know is lovely, or I think is a great company member, and someone will just not like them. And sometimes it's for no rhyme or reason, or they might get an energy or a vibe about someone that I believe they're misreading, and so they might say, "Ooh, I'm getting a really funny energy from them: what are they like?" And I say, "No, they're one of the nicest people I've ever met." Or I know that they're a brilliant company member, and I didn't think that they were having that kind of energy when they came into the room, but people just have different reactions to people and we all experience people in different ways. So my job is to be a buffer there and to try and mitigate that, if I think that somebody's experiencing somebody in a different way to how I think they're coming across.

However, Jim Arnold has seen an increasingly uncompromising attitude from auditionees around their own behaviour:

Jim Arnold: A performer's job is to try and come in and be the best version of themselves and want to be employable. There's a prevalence at the moment for "take me or leave me." And I think, but we all adapt ourselves to try and behave well so that people want to employ us, so why wouldn't it be the same for a performer coming to an audition? Why wouldn't someone want to come in and be the best version of themselves, and be friendly and open, and listen, and want to be playful, rather than going, "No, this is me. Take me or leave me."

Shaun Aquilina: Are you seeing that "take me or leave me" attitude in auditions?

Jim Arnold: Sometimes, sometimes. And sometimes people come in and are incredibly chatty, and the director will be slightly not loving that kind of energy. And then other people come in and are having a bad day and are not being as talkative or as friendly as I know that they are usually. Or some people are coming in, and I know that they've been a terrible company member, or I've just heard or had a reference that someone's not great, but they are incredibly charming in the room. So it's very difficult to read from that ten or fifteen minutes what people are like, but you get a good idea from it. And if you see them multiple times throughout the process, you do get an idea. For instance, in a movement call, are they being loud because they're covering up their inability to do what they're being asked to do? So they're shouting and making jokes and being loud, whereas someone working away diligently in the corner, you notice, and you see, ok it's a quiet energy, but it's determination, and they just want to get on with the job and make sure they're doing a good job.

As I mentioned in the opening, of all our creatives, casting directors are likely to spend the most time in auditions. Jim Arnold says that gives them a lot of experience in assessing an auditionee's attitude and personality:

Jim Arnold: You can read people's energy, I believe, and you become quite attuned to that. Certainly, when you're in auditions all the time. Some creative teams, if they're the resident team on a long running show, they only go into auditions once a year, whereas I'm in auditions for different shows with different people, and you become quite attuned to how people behave and you adapt yourself so that you can try and mitigate or help advise, depending on the situation that arises. I've had auditions that have gone terribly because someone has come in and has had a disagreement with the director, and they started having an argument, in an audition. And I've had to step in at that point and say, "I'm really sorry, I think we should probably move on. Can we get on with scenes or the singing" and then I try to bring the audition to a conclusion. And sometimes they're having such a good time with the actor that it runs on and on, and I have to step in and say, "I'm really sorry, we don't have any more time but thank you so much." So you do become attuned to reading people's energy.

Jim Arnold showed considerable compassion towards auditionees. If he has a difficult encounter with someone, he's more interested in understanding what has happened to lead to that behaviour:

Jim Arnold: Sometimes the experience you've had as a casting director tells you that that person is just not having a good day. It's not necessarily about them as a person and the way that they would normally behave. And you kind of go, "What's happened?" And that's why it's important to have a good runner because you can ask them, "How were they outside? Were they okay, were they chatty? Did they seem like they were upset? Any idea what's going on? Did they say anything to you?" Because you want to know if that person's ok, you want to just check. And then sometimes they'll have told the runner outside, "Oh, my dog's just died," and then you can understand. But sometimes it's about context, and again, that's part of my job to try and work out the context and why that person is behaving that way. And sometimes it's because they just have the attitude of "take me or leave me" and then the director has to decide whether they want to have that energy in the rehearsal room or in a company.

And the panel can affect the attitude of the actor. Jim Arnold says it's part of an actor's job to match and mirror energies in performance, so what might seem like a difficult attitude could be a reflection of the atmosphere created by the panel:

Jim Arnold: To be fair, sometimes the actor is reading the energy from the room that they're coming into, and then their behaviour changes. Because they're so used to adapting themselves and changing their energy to meet the needs of whatever they're doing professionally, if the director's having a bad day, or the musical director's not talking, they come in and they're matching the same energy. So then it's not just about the actors coming in and how they behave, it's also about the way the panel behaves, and the energy within the room that they're coming into. So it's a two-way street, definitely. It is very subtle. And can be easily misread on both sides. And so again, my job, hopefully, is to try and be that buffer so that I can help guide people and say, "Ok, well, actually, I think it was this" or "I know that they behave this way usually so I think, perhaps, we're misreading that," or actually "No, I do agree with you, that was a very strange energy. Let me see if I can find out the reasons for it," etc., etc. And sometimes there's a myriad of reasons for why people are behaving a certain way – on the panel, and the actor in the room – and the synergy of when it comes together, and people are getting on with each other and having a good experience, that's the best auditions because you can feel that energy and the fizz of that in the room. And often you know that that person's going to get the job. And that's the exciting thing about it all.

We've looked at several qualities in an auditionee in the room, including their ability to perform the material, artistry, taking direction, professionalism and being a nice person. I suggested to Stuart Burt that the ideal auditionee brings all of these qualities together:

> **Shaun Aquilina**: It sounds to me like you're looking for layers in your auditionees: they know their technical ability and how to employ it; they know their motivation to be in the production; and on top of that, they bring a human element of "Hi, I'm in a room, you're in a room, let's have a good experience."

> **Stuart Burt**: That's a really great way to put it, Shaun. It's like that's your base level, and then all this other stuff, and how you are, and how you interact with us, that's the beautiful top notes.

Casting decisions

Finally, the panel must decide who they want to employ. I suggested to Jim Arnold that it might be a strange moment for a casting director, having taken so many decisions early in the process, now to give the final decisions over to the panel:

> **Jim Arnold**: When you're doing the preparation, it's very much about your decisions and your choices. And then when you get to the auditions, you have to take a step back. You're there to advise, you're there to give your opinion, but you're not there to make the decisions and the choices in the end. So it does shift somewhat.

Stuart Burt agrees and says that the casting director's role becomes more about enabling the dance, music and direction departments to meet their needs:

> **Stuart Burt**: Ultimately, when we're putting a cast together, it's all about the trade-off between the different departments. And when it gets to those points, as a casting director, you become slightly more passive because you are there as a mediator trying to put these things together. But that's something for them to work through. It's a continual trade between different departments, like, "Well, but you've got the actor you wanted so I need the dancer." And you're gonna go, "Well, ok, I've got that so you can have this." And that's what it becomes part of.

However, the panel may not have found the right performers. Jim Arnold says it's then down to the casting director to decipher why that is and guide the process further:

> **Jim Arnold**: If they're saying, "Oh, I'm not quite finding this," or "There's something else that I'm not seeing," I have to respond to that. They haven't necessarily imparted it to me but I'm starting to sense it through the way they're talking about people. I previously worked for a casting director who called it "triangulation." You meet lots of actors, bringing the sides of the triangle in to try to zero in on who it is you are looking for. But then sometimes there's nobody left in the middle of that triangle, and you have to recalibrate and look for more candidates. But by that

point, as you've sat in the auditions and you've listened to the panel talk about the auditionees they've already met, you have a better understanding of what they want. I try to have a holistic approach and serve the needs of the show, as opposed to imposing my will or my opinion on everybody else, but sometimes there are moments where you say, "Look, I have done a really extensive search: without searching further afield and spending a lot more money on doing open calls and really going for it, these are the people that I think are the best people we will find, who are available, and would like to do it." And that's an important point to make sure the panel are understanding. Or, happily, sometimes you sit there and you've nailed it. And people are coming in and the panel's going, "I love everybody. It's going to be a really difficult decision."

Returning to the selection process, as Stuart Burt mentioned, the different departments need to ensure the cast will deliver on their part of the production, whether that's the dance, vocals or drama. David Grindrod says the decisions come down to one thing:

David Grindrod: It's the art of compromise. I'll do little bits of, "But if you have that one, we can have that one" or "that one gives you that, and that one gives you that, so perhaps we can put that together but they would be a good cover . . ." So you go through and it's a bit of a game to put all the pieces into place. But it's talking to each other! And if you've got a nice panel, it's fun. I've just been in a situation now where we have to have a dancing ensemble, but of course they need some vocals out of them, and the MD has gone, "Oh, let him [the choreographer or director] do that, I'll sort this out another way, because they can't give me the vocals that I need." But nobody's going to fall out about anything, they'll do the art of compromise.

Though a relationship has been built with each auditionee, Stuart Burt says the decision process becomes much more objective, looking at the complete casting picture:

Stuart Burt: When you get to the final stage and they've spent time with you through different phases, it really becomes less personal. It becomes quite functional of putting a company together, because every single jigsaw piece influences other things. And so it becomes less about the individual, and more about the function and what's best for the show, what's best for the company.

And one of the biggest factors in casting shows today is finding covers. We'll see this come up again and again. David Grindrod says choosing the ensemble/cover roles is harder than deciding on principals:

David Grindrod: Of course, once you've got the principals, you've got to get all the ensemble who then have to cover. And so you've got to get two covers out of every ensemble member, somewhere along the line, so that is more problematic than finding the principal, actually.

Directors are the creative heads of a production. Though they can be seen as having the final word on many things, including casting, David Grindrod says it's usually more collaborative than that:

David Grindrod: The directors that I've worked with wouldn't normally take it away and make all the decisions themselves. They'd normally have an affinity with a choreographer or the musical supervisor.

Stuart Burt says some directors do take charge of the casting, but most are looking to collaborate and defer to the expertise of their colleagues on the panel:

Stuart Burt: I think that there are definitely directors who just want what they want, and they will to be quite strong with that. But the majority of people that I work with are very kind, pragmatic people, and trust the reason why they've hired this choreographer, trust the reason why they've hired this movement director or musical supervisor, and so it has to be wholly collaborative. It's not always but most people are collaborative, for sure.

As well as the creative team, the producers may want some input on the decisions:

David Grindrod: The producers that I work with always come around for the finals – it's their name on the line and they have to be happy, as well. They will have a say but they will also go along with the panel. Again, it's all the art of compromise, it's talking to each other, making sure the shape is right.

Stuart Burt says the level of influence the producer has on casting can depend on the type of producer you're working with:

Stuart Burt: The producers do have a say but a lot of producers aren't really creative producers. They're more financial producers. So I think that they can say what they think. I mean, there's some great creative producers like Adam Speers, Sonia Friedman, etc. But I think the financial producers' input can be taken with a bit of a pinch of salt.

Ultimately, what does the panel want from their casting? Pippa Ailion summed it up:

Pippa Ailion: I think it's about making the best production with the best cast that's available. People are going to pay a lot of money to come and see the production. Tickets today are very expensive. And so you have to give the audience a magical, memorable, exciting evening in the theatre. It has to be a special event. So you have to create something that is magic and you need the cast to be an integral part of the whole. So they've got to be good. You need the creative team to be the best and to get on with each other, which doesn't always happen. And then you need the cast to form a good company. There are so many components.

David Grindrod is also looking for those performances where all the parts of the production work together to create a magical evening:

David Grindrod: When we did *Hairspray*, that first performance at the Shaftesbury [Theatre, London], I always think of a plane taking off: you start the show, and you just go, "Oh, my God, this is going really well… Oh, my God, it really is going well! . . . Oh, my God! We're taking off!" And by the end of the show you're whooping away, going, "This is amazing!" I call it, when all the planets align. It's that thing of when everything comes together – sets, costumes, music, lighting – wow! And you know they don't often happen but when they do, they're very exciting!

Casting directors carry out a huge amount of work to filter through potential auditionees, deliver them to the casting panel and create a positive audition experience on both sides of the table. We've seen a lot of discussion about what makes an auditionee right for the role, covering layers of ability and attitudes. Now we'll turn to the contexts for casting, which change depending on the status of a production.

New shows, new productions and re-casting

In the West End right now, you could see a new production of a new show, a new production of an old show, shows that have come over from Broadway, and long-running productions. These all have their own casting requirements, and the creativity and openness available to them vary.

For new shows, the casting process can begin, informally, before any auditions, at the workshop stage:

David Grindrod: If a producer or a composer or a creative team are worth their salt, they will have started on workshops. So you would have done one or two or three workshops prior to even going out to Spotlight on a big trawl. Normally, the first workshop is doing a few scenes or doing a couple of numbers. Normally, you bring in the kind of people that, perhaps, you know won't be right for the show but they're right for a workshop. So some people are very workshop orientated, and they enjoy doing workshops, but they know they're not right for the role and so it's quite good. It sounds a bit stupid but it gives the creative team an idea of how they're going to sound, what they want, what they don't want, it gives them something like that. For something like *Back to the Future*, I think we did four workshops. And they gradually got bigger and bigger and bigger and that was partly for the creative team and partly for investors and theatre owners. And those big workshops have bits of set in, and all sorts of things like that as well. And then the more you then start to work out what you want, then you can start to go to Spotlight or put a breakdown at certain agents, or however you do it. You start small to go big and then once you've kind of got an idea of what you're looking for, and/or the theatre is being confirmed, or investors have been confirmed, then dates are being confirmed, then you can go forward with a much broader aspect of a breakdown.

Pippa Ailion says that when auditioning for a new show, there's an unknown quality to what the director wants from the actors. That makes the casting much more flexible and responsive, and auditionees have a greater opportunity to shape a character:

Pippa Ailion: Casting requirements for a brand new show evolve with each casting session. And often it's what the auditionee brings into the room that is considered, embraced and developed. With a new show, the director doesn't really know what they're looking for to start with. And you have to go along with that. You could have brought in all these wonderfully talented actors and then suddenly the whole thing turns on its head. And then you're looking for someone completely different. That's what's exciting, that's what's creative about it. I fought very long and hard to get casting included as part of the creative team. So we weren't just seen as a side appendage. I'm in right at the beginning with the director, the producer, choreographer, the musical director, and I'm part of all the creative discussions, and we move forward together.

The panel on a new production is likely to be looking for auditionees with creativity, flair, imagination and the integrity to explore the piece and contribute to the creative process. Stuart Burt says that's exciting:

Stuart Burt: We're casting the Live Aid musical *Just For One Day* at the moment, and again, it's about points of view, it's about people with voices and points of view, on top of their talent. And when we were casting *Sunset Boulevard*, Jamie [Lloyd, Director] just went, "I don't know what this is going to be or where we're casting it, it happened so quickly." He was like, and he always says this to me, "Just bring me cool people" and that's it. Which is such a gift for me.

Long-running shows can be different because, often, there will be an expectation or a specification for each character. Pippa Ailion calls this 'the mould': the external characteristics such as look, sound and physicality. But there's also an inner life to the character, what they think, what they feel, how they act and how they relate to other characters. This is what Pippa Ailion calls 'the essence':

Pippa Ailion: If you're doing a long-running show, there is a mould. It's lovely to work on brand new productions, and having worked on original productions like *Billy Elliot* and *We Will Rock You*, you create the mould. Now, obviously, there are a lot of actors that fit a mould. And it's wonderful when a director is happy to explore a little left field, that's very helpful, but there is a mould. When you make a list, you're looking for the essence of that character in that actor. And so many different actors could fit that role who are so different but they have an essence of what you're looking for. And it's exciting, because if you were to look at a list without knowing what the role was, you'd say, "But they're so different, they're so diverse," and that's what I love.

Some shows adhere to their moulds more closely than others. Stuart Burt gave some examples:

Stuart Burt: There are certain shows I do which probably have more of a template, and that is stuff like *Sister Act* or *Mrs. Doubtfire . . . & Juliet* to a certain extent . . . there's a template of how those casts are, and we will try and cast slightly more like for like.

David Grindrod says there can be a level of expectation around what an older show or production will be:

David Grindrod: I suppose the older shows, those characters are definitely fixed with what they've got to be and what they've got to produce and what they've got to do. So there's no kind of flexibility in that, it is what it is. Sometimes, there's a twist to it, like the recent *Oklahoma!*, [Daniel Fish's Broadway production that came to London in 2022/3] but those big shows that I did for English National Opera, they were "the show".

However, there can also be creative takes on older shows when they come back in a new production. Stuart Burt is involved with shows that sustain that level of creativity through successive re-castings:

Stuart Burt: With stuff like *Standing at the Sky's Edge*, which we've started recasting again, and even with *Cabaret* where we're now in year three, there is still flexibility in the re-casting, and we can bring new types of people into these roles. It's not like for like, in any way. So even when creating *Cabaret*, we literally didn't know what we were making. We knew we were doing *Cabaret* but we didn't know what the people who lived there looked like and what they would bring, so that was completely open season. And it continues to be so, even into year three, where we're like, well, we know that Bobby has to be a beautiful dancer but that's it. In terms of age, body shape, ethnicity, sexuality, gender, that is open. We just know they need to be able to deliver on certain physical moments. So there's a beautiful movement. And then we redesign the costumes for every single new person and they work collaboratively with the designer, Tom Scott, to express what they want to bring to the Club, which is rare. That doesn't suit all shows. If you're going to do *42nd Street*, you're probably going to have to be a certain type of person with a certain type of skill set. But I think the work I seem to be doing, with the people I work with, is about exploration with people. We take people's hands and we create something together. That's the type of work that I seem to have fallen into.

I asked David Grindrod if he agreed with the idea of 'the mould and the essence' in ongoing shows. He did, and observed that though there are many different auditionees who can play a role, the production remains consistent:

David Grindrod: I was doing the *Mamma Mia!*'s in the States, and I had five productions on! And I had three directors across these five productions. And in the States you do big audition rounds, so you do New York, you do Chicago, you do LA, you do somewhere else, and you draw up big lists of people that could play certain roles, because the contracts there are rolling contracts, and the ensemble artists can give you four weeks' notice at any time, so you have to slip people in really quickly. And it was really interesting going around doing that show. It's the same show, three different directors. There was hardly any arguing about who they liked or who they didn't like, and nobody really crossed and wanted the same person for different productions, they all had their own tastes. But in the end, the show was exactly the same. That's what I found really fascinating!

Shaun Aquilina: Are you able to see what those performers had in common that allowed the show to become the same?

David Grindrod: I suppose it is an essence. We called it the *Mamma Mia!* Factor, whatever that is. But I always find it fascinating that, even though I'm supervising the casting, I can go, "Ok, I'll go with that because I trust you," and I have to say it never really failed at all. It was fascinating.

Shaun Aquilina: It's been described to me as performers who have the mould and the essence: the mould is those characteristics we expect to see and hear, and the essence is the inner life of the character, would you go agree with that?

David Grindrod: Yeah, yeah, yeah. Absolutely. What you can't do, and what is very difficult for the resident teams, is when you're putting a new company into a fixed show, you can't say, "And on that note you go there, and on that one you go there, and that's what that is." They're very clever in finding a way to talk to the actor so that the actor comes up with that themselves, even though you're guiding them to it. Because certain things have to happen – you've got to stand in that spot because the track's going to start there and this special light's going to come on you – but you have to give the actor the lead for them to find out why they are in that position.

Our final casting context looks at what happens when a Broadway show comes across to the West End. Stuart Burt says, in his experience, there's more likely to be a 'mould and essence' casting that re-creates the New York production:

Stuart Burt: I've not worked with lots of American creative teams but I feel like there's less flexibility while working with American creative teams than there is with British creative teams. And transfers, or remounting stuff over here, I think they really want a like for like casting. They will continually reference, for example, "John," who played it in the original cast. So you have to know what your limitations are. But it's also my job to try and provoke and push to see what's possible, because that's more interesting for me to be honest, selfishly. So although I know exactly what they're looking for, I'll always try and provoke them by showing them something that they didn't think they were looking for.

Pippa Ailion says it can be difficult to work with American creative teams because of a lack of knowledge of the way the West End works and knowledge of its performers.

Pippa Ailion: My job, I always think, is to try and guide them to where I think they should be. Now it doesn't always work. You have to respect that a director and their team have the final say. UK directors know the talent pool but when you have a creative team coming from the States, they don't know the talent pool. And they don't always understand the workings of the West End, and the hierarchical structure. Because they don't know the actors and the actor's history, although they have their CV, they would say, "Will he swing?" And you say, "No he's just played three lead roles, he won't swing," and they don't get it sometimes, and that's quite frustrating.

It's also possible that Broadway shows will appoint a resident, or associate, director at the very beginning of the audition process. Pippa Ailion says that's quite a recent development:

Pippa Ailion: Today, more and more resident directors are assigned to a project before it starts, which is a fairly new occurrence. Before, they would come on board after the casting is completed, but more and more today on the big musicals, not so much on the UK musicals, but on the big American musicals there is an associate director or a resident director assigned to that production before we start the casting process. They've gone over to New York, and watched the show, had conversations with the director, the choreographer, musical team, and then they come and sit in on our auditions. However, I prefer to do pre-screens on our own and collect the talent, first.

The creative team's availability also becomes an issue. Pippa Ailion is expecting casting for one Broadway show, now in the West End, to take several months:

Pippa Ailion: I've been casting *MJ: The Musical* [see Chapter 3] and we started in April. We did a whole load of auditions. The team came over in May. We showed them everyone. We completed a significant amount of the casting but we didn't cast it all. So then we had another whole round of auditions in September and early October. The audition process for *MJ* started in March/April and will finish probably in December. I prefer to try and do it in one block but when you're working with American creative teams they don't ever really believe we have the talent here to cast the show and so continue on until the very last moment and then realise that perhaps we did bring in the best candidates first.

US supervisory teams are becoming more common and we'll see how they affect the casting of shows such as *MJ* and *Wicked*, in later chapters. We'll also see how Broadway performers approach their auditions, in contrast to those in the West End. For now, here's David Grindrod's assessment of auditionees in the United States:

David Grindrod: The Americans come in, and it's a job. It's absolutely a job. That's what it is. "I've got this song to sing, I can also do this song, I can do this, I can do this, I've got my book, I can do that, I can do that." They bash through and you just go, "Whoa!" And it was so funny when I was doing the auditions for the Broadway company, I'd say to the actors, "Right, start to read the scene." "So how do you want me to do it?" I said, "No, you do it, and I will tell you." "But you gotta tell me what you want." "No, you just start it and we'll start to play." Well, they couldn't cope with that, at all, it was just so weird to them. And then in the end, by the time we'd done it for all those years, they go, "Oh they're the mad Brits that want you to improvise and do all this business. Oh yeah, okay, we'll get on with it." And they did in the end, God bless them! But it was a definite mind change. Here, everybody's quirky and fun, and it's the way we're trained, we'll play more, whereas the Americans are "Right! What do you want me to do?" It was fun, but they got used to me in the end.

Commercial casting

Commercial casting – putting celebrities into shows – is common practice. It has its supporters and detractors, but I wanted to know how our casting directors feel about it and gain more insight into the practice. David Grindrod remembers the boom in commercial casting in the 1990s:

David Grindrod: Well, I started it! I started it with *Chicago*.

The West End revival of *Chicago* saw lead roles going to musical theatre veterans who were also celebrities, such as Maria Friedman, Ruthie Henshall and John Barrowman. But also cast were celebrities unassociated with musical theatre, such as Christine Brinkley (Roxie Hart), TV personality Jerry Springer (Billy Flynn) and Olympic figure skating champion Robin Cousins (Billy Flynn).

Shaun Aquilina: Are you talking about the late 1990s? Because I remember the *Chicago* posters around London and each time a new cast came in, the celebrities on the posters would change, and you'd have a new Roxie or Velma or Billy.

David Grindrod: Yeah, that was me, that was me.

Shaun Aquilina: So, what was your thinking behind getting that started?

David Grindrod: Well, it was the producers! So we put the show together, which was fine, and then the Weisslers [husband and wife producers, Barry and Fran Weissler] suddenly said to me, "We need names!" And back then I was going "Oh, please, how could you? Oh, how demeaning! I can't do things like this." And then I had to go, well, if they want it, let's see what we can do. And of those people on those posters, some worked, and some were absolutely dreadful and it was just like, "Oh, my God, what have we done?" But some worked, and it gave a lot of joy to a public that wouldn't normally come to the theatre, but they would come to see their stars. And a show like *Chicago* can take that, there are definite characters which you can do it with. And other shows you do have to have a bit more training to make that star vehicle work. So when we did *Joseph* at the Palladium in the early nineties with Jason [Donovan], to get him to come on stage, it was like getting Harry Styles to do it today. That's how big it was for him to do it. And the roads around the Palladium were closed after every performance, because he used to go out and sign autographs, and we had security, we had police, it was total rock star stuff, and that was 1991 when I did that. And so that for me was the start of those star names coming into it.

David Grindrod says that, today, it's the theatre owners who are really pushing for commercial casting:

David Grindrod: It gets people into the theatre, it can earn a bit of money for the producers. The theatre owners are the ones now that are saying, "Who's in it?" And they're saying, "Who's in it" because at the moment the West End theatres are absolutely packed, you cannot get any theatres, but they will move for a name. And all of a sudden, if you're getting a big name like Ken Brannagh, or whoever it is, all of a sudden, doors open. So that's what the theatre owners are looking for.

Stuart Burt has been involved in commercial casting for much of his career. He fully backs it:

Stuart Burt: Big fan, always have been. I'm a commercial casting director, I was in-house at ATG [Ambassador Theatre Group] for ten years and we did massive commercial casting. I've got posters of everybody who was in "Pinter at the Pinter" [a season of Harold Pinter plays performed at the Harold Pinter Theatre, in 2018–19] next to me in my office, which is all famous faces, and the truth is that casting a star in something will hopefully ensure its success and sellability, and keep hundreds of people employed. And it can be done well. And it can be done terribly. So just try and do it well.

To do it well, David Grindrod says you have to be clever:

David Grindrod: You have to be canny with the casting and who you put around them. And I always say it's good if they go into the lesser roles where they can just do their own thing, and we can then put other people around them to be a safeguard.

Stuart Burt returned to the theme of the artist knowing themselves. He says if that's in place, the commercial castings can work brilliantly:

Stuart Burt: It's about the artist, and the artist having self-awareness of what they're capable of. Because sometimes, you see celebrity castings and you're like, "Did they not know their limitations?" And I have to say that when I was working in a different company and I had to do what I was told, I definitely cast people that I think were miscast and couldn't really do it. But I think why a lot of stars want to do theatre is because they can play something that they don't normally get cast as. They can play quite similar to themselves in TV stuff but I think they get to explore really, very different personalities on stage. When we did *The Homecoming*, John Simm was this absolutely terrifying, malevolent force on stage, and I don't think he really had the opportunity to play that before. And I think that's what appealed to him. So going against what they're kind of known for can be really interesting. We've just cast Ruth Jones as Mother Superior in *Sister Act* and yes, I think it's just so perfect because people love her. She's so well loved as Nessa [in the TV comedy *Gavin and Stacey*], and here she is in a habit, and it just feels right. You go, "Gosh! That feels good," and you can't quite put your finger on it but you're like, Oh, that pleases me. I know what that is, and it looks fun.

TV casting

If you can't cast a star, what about creating a star and casting them at the same time? That's the premise for the casting shows that have become such reality TV successes. David Grindrod was behind several reality casting shows on UK television, including: *Superstar*, *Over the Rainbow*, *Any Dream Will Do*, *How Do You Solve a Problem Like Maria?* and, most recently, *Mamma Mia: I Have a Dream*. He says they attracted huge numbers of auditionees:

David Grindrod: When we did the Nancys [in *I'd Do Anything*], there were thousands of people coming through. I had ten rooms going at one time with casting directors in there. And then if they got through those rooms, they'd then come to me. But that was a big thing, and we all learned on the hoof. And we didn't do too badly with who we got!

One of the features of the TV programmes is that the audition panel often included the show's composer. This led David Grindrod to give some strong advice for any auditionee who finds themselves in that situation:

David Grindrod: Those people don't kind of come in until the end, because they have trust in their director, their MDs, etc. Someone like Andrew [Lloyd Webber], he likes "a project." So all of a sudden, you go, "Andrew, I've got a problem." "Ooh, marvellous!" he says. So in he trots and he then enjoys working with them. And he does enjoy working with new, young talent, and that came out of the TV shows, when he became far more involved with the process of an audition, etc. But in the end it's so kind of weird when you're dealing with the composer, and it's the same with ABBA, with Benny and Bjorn, it's a case of: don't change the notes! Don't change the notes in front of the composer, it's not a thing to do! Don't do that riff, cause he or she or they didn't write it, so don't put it in when they're in the room. It's the basics of that really.

TV casting shows have been so successful that I wondered if they had influenced David Grindrod's process when he returned to traditional theatre casting:

David Grindrod: Yeah, I think it did. I think it all helps to see what else is out there. The thing is as well, it's always a joy to do open calls but the trouble is now, they cost so much money. But when we did the TV shows, we found a Jessie Buckley, or we found a Sam Barkes, or we found a Jodie Prenger, and that was really exciting. I'm sure those kids would have come through somewhere, but we have the opportunity to find them, and they have the opportunity to come to us and see what they could do.

This led us to discuss open calls and how they operate in the casting process today. David Grindrod said the important element is training:

David Grindrod: You will find now that anybody that really comes to me at an open call has not necessarily got an agent but they have had some form of training. And even on those open calls, if I feel they haven't had those forms of training, or some level of training that we can do something with, they won't get through. We're doing the ABBA one at the moment [*Mamma Mia: I Have a Dream*] and there was a girl who worked in a factory in Margate, the blonde girl, Maisie. She came in, and she's an enthusiastic amateur, that's what she is. But she just had this quality, this amazing soprano voice, where I just went, "What the – ?! Where did that come from?" And then I worked with her, you don't see me, but I worked with her a lot, thinking, "Am I sure? Am I sure?" And I was! And we're now sending her to college, funnily enough, the TV show is, to expand on those other skills. But she has got a God-given voice that she didn't realise she had. And that's very exciting.

David Grindrod says the TV casting process also sharpened his instinct for assessing auditionees:

David Grindrod: I refined it more doing the TV shows because that is really quick. You are seeing people really quickly and putting them through or not putting them through, so you have to concentrate really hard. For those, of course, it's also: are they good for television? Are they good for theatre? How does that work out? What do we need? And so I found that when I first did them, that really was a skill I hadn't refined. And to me, fifteen years ago, that was a big thing that I had to come up with. So there are moments when you can instantly go, "Ooh, they're really interesting."

Great auditions

All our casting directors have seen auditionees perform so brilliantly that they left no doubt that they were right for the role. These auditionees also embodied many of the qualities discussed throughout this chapter, around what makes a great audition. We start with David Grindrod:

David Grindrod: Jessie Buckley came in for *Oliver!*. We were at County Hall, in London, and the researcher said to me, "There's this girl from southern Ireland. She's been turned down by two drama schools, just to let you know that's the background. But she stayed over today to do this open call." And in walks this Irish girl with fiery red hair, curls and everything else, and just sings up a storm. And you're just going, "Wow! I can't believe that you've been turned down by two drama colleges" and she said, "Well, yes, I have." And I said, "Well, this Drama College ain't gonna turn you down! There's just something about you which I think is amazing." And so it's those sorts of auditions that you remember.

Jessie Buckley would subsequently gain a place at RADA, receive Oscar and BAFTA nominations for her screen acting, and win an Olivier for playing Sally Bowles. But it's not just new talent that makes an impact in auditions. Some of the West End's most high-profile stars occasionally have to return to the audition room:

David Grindrod: When we put Michael Ball into *Hairspray*, all those years ago, it was a show he really, really, really wanted to do but I said, "You've got to audition." And he hadn't auditioned for twenty years, or whatever it was, and bless him, he was really, really nervous. And you see then the vulnerability of those marvellous performers. And of course he did the audition, and was spectacular, and the rest is history. But you're there at the moment when you see them as a vulnerable child, still going back to nerves and making sure everything's all right, and I was literally holding on to him before he went into the room, because it's the whole thing about wanting the job, doing a good job, and nerves.

When an auditionee is brilliant, the panel can be tempted to offer them the job on the spot. David Grindrod has seen that happen too:

David Grindrod: Yes, and then you have to tell them to stop it. They get carried away. And you say to the auditionee, "I'll just come back to you in a minute, that'll be lovely, thank you very much." Not because you don't want that to happen, it's always great when it does happen, but there's so many other bits and pieces to put into place that you have to hold on a minute. Or you can do that if you send the auditionee out of the room, and then everybody agrees, and then you bring them back in again. So you can offer the job but it can't be without consultation with everybody else. But that doesn't normally happen because you normally go back and then an offer is made, so the creative team don't actually see the offer being made, funnily enough. And it's nice for them to have the opportunity to go, "Come into our show."

Pippa Ailion remembers seeing Rachel Tucker before she trained at the Royal Academy of Music. Rachel has gone on to play Elphaba in the West End and originate roles in *Come From Away* on the West End and its Broadway transfer. Pippa Ailion says she was a raw talent but already sang in a way that connected to the material and the audience:

Pippa Ailion: This is going back a long, long time. Rachel Tucker. I was doing a production of *Rent* for Dublin. And I was over there doing an open audition and this eighteen-year-old walked into the audition room with a voice to die for. No discipline, no polished acting skills, lots of great instincts but really all over the place, but this amazing voice. And we took a chance on her, and that was Rachel Tucker, and I've cast her so many times since.

Shaun Aquilina: When you say "amazing voice", was that an amazing sound or was it that she connected with people and told a story?

Pippa Ailion: She connected with people, she told a story and made it completely her own, and she thrilled you when she sang. It was thrilling. Just the sound she made, the energy, the commitment and the joy exuding from her whilst singing.

Pippa Ailion also described finding two young performers who have gone on to have outstanding careers:

Pippa Ailion: Jamie Muscato was sixteen when I first noticed him in a talent competition I was judging. He won it! A thrilling, really mature voice for someone so young. We kept in touch and I gave him his first professional job in the original UK production of *Spring Awakening*, found him an agent and again have cast him many times since then. He has played the lead in *Moulin Rouge* for me and now is playing a lead in *Natasha Pierre and the Great Comet of 1816*. Alexia Khadime is another who came for her first audition at fourteen. Another extraordinary thrilling voice for her age. We kept in touch and at the age of sixteen, she did a short tour for me in *Leader of The Pack* and at seventeen, she made her West End debut in *The Lion King* as a Nala cover and the rest is history! She went on to play the lead role of Nala, the first Elphaba of colour, Nabalungi in the original UK production of *The Book of Mormon* and Rita Marley in *One Love*.

Stuart Burt remembers casting two different productions of the same show and the electricity that went through the panel when a young actor walked in to perform for them:

Stuart Burt: It happened twice and it goes back to *Sky's Edge*. When we created it originally, which was for 2019 in Sheffield, we found this incredible young graduate called Adam Hugill to play the role of Jimmy. He'd never done a musical before, it was his stage debut, but he was from outside Sheffield, and he was absolutely magnificent, and he won The Stage Debut Award for Best Actor in a musical. And then he chose not to return for the remount in 2022, so we were like, "Oh my God! How do we recast Jimmy?" Because Adam created it. And then Sam, who's playing it at the moment, walked into the room, and I remember sitting next to our choreographer, Lynne Page [see Chapter 2] who was then next to [director] Rob Hastie and within seconds, we all just held one another's hands because we knew we'd found Jimmy. Because he was just so perfect. I don't know if you saw *Sky's Edge*, there was an authenticity and a reality about it, and it was just that, it was the perfect meeting of actor and role and time. And that was really special. It was the right person, the right role, and we were absolutely terrified, and then he walked in, and within seconds – I think he probably said his first couple of lines, he hadn't even sung yet – we were like, Thank God, we've found him. And it's when an actor comes in, and just by them being themselves, they tell you you're going to cast them.

Shaun Aquilina: And did he exhibit those things you were talking about earlier? Was he an artist in command of himself and his abilities?

Stuart Burt: There was a closeness between the artist and the character. It felt so natural and there was nothing laboured about it because I think he is ultimately quite like Jimmy. So it was just exactly what we were looking for. I mean, there's luck involved in that, by the way. So obviously, I invited him in but I invited him in on the basis of a self tape, and like I said, he'd never been in a musical before. And I love this story: so when we cast him, he started going around old people's homes and singing on his guitar to get used to singing in front of people, which made us love him even more.

Finally, Jim Arnold remembers another auditionee who would go on to lead the cast of *Wicked*. This example led us to consider star quality and what that is in a performer, and how some performers have it early on but others can discover it as they develop:

Jim Arnold: I remember Alice Fearn coming in for Standby Elphaba, and she was a star from the beginning; the first time she sang "Defying Gravity", it gave me goosebumps, and she just got better and better every time she came in for recalls, and I just had this strong feeling she was going to get the role that year. And then there are other people who you've seen who you remember when they graduated, and they were still slightly unformed as performers, or they haven't had the experience to know how to get through the audition process without slightly falling apart in one way or another. And then, a few years later, you suddenly see them come into their own, and they come into the room, and it's just this incredible force that they're bringing to the audition process. Those things are incredible to observe, when those people come in and they just blow you away.

Shaun Aquilina: Is it possible to say what star quality is?

Jim Arnold: I think it's intangible but also it's a synergy of vocal ability, the ability to tell a story, the energy they're bringing to it, the determination, the way that they come in and they're not nervous – or they might be nervous, but they're hiding that – and they just grab the opportunity and go, "This is mine." It's a combination of all those things and you feel it as people come into the room. And we talk about the "X Factor" or star quality but it's just something that you can feel. It's subtle, it's intangible, but it's there. And a lot of people have that and some people grow into that, as well. Some people have it from when they were very young, or the minute they graduate, and other people you wouldn't necessarily think have that kind of star quality, suddenly they grow, the more experience they get, the more they do, the more they grow into it, and then they come into the room a few years after you first meet them, and you go, "Wow! This is just incredible. What you've learned, what you're bringing to it now, is so far from where you started and it's wonderful to see."

Conclusion

Auditions are a big process. We've started at the beginning with the casting directors and their extensive work to put together a breakdown, sift through thousands and thousands of potential auditionees on paper, on screen, and then in person, and then put together a cast. We've heard how their work is driven by the needs of the show. That's vital. And David Grindrod says auditionees need to remember that and be flexible and prepared to offer more:

David Grindrod: Keep to the brief. If we ask for two contrasting songs in the style of "x" that's what you bring in. But you don't just bring two in, you bring your book in, bring everything in because then the MD or whoever could go, "Have you got anything else to show me?" So that's always there. It's the same with the dance calls: bring your sneakers in but bring a proper dance shoe or a tap or something, bring everything with you, be prepared to do whatever.

Auditionees need to show they're great at what they do and that what they do is right for the show. They often have to bring the essence and the mould. But they also need to show they're creative, can take direction, are generous to other performers, and that they're nice to have in a rehearsal room. Stuart Burt sympathises and says it's a lot to deliver:

Stuart Burt: I think it's really tricky for a performer because not only have you got to walk into a space that you might have never walked into and meet people and try to remember their names, you've got to try and remember your name, you've got to try and remember the song that you've chosen, the words, you've got to try very instinctively to go, how big is the space, where am I going to stand, etc., but you also have to be open and listening because we will ask you questions. I like to think that I know every single person coming in, so I will say, "Oh, how was your time at the Union Theatre, on *Bells are Ringing*", or "How was Guildford [School of Acting]?", or "Oh my gosh, that is an absolutely beautiful jacket, where's that from?" You have to be open to having a conversation. So I try to have some sort of chat with everybody at some point, because it's not only the performance level, it's like, who are you as a human being?

So what is a 'good audition'? Here's Stuart Burt again:

Stuart Burt: I think what a good audition is, is someone who just walks into the space and is just happy to be there, and share a bit of themselves, and walk out. That is the best audition in the world. It is so easy. And what gets in the way is nerves and second guessing, and I always say, if you walk in, take the space which is allowed to you – and never forget, I asked to spend time with you – you're already on a win. So come in, share yourself and leave, and just feel that you've done a good job. And then don't think about what the job is. You've heard the phrase "win the room, don't win the job" – that's it. Because the other stuff gets in the way, and I can see when you walk into the room that you already pictured getting a phone call from your agent, and then you telling your mum and dad, it's there, and that comes in the room with you, and you can sense that. So I think what makes a great auditionee and a great performer is someone who just is happy to be there and free to share that something of themselves.

Jim Arnold agrees and emphasises the total engagement of the performer in what they're being asked to do:

Jim Arnold: I think it's having the confidence to know what you're capable of, and being able to show that, and bring that to the table when you go into that audition, with whatever you're being asked to do. There's a quote which feeds into that: "amateurs are people who practice until they get it right; professionals are people who practice until they can't get it wrong." And I think star quality is about people who are so confident in their ability and know how to use their body and their voice and their intellect and their feelings, and bring it all to the table, who are able to then create that character and create that story, and are able to adapt it and play, all of those things we've talked about, those are the people who are stars. And it doesn't matter what you consider to be a star, whether it's people who are really famous, or who earn a lot of money; in my eyes a star is the person that can do all of what we've talked about and have the confidence to shine.

Shaun Aquilina: I like that idea that you are using your intellect and your emotions and employing those in the same way you use your voice and your body, to perform, to tell a story, to realise the material.

Jim Arnold: And it's a synergy of all of those things. You can't just put your finger on one thing, it's all of those things added up to making someone have that confidence to be able to come into the room and own the room and create a character that is exciting to watch.

And to find out how auditionees do that, we need to hear from the rest of the creative team behind the table. We start with the choreographers.

2 Choreographers

Sir Matthew Bourne is one of the world's leading theatrical choreographers and directors. For nearly forty years, he has created dance work for musicals, ballet and his own companies, including the world's longest-running ballet production, Swan Lake. *His work in musical theatre includes choreography for* Oliver! *(London Palladium, 1994),* My Fair Lady *(The National and Theatre Royal, Drury Lane, 2001) and* Mary Poppins *(with Stephen Mear), a production that has included runs in London, Broadway, a UK tour, a US tour, Australia, Mexico and Vienna. He has directed* Oliver! *(2024) and* Stephen Sondheim's Old Friends. *He is the only British director to have received the Tony Awards for both Best Choreographer and Best Director of a Musical. He has also won a record nine Olivier Awards, including two for* Mary Poppins *with co-choreographer Stephen Mear (2005 and 2020) and for* My Fair Lady. *He was given the UK Theatre Award for Outstanding Contribution to British Theatre in 2015. He was knighted in 2016.*

Bill Deamer is a choreographer and director working in theatre, television and film both in the UK and internationally. Productions include Hello, Dolly! *(The London Palladium, 2024),* 42nd Street *(Sadler's Wells Theatre & International tour 2023/4),* The Corn Is Green *(National Theatre),* Cats – Tap Choreography *(The London Palladium and international tours),* The Boy Friend *(Menier Chocolate Factory),* The Sound of Music *(50th Anniversary UK tour),* Evita *(The Dominion Theatre),* Saturday Night Fever *(UK/European revival) and the acclaimed* Follies *at the National Theatre, which won the 2018 Olivier Award for Best Musical Revival. Bill was awarded the Olivier for Best Theatre Choreographer for* Top Hat *(The Aldwych Theatre 2013). As a director, his productions include* Holiday Inn *(Theatre Orb, Tokyo, 2025),* Oklahoma! In Concert *(Theatre Royal, Drury Lane, 2024),* Follies in Concert *(London Palladium) and* Fred Astaire: His Daughter's Tribute *(London Palladium). Bill's TV work includes* So You Think You Can Dance *and professional group routines, Charlestons and show dances for BBC's* Strictly Come Dancing.

Stephen Mear CBE is a choreographer and director whose work has been enjoyed in some of the most prestigious theatres in the world. His productions include Funny Girl *(Director and Choreographer, Marigny Theatre, Paris),* Guys and Dolls *(Director and Choreographer, The Royal Albert Hall),* 42nd Street *(Director and Choreographer, Theatre Du Chatelet, Paris),* Sunset Boulevard *(English National Opera, 2016, and Broadway, 2017),* Gypsy *(Chichester Festival Theatre, 2014, and The Savoy Theatre, 2015),* Die Fledermaus *(The Metropolitan Opera, New York),* Kiss Me, Kate *(Chichester Festival Theatre and The Old Vic),* Crazy For You *(Regent's Park Open Air Theatre and Novello Theatre) and* Sweet Charity *(Menier Chocolate Factory and The*

Theatre Royal, Haymarket). He has received three Olivier Awards for Best Theatre Choreographer, for Hello, Dolly! *in 2016 and* Mary Poppins, *with joint choreographer Sir Matthew Bourne, as noted above. He also enjoyed a close working relationship with comedian Victoria Wood, including her 2009 Christmas Special watched by nearly 7.5 million viewers. He was awarded the CBE in 2020 for services to dance.*

Lynne Page is a choreographer and movement director who works internationally in musical theatre, film, TV, opera, plays and commercial music. Her choreography for La Cage Aux Folles *was seen on Broadway and the West End and was nominated for a Tony Award, Drama Desk Award and an Olivier Award. She has also choreographed* Tammy Faye *(Almeida and Broadway),* A Little Night Music *(Menier Chocolate Factory and Broadway),* Funny Girl, Tell Me on a Sunday *and* Standing at the Sky's Edge *(Sheffield Crucible and National Theatre), for which she received another Olivier nomination. Lynne choreographed the highly successful film biography of Judy Garland,* Judy, *starring Renée Zellweger.*

Introduction

In this chapter, we are going to see how some of the industry's leading choreographers select their performers. Technique is very important to them, and so I'll ask what makes a good technique and how clear that is in an audition. Passion is at the forefront too, both in the performance of an audition routine and in the auditionee's attitude to dance and theatre more generally. And story-telling which, for all our choreographers, is the primary reason for dance in musical theatre.

Dance requirements vary from show to show and role to role. We'll discuss the full range, from the precise and uniform ensemble to the technically highly skilled individual, to the character-actor who dances and the actor who tells stories through movement and gesture. We'll also investigate the non-dance factors that lead to an auditionee being successful. These include the ability to cover other roles in the production (increasingly influential in casting decisions), their creative input in the rehearsal room and the benefit and wellbeing they might bring to the company.

I also wanted to understand the creative vision of our choreographers, many of whom also direct, and what they believe dance, movement and theatre can be. Sharing that vision in auditions and rehearsals is something that our choreographers, and indeed all our creatives, value.

We begin with the importance of the audition process.

Getting the casting right

All our choreographers stated how vital it is to get the right performers. Lynne Page put it most directly:

Lynne Page: Casting is everything. I mean it really is. You want absolutely the best people for the job. If you have a potentially great show but not a great cast, you're not going to realise that great show. But then, even with a show that's less strong, if you've got a fantastic cast, it will just lift it off the ground.

Lynne Page recalled one particular production where the performers made a huge difference:

Lynne Page: I'm really proud of *Spring Awakening* – it is quite a dividing show for people because some people love it, some people think it doesn't make sense – but I feel like in the past version I did, the cast was so compelling that it was just everything. And it was so esoteric in what they could put across because we got these extraordinary young performers. So the performer is everything.

Bill Deamer agreed on the importance of casting because he knows that miscasting can lead to problems once the production moves into rehearsals and performances:

Bill Deamer: I always keep an open mind when casting. We are always on the lookout for new talent and there are always some amazing people to audition. We are lucky in the UK to have some of the very best casting directors who really work hard to bring the best talent into the audition room. It is vital to get the casting right from the word go.

Stephen Mear doesn't even wait until the auditions begin. He's actively looking for new and talented performers:

Stephen Mear: I like to go see shows and see people and go, "Oh my god, they're amazing! Wow, I've never seen them before!" I'm patron of so many colleges because I feel that's my job. I try to go to as many as I can during the year because I want to know who's coming out of colleges. I think I had twelve kids straight out of college in *42nd Street*. Brilliant kids, as well. And two of them came to do *La Cage aux Folles* with me, afterwards, and played the two young leads. So, I love finding talent and seeing who they are, and I think any choreographer or director should be doing the same thing.

This strategy of finding performers before auditions begin raised a related point: how often do performers get invited back by a choreographer, like the two young leads mentioned above? Stephen Mear says it's something he's often accused of but, in reality, there's more of a balance:

Stephen Mear: People used to say to me, "You use all the same people" and I don't! I use a handful of the same people in every show, not exactly the same people but people that work with me, just to keep the discipline there, and because they're good and brilliant. But I love getting new people into a show, it's so exciting. When I did *42nd Street* in Paris last year, we did massive auditions that went on for ages, and the amount of people that stood out because they were brilliant, who I didn't know, was so exciting for me.

Lynne Page admits she would like to use more of the same people, but it often isn't right for the production:

> **Lynne Page**: I've got so many performers I absolutely love. There's a performer called Joel Montague who is one of my favourite performers, he was my Eddie in *Funny Girl*, but I haven't yet been able to get him into another show because I haven't had a show that's got a part for him. So, absolutely I would use so many performers I love but unless the show is right or they are right for the part, there's nothing I can do.

Once auditions are underway, it's time to start seeing performers. Stephen Mear says he goes into the process clear and focused:

> **Stephen Mear**: I always know what I'm looking for in an ensemble when I'm casting. And I've always been able to spot passion, professionalism, ability. Even when I was a dancer, I'd look at people and I was well aware of why people were getting things.

Bill Deamer agrees that there's a distinct difference between performers who meet the required standard and those who do not:

> **Bill Deamer**: In this country we have some absolutely wonderful, top class performers. There are also performers who don't quite make the grade. We also have an abundance of new young talent which we must nurture for the future. There's not much middle ground, at the moment. And I think that is because there is a requirement for triple threat performers. The days of "the dance" and "the song" and "the acting" being separate, has gone. It really has gone. And anyone coming into the business should really adhere to that. You can't be a jack of all trades, a master of none. You've got to be able to do all three.

Technique

Often, the first attribute our choreographers look for is technique. Stephen Mear explained what that means to him:

> **Stephen Mear**: You know when people have got good techniques, you can see it straight away.

> **Shaun Aquilina**: What do you see?

> **Stephen Mear**: Sharpness. Quick people that can pirouette and do things like that and tricks. I'm not just asking anybody to whack their legs up, I'm not a big whack-leg person, but anybody who's got pirouettes and turns and tricks that are beautifully done and presented, that's always great to look at.

Bill Deamer explained that technique is so important because he wants dancers to take his choreography and make it live:

Bill Deamer: Above anything they have to have a technique. Because if they don't have a dance technique – ballet, jazz technique, certainly a tap technique for me as well – there's no body to hang the suit on. They've got to be able to take what I'm doing and take it further.

And so, in auditions, Bill Deamer watches the dancers closely. He agrees with Stephen Mear that technique is instantly visible:

Bill Deamer: When I take an audition I always have my associate teach, and while she's teaching, I'm walking the room, and I'm watching to see how people take to the choreography: their approach, their eye line, there are so many things, people don't realise that I'm watching from the moment they walk in the room, how they take to it. And it's a clear case of "they're going to get it or they're not." Then some you re-consider, "Hmm . . . yeah, that's possible, let's recall and let's see them again and work in another style." But I can immediately tell the dancers with technique.

Many musical theatre dancers will have trained in ballet. It's often seen as foundational and taught in most, if not all, conservatoire MT courses. Stephen Mear agrees with its importance, though it's not necessarily decisive for him in an audition:

Stephen Mear: I think ballet training is such a strong base to any technique, any sort of formal technique. Finding your centre, pirouetting, spotting, it's being in control, so I do think ballet is such a main thing to get hold of. I didn't think so at the beginning, because I was a tap dancer, but I desperately needed it and it helped tremendously.

Shaun Aquilina: And when you make decisions on your dancers for a show, are you more likely to pick the people who are ballet trained?

Stephen Mear: Not really, but as long as they've got a good technique. I think most of the people I've worked with are triple threat. I do love a good old triple threat more than anything! There's some great techniques being taught at colleges now, amazing techniques. For some reason, their bodies are doing a lot more than our bodies used to do.

Lynne Page was equally in favour of ballet training, though again, there is more than that to be seen in an audition:

Lynne Page: My perfect dancer would be somebody that's got an extraordinary, strong technique, and that means they've got a very good base of classical training. But I'm also a huge fan of contemporary dance, I always try and incorporate that in a lot of my work, so if I really ask them to fall to the floor or be quite angular or throw themselves off centre, they've got that in their bodies, as well. Then, if they've got some kind of specialty, like some little gem that they can bring to the table, occasionally there's something spectacular that they do that's unique. And then if they can tap, I quite often get tap in my shows but in quite an unorthodox way. I love strong, visceral, powerful dance-based actors that have got loads of muscularity. That's my favourite.

So our choreographers agreed on the importance of ballet but also agreed that there is more than ballet when it comes to dance in musical theatre. Matthew Bourne offered another reason why ballet is so useful in MT, and this was less to do with technique and more about the style of performance. He began by reflecting on the performers he selects for his dance company and those he selects for an MT production:

Matthew Bourne: There is more crossover than you think, actually, because the sort of dance productions that I do are very much narrative based. When I started out, I used to say we were a contemporary dance theatre company but, strangely, over the years, the sort of dancers that I go for more are less contemporary dancers, more MT dancers or ballet dancers, because ballet and MT have something very similar about them: they're about giving, telling a story, sending that out to an audience, whereas contemporary dance is often so internal, it's not about performing for an audience, it's about the audience having to come to you a little bit. So ballet and musical theatre have very similar approaches in their style.

I put this idea to Lynne Page, and she agreed:

Lynne Page: Exactly right. I do agree with that. I absolutely do agree with that. Yes, musical theatre and ballet are super presentational, and that has its purpose. But you can absolutely turn inward, because contemporary dance is a lot more low to the floor, it's a lot more internal. You don't generally go "ta-da!" with contemporary dance! But if you start to mix all those styles together within the same show, it can look really interesting. And finding dancers or performers that can do that means you've got a greater vocabulary to create a show.

Mixing styles and having a greater dance vocabulary both point towards a creative freedom which allows the choreographers to produce their best work, as does Bill Deamer's earlier point about technique being a 'body to hang the suit on'. And so it's important to remember that at an audition, choreographers are assessing whether a performer is of a standard to deliver, develop and even enhance their creative vision.

The other aspect of technique is the ability to meet the physical demands of a performance run and the MT standard of eight shows a week. Matthew Bourne and I discussed this, particularly because of the difficulties it caused his dance company when they moved *Swan Lake* into the West End:

Matthew Bourne: I think the story of *Swan Lake* going into the West End is a really unique and unusual one, because the kind of dancers I had in *Swan Lake* originally were people from the dance world who just don't do that many shows, nowhere near. If they're in a dance company, they do two or three shows a week, maybe, occasionally, with long gaps, that's the state of the industry, really. To suddenly do that many shows without proper cover or understudies was a shock to the system of all of us, really, we didn't really know how to do it. Whereas MT people, you know that's what you're going into, that's what it is. Eight shows a week can be quite inhuman at times, depending on what the show is. It's a different way of living, you may not want to speak all day if you're going to sing all night, that kind of thing. A lot of sacrifices need to be made.

Shaun Aquilina: And is that something you're aware of in audition?

Matthew Bourne: Difficult to see all those things in an audition. I mean, you can work people really hard and see if they flag, I suppose you can do that. [This was said with a look that suggested "I suppose you could, but I wouldn't."] But that's different to doing something over a long period of time, and whether someone's got the ability to do it. For my own company, there's a massive demand to be in the shows that I do, particularly something like *Swan Lake*, but I always say in the auditions, "I know you really want to be in this and it may be something you've grown up seeing, and it's your dream show, but it's really hard work, and it isn't for everyone, and ask yourself if this is what you want."

Shaun Aquilina: Do you have those conversations with MT people as well?

Matthew Bourne: Well, they tend to already know. I'm often dealing with people who don't really realise what it takes, the stamina needed. But you very rarely get that sort of person in a musical theatre company who is not pulling their weight. They already know, they've always known, what it requires. Very rarely do you ever encounter someone who's lazy or doesn't want to be there.

So a dancer's technique is directly linked to the priorities of the production: can they achieve the creative vision set by the choreographer, and can they meet the demands of the performance run? Ballet is seen as foundational, providing key aspects of physical control, balance, and support, but more than ballet is needed: what's needed is whatever the production calls for. And there are tricks and specialisms to be enjoyed too, which enhance the production. But now we move on to the part of musical theatre dance that all our choreographers considered to be the most important.

Storytelling

For our choreographers, the purpose of dance and movement on stage is to tell a story. Driving the narrative forward and revealing more about the characters and their relationships are the reasons our choreographers create their work:

Stephen Mear: That's a massive thing for me. I'm glad you said that: storytelling is so important to me. Not just "to dance", with nothing behind the eyes; I love storytelling. I love telling stories through dance, it's brilliant.

Matthew Bourne sees dance as another layer of communication with the audience. It enhances the whole performance and should be something to which the entire cast contributes:

Matthew Bourne: Good theatrical dancing is about telling a story. And what can you add to the bigger picture of the piece, to the whole, through the movement, through your particular skills, I think is very important. And I think all theatrical dance is like that. Whether you're the lead character, or you're a supporting character, or you're the ensemble, you're all feeding into that story, you're all trying to get the audience to be able to understand what it is. Particularly in nonverbal theatre, which a lot of MT theatre is, there are long sequences, sometimes, with no words, no dialogue, but through a dance number, you are often trying to forward the plot and keep telling that story. So I think everyone has to feed into it.

Bill Deamer believes that dance in musicals has advanced in recent years in its narrative capabilities, a development he noticed while working on *Follies* in 2017. However, he ended with a reminder that to make those advances in storytelling requires the strong techniques mentioned earlier:

Bill Deamer: We've gone so much further now with movement and that's what makes it exciting. When I went to the National Theatre and choreographed *Follies* with director Dominic Cooke, I was working with an incredible creative team. We had Stephen Sondheim in the room with us and orchestrator Jonathan Tunick, and to see all those disciplines come together in such an incredible show, with a line-up of brilliant actors, I cannot stress how important it is for a creative team to collaborate and work together. It was a wonderful experience that showed how far musical theatre has progressed and how powerful it can be. You can do so much more in musicals now and when people dare to take chances, magic happens. But to do that in choreography you must have a discipline.

Without a narrative underpinning, theatrical dance risks becoming an adornment that lacks substance, as Lynne Page commented:

Lynne Page: Even if you get a more dance heavy number in a musical, unless it's clear what story you're telling through that number, it becomes decorative. Whereas you can do a huge production number but if the audience understands the story that's going on throughout that production number as well, then, win-win! Actors that can really connect with that are so exciting.

The pleasure of a dance spectacle was in no way dismissed, as Matthew Bourne commented, but acknowledged to be something different from purposeful, narrative-driven theatrical dance:

Matthew Bourne: There are musicals like that, obviously, where that kind of thing can be great, I don't have a downer on it, I actually enjoy that sometimes where it is a number for the pleasure of being a number. And, as Stephen [Mear] said, things like *42nd Street* and a great bit of unison tap is joyful and thrilling and I love it. But I think good theatrical dancing, which is a slightly different thing, maybe, is about feeding into the story and how can you deliver that story better.

And it isn't only dance. Movement work adds its own layer of expression and emotion to the story:

Lynne Page: I particularly remember a sequence that was quite personal. I had an idea of trying to do something which was quite sad about a couple that couldn't communicate. And I did a workshop with some older actors where they'd been in a marriage for a very, very long time, and they got to that point of stasis, of not being able to communicate. And it was just an exercise of trying to talk to each other but with hand gestures. It was very small and delicate. It was like a conversation across the table but just using hand gestures. And that can look really boring if you're just moving your hands but if you've got an actor that can be trying to talk through their hands, and that talking just not work, it can be one of the most moving things in the world. So I did that exercise quite a lot for *Standing at the Sky's Edge*, and in the end found a couple of actors that were just extraordinary.

So performers in dance and movement auditions must tell the story the choreographer is trying to put across. They need to show a desire and an ability to connect with an audience and communicate a narrative to them. For Lynne Page, that also means finding performers who are willing to open up in the audition room:

Lynne Page: Vulnerability is key. It means they're not resistant, and I don't think some actors are resistant on purpose, they just haven't got over that barrier where they can be vulnerable, a fear of not feeling comfortable, a fear of looking silly, all of those things. But if they can invest, then you can create something really interesting with them.

Physicality

The physical looks and type of dancers now on the West End have developed and changed, so I was interested to know how our choreographers viewed that. They were enthusiastic; however, they acknowledged that some shows still require a particular look and physique:

Stephen Mear: I think that's brilliant because I've worked for Victoria Wood for years, choreographing her stuff, so I always had loads of body shapes. I did *The Witches of Eastwick* at the National which is all shapes and sizes and diversity, which is brilliant. But *Crazy For You*, *42nd Street*, you can't do that, really. They were meant to be chorus and that period. And the *42nd Street* ladies were curvier in those days, and they always look cute and that, but it's different depending on what show. If you want to do an Apache or something, you've got to have somebody that's strong or can lift, etc. so it depends what you're looking for. But I love characters, I love choreographing on characters, you can't beat it, because then half the audience think they can do it!

Stephen Mear also pointed out that there are shows where a dancer's look isn't only about style and period; it's relevant to the narrative:

Stephen Mear: *A Chorus Line* needs a certain look because that's the whole thing about it, they pour their hearts out and then at the end they're just in a line, in gold. There are certain shows that need showgirls and then there are certain shows that need loads of characters.

Casting also dictates which kind of performers can be used, particularly in the ensemble who can be playing multiple roles, as well as covering the principals. Bill Deamer encountered this when working on *42nd Street*:

Bill Deamer: In *42nd Street*, we have what I call "reality scenes", like the train station scene is a real scene, it takes place in a railway station; you also have the big show numbers like "Dames". It's finding the balance between the two. So actresses that are fine in their character roles have also got to become showgirls. You must always consider what's going to work for the show. Nowadays we look for real people. Just be yourself and you will be fine.

Casting non-traditional looking dancers can also add surprise and excitement to a production. Lynne Page spoke about this after recounting an experience on the more traditional side:

Lynne Page: I shot the film *Judy* and it was of a time period when she classically had the Feather Girls, and they were of that era, very tall, very slim, and that was part of the casting requirements of the film. If you've got free reign in the musical, I would say, actually, the gem of somebody that, to traditionally look at them, they don't come in presenting a perfect dancer's physique but actually they can really, really move, that's incredibly special. So I think talent overrides anything else.

And Matthew Bourne – who so often during his interview had his eye on the production as a whole – reminded me that any performer on the stage contributes to the theatrical truth and reality of that stage. And so the physical types the audience sees are so important to the overall impact of the production:

Matthew Bourne: With limited casting numbers at the moment, you're often telling a story where you've got to represent the world that this story is in with less people, so the more shapes and sizes and different types of people you have within your production makes it feel more like the world of that piece. If everyone looks a bit the same, you start to question it, unless it's relevant to the piece. *A Chorus Line*, for example, that is an example where I think you do want everyone to look like they're a dancer, because that's what it's about. They are auditioning to be in a Broadway show so lots of different shapes and sizes maybe not great in that show. But *Oliver!*, or any number of shows actually, most shows now, it's really a pleasure to see a real variety of people and ages as well. I think it's a really good thing, but it's specific to the show.

To bring this back to auditions, we see again that the casting decisions are rooted in what's right for the production, not just who's talented enough to get the job.

Individuality, uniformity and character

As we saw above, the presence of any performer on stage affects the whole picture being presented to an audience. Another aspect of this is the dynamic between a performer's individuality, personality and expressiveness, and the requirement for them to subsume that individuality into the larger group, ensemble or cast. This is clear in the vocal parts of a show where the riffs, timing and phrasing a singer might use to enhance a solo song would weaken an ensemble because the sound wouldn't be unified. And it's the same in dance. There are moments for dancers to shine as individuals, and there are moments when they need to form part of a unified group:

> **Stephen Mear**: I love individuality, if it's a show that's got individuals in. If it is something like *Crazy For You* or *Singin' in the Rain* where you've got to do those line-ups of big numbers, it's no good somebody else popping their head and trying to stand out, especially when the main part is Peggy Sawyer [*42nd Street*] who stands out anyway – it takes away from that story. I've got a couple of dancers that are my favourites that I love, and one of them drove me mad for popping her head, only because she was an individual, that's what she was, wasn't done on purpose, she was meant to be an individual, so I always got her jobs where she had a character part, as well, so she stood out in her own right.

Our choreographers are clear about the distinction between individual and ensemble performances when they're auditioning or rehearsing:

> **Stephen Mear**: I'll always tell them what I want, or you're allowed to be individual, you're allowed to give a bit more of yourself in this because it's an outdoors number, it's not where you're in "a show", it's where we're in the station in *42nd Street*, they're all characters running through the station, they're not in the show mode, as it were.

For Bill Deamer, a performer's ability to switch between those two modes is vital in auditions:

> **Bill Deamer**: I say to the actors: we're looking for individual characters who can then come together as a chorus line. And if you say that from the word go, they get it. Listen to the music – which is very important! – listen to the music and the way I'm using the music and then just be yourself. And then we'll dance it, and then I step in, and I say, "Right, let's do it again." And I may correct a few things, work through what the routine is about, and then I really tighten everything up, and you can see both worlds coming together, the dancer and the actor. And that's really important, that actors can live in both worlds.

> **Shaun Aquilina**: Both worlds, as in both the individual and the ensemble?

> **Bill Deamer**: Absolutely, absolutely. 100 per cent.

Some productions are more concerned with movement than dance, and then it's up to the auditionee to show characterful movement that, again, brings the production to life:

Matthew Bourne: Doing something like *Oliver!*, which I've just done, it's all very character based. It's not about dancing. It's not about dance technique. It's about movement that has its particular characters running through it. So you almost want people to do it in a different way, you don't want unison, you don't want clarity, in that sense. You want everyone to be a bit different. And it's the same working with young people: children are always going to move in a slightly different way and that's the charm of it. So, in some ways, that production is a little easier because you want that difference in people. Some productions, like if you're doing *Hello, Dolly!*, or *A Chorus Line*, or something like that, that maybe requires unison, precision of choreography. Obviously, you'd be struggling a bit if you didn't have those people who could do that. And that's where you're looking for the triple threats or at least the double threats of singing and dancing.

An important aspect of characterful movement is that it is natural and born out of the characters and their situation. For Matthew Bourne, this natural expression is vital to the success of musical theatre and its impact on the audience:

Matthew Bourne: You want the dancing and the singing to come out of a natural situation and feel like it's the only answer, the only way to go, and that it makes sense, especially in a musical that's not sung through, a musical that's got a book. Fred Astair made walking look like a dance and then he would just pick something up and throw it around, and it all looked like it was made up on the spot. That's a nice thing to have in a musical, it makes people accept it more.

I asked how a panel spots that in an audition:

Matthew Bourne: Sometimes it's just instinct. It's someone who makes you smile. Someone who does something in such a quirky way that you just think, oh, love them! It's hard to be specific but it's often just them, it's who they are, that appeals to you. I know for a fact that every director I've worked with, the people they love the most are the ones who are the most natural. But how do you be natural? It's very, very difficult. They want people to make mistakes, they like people making mistakes, they like people messing up and making a joke about it, I think that always goes down really well. I'm not saying come in and make loads of mistakes but it just shows humanity and that the person's a real person, and I think directors love that. And I think we are looking for the individual often, we're looking for diversity within our casting, we're looking for all kinds of diversity. And I think that's very appealing to audiences today. And appealing to be working with people who don't just stand there and wait to be told what to do, they have a viewpoint. That's maybe the way things have changed over the years, in a good way.

Other attributes of the performer

There are other attributes that affect our choreographers' decisions on whether to take a performer forward in an audition. Bill Deamer wants to see spontaneity and warns against learning routines so well that the performance lacks vitality:

> **Bill Deamer**: With a first-round dance audition, when you've worked the first two days of auditions and you're continuing to see people over the coming weeks, the audition routine gets learnt by dancers before they come into the room. People go away and they learn it. Which sometimes doesn't work, because by the time they're there in front of you, they know it so well, they're just going through the steps, nothing's going on behind the eyes because they haven't gone through the process of learning it with me or an associate. So, you must be careful of that one too.

There's also the question of style. In the first chapter, casting director David Grindrod defined two distinct styles of choreography, earthbound and airbound. When I put this to our choreographers, Matthew Bourne said a mix of the two is ideal:

> **Matthew Bourne**: Hopefully, a bit of both, depending on what you're doing. I do like earthy, into the ground, movement, but I also like a bit of flying around the stage, so I think a combination of the two is rather good.

Bill Deamer had a more candid assessment:

> **Bill Deamer**: Well, that's a casting director's way of looking at it. A mix of the two is certainly good. But I think that choreographically, it depends on what style of dance you're doing and the demands of the show.

Some of our choreographers identified with having their own particular styles:

> **Bill Deamer**: A lot of the West End performers have worked with me, they know my style. And youngsters coming in, there are certain musical theatre schools that pick up on that style and start to use it so that when they come to audition for me, they've got a rough idea of what I do.

And for Bill Deamer, this goes further in an audition when a performer not only understands the style of his work but his creative vision, too:

> **Bill Deamer**: There's an intelligence, there's an understanding, of what I want to say with my choreography. Sometimes I've seen someone who's maybe not got the best technique but they really do understand the style of what I want.

We'll see again later how understanding the vision of the creative team can be hugely important to an auditionee's success.

Stephen Mear's training remains key to his style of choreography, but it's something that can challenge performers when they audition for him:

Stephen Mear: I was trained in Matt Mattox, his form of jazz. There's also Luigi Jazz, there's loads of different styles of jazz. But Matt Mattox is isolation so it's fabulous for your coordination and your brain. And I put that into a lot of my choreography. Some people have been told they're brilliant at college and they've come in the room and I've thought, err, well actually they're not, they're not disciplined enough to do my stuff. They're alright doing their own, if you say to them, "Everybody just do eight counts of your own at the end," but I very rarely do.

Lynne Page says her work is so contrasting that she doesn't have a choreographic style:

Lynne Page: No, I don't think I do! No! I mean I might have some familiar traits but I think every job is different, and what is required on every project is very different. So I may have similar approaches in the fact that I'll always want the performance to connect with narrative but performers that I would audition for *Spring Awakening* would be very different to my current project, *Tammy Faye*. So no, I think it varies project to project.

Lynne Page did discuss the need she felt to project strong female personas on stage:

Lynne Page: I suppose if there really is anything that I would lean into it's that I always want the women to be more than just decorative. I don't often do shows where I just need beautiful women to do something quite light. I really want . . . I mean, maybe this is from my own politics or my own standpoint . . . I want the women to be as visible and as viscerally strong as the men. So, I am interested in very, very strong female performers.

Finally, our choreographers also assess the auditionee's personality. As with the Casting Directors in Chapter 1, they expressed a clear preference for auditionees who are nice to work with:

Stephen Mear: I've got this thing: even if it might take them a little bit longer to get it, I'd rather give that to them than to someone that's brilliant technically but is a pain in the arse, because there are those about that keep getting jobs. And I would rather have somebody that's going to take a couple of weeks longer but I know will get it, because of how passionate they are and how lovely they would be in a company.

Bill Deamer agrees and says he considers the closeness of working together through rehearsals. But he also gives auditionees some allowance because of the pressure they're under:

Bill Deamer: When people walk into the room, I'm also thinking, do I want to spend the next two, three months working with this person? Do I want them in the room being part of the creative process, working with me? That's where people really do have to be themselves, and that's all I can ask. And it is difficult:

you want the job. And the nerves are there, and when those nerves are there, people do tend to push, but that's fine, I understand that, I get it.

So, there are many elements to consider when deciding on an auditionee, including technique, performance, individuality, understanding, and being nice to work with. But I wanted to know which are the most important when our choreographers make their decisions.

Principal values

When it came to the principal values for choosing an auditionee, there is one thing Stephen Mear looks for above all:

> **Stephen Mear**: I love seeing people who have got passion when they dance, you can't beat it, you'll just be drawn to that person in a room. I love a strong technique. A technique is very important. But not just somebody that can whack their legs up, somebody that dances from the soul and dances from the heart. You can't teach that. So that's my thing I look for the most: passion.

That isn't just passion in performance; it's about the auditionee's whole approach:

> **Stephen Mear**: I think it's looking at someone that comes in the room, means business, they want to be there, they're passionate about the show or they want to work with this creative team. It's something about being hungry but being good. And you can see it straight away.

Bill Deamer also wants to see passion in his auditionees but spoke about two other aspects first:

> **Bill Deamer**: The main two are technique and musicality. They're the main two for me. But the times I've written at an audition, at a recall: "Shame: deadeye!" Because it's not coming from anywhere.

On that last sentence, Bill indicated his core. Core engagement is very important to him, and he recounted an experience of working on the new tour of *Cats* to show why:

> **Bill Deamer**: Yesterday, I was rehearsing the Gumbie Cat-Jennyanydots [Bill created the new choreography for it, for the 2014 London Palladium production]. I went to see the young group of new cats who go out on an international tour in a couple of weeks with this amazing show and they danced the number for me and my first note was "none of you are using your centres." And it is something that is happening with today's generation, it all comes from the arm, there's nothing central, which in acting and singing is a no-no, and in choreography it's a definite no-no. It must come from the centre within, otherwise it's just arms and legs moving. I gave them the note, and it's a tap number, and we were going through it bit by bit, and as we were doing this – I wasn't making a point of correcting the

actual tap beats with the feet, I was talking about the arm lines and the structure of the body and where it should be – the actual fact is that the tap became right on point because it was coming from somewhere.

Shaun Aquilina: So that core engagement is both a physical and an emotional engagement?

Bill Deamer: Absolutely! And as soon as that light goes on in your core, you're in control.

Lynne Page shares some of the values discussed by Bill Deamer and Stephen Mear, particularly the emotional engagement:

Lynne Page: I suppose it's just if they move you. That's a weird, dark art, really, isn't it? But I can usually see whether somebody is putting in their heart and soul, and can think the thoughts whilst doing the movement. And if they can inhabit the movement, then it becomes very moving. But usually, I can tell when an actor is really invested in movement, and you get something from it. Sometimes, it's unfortunate that some actors are taught to brilliantly act but then they almost shut down when they move. I try and release them – it's exactly the same process, they're just telling a story in a different way – and the actors that can connect with that are usually the ones that are really exciting to work with.

But Lynne Page also looks for the interesting individual as part of making the entire stage hold the audience's attention:

Lynne Page: It'll be a combination of technique and drive and some kind of pizzazz depending on the show. And charisma. I always feel that wherever the audience looks on the stage they want to be interested in that person. I often make work where the story is always integrated and therefore you cannot afford to have anybody on stage that if an audience member casts their eye on them, even if they're at the back, that they are not fully interested in that performer. So often I have quite a mixed bag of performers, because each one has to do something collectively, but they all have to be unique. So there's just got to be something about them that draws your eye.

Matthew Bourne spoke about passion too, but for him, it's passion to communicate, and that is at the root of the whole theatrical experience:

Matthew Bourne: What I can tell in a performer is how passionate they are about movement, and the passion of that is wanting to convey that to somebody else. For me, that's the beginning of acting. It's the beginning of storytelling. It's the beginning of connecting with an audience. You can see that in an audition. It's not about people who are in your face all the time. And it's not always about smiling and showing your teeth. It's a sincerity, I think, that you're looking for, an integrity and a sincerity in the movement. That tells you a lot, in a short space of time.

Our choreographers' principal values are passion, expression, communication and emotion; they want to see those in their auditionees because sharing those values as well as sharing an artistic vision is more likely to lead to a successful collaboration.

Musical theatre isn't only an art form, though; it's an industry and, as such, has to deal with the pressures and challenges of the real world, to which we now turn.

Background checks and references

As we saw in Chapter 1, forming a company that will support each other and enhance the production is highly desirable. For the creative team, a key part of this is the rehearsal period, often an intense, collaborative and creative period of working closely with the performers. And there's the performance run to consider, too. Stephen Mear is so strict on getting the right people that bad behaviour outweighs any level of talent and ability:

Stephen Mear: I do backup checks on all of them. I talk to the colleges, if they're straight out of college, their teachers, you know. You only need a couple of bad apples in a company and it starts to go through the rest. And especially if it's a principal. That's a big no-no. Because principals lead a company. I've only had one or two but I had a big go at them, because then the ensemble think they can behave like idiots as well, and that doesn't work for me.

Shaun Aquilina: So how big a no-no? Let's say you've got a very passionate, very capable person, but they're not living up to those company standards.

Stephen Mear: Massive, 100 per cent no-no.

Shaun Aquilina: So, out?

Stephen Mear: Out.

Lynne Page agrees that how a performer behaves in a company is decisive for future work. She says that it's something that has become even more valued in recent years:

Lynne Page: Hugely important. I feel like the industry is very small and, right now, especially within the Broadway community and West End even post Covid, there is way more emphasis on a collective kindness within companies. So if anybody has been unkind on a project before or, especially in America at the moment, if they've missed too many shows, if somebody has behaved in a way that is not going to be positive moving forward, the creative team will know about that and that can often be the difference of whether that person gets a contract or not.

The other choreographers reinforced this idea of a small industry where bad reputations spread quickly. Here's Bill Deamer:

Bill Deamer: We all have our own little red book, and we all talk, all choreographers and directors talk. That's all you need to know.

And Stephen Mear:

Stephen Mear: It's a small business. I don't care what anyone says, it's a very small business, all us choreographers and directors speak to each other all the time. I get phone calls all the time about shows and what's so-and-so like, and likewise, so just keep that in the back of your mind.

Those checks and references are a process, though. Lynne Page always wants to hear what the auditionee has to say:

Lynne Page: If somebody's had a bad time on their previous show, it's an investigation, because there's always two sides and you always will hear the performer's voice as well. Sometimes those conversations go, "Well, I was really unhappy on that job," and you go, "Ok, right, on this one, things will be different."

There are also times when the auditionees are observed before they enter the room. Matthew Bourne recalled an example of an auditionee ruining their opportunity because of their behaviour before they went in:

Matthew Bourne: When we were casting *Oliver!*, someone in the green room, waiting to come in and audition, asked one of our leading actors why he was auditioning for this little part, "Oh, is that all you can get?" kind of thing. And I just heard very bad vibes about this performer that didn't come across in the room but from everything I'd heard they said in the green room: putting down other actors, putting the show down a bit like "what are we here for?" and being negative! Obviously, you don't want that! That's a no-no, straight away. So even when you're not in the room, it's good to be positive, because you never know who's overhearing you.

And there are other ways to find out about performers and get to know who might be forming the company. Matthew Bourne uses social media:

Matthew Bourne: I'm nosey! If I'm considering someone for a show, I tend to look them up on Instagram and get a sense of who they are a bit from that, what sort of things they post. Sometimes you get a sense of their career a little bit, "Oh, they've done this. Oh, they did that, and they went to . . ." or they're friends with that person. I think putting a company together is not just about individual talents, the word company is very important, and I think you want people who are going to get on with each other, are going to be nice to work with, who are going to be a great team, who are going to look after each other during a long run. So in the limited time that you have, something like Instagram is quite useful for a snapshot of people's lives.

So a significant part of getting the right person for the job is getting someone who will strengthen the company as a whole, and because that's more difficult to measure in an audition than someone's abilities in singing, dancing and acting, creatives often look elsewhere to ensure they're offering jobs to the right people.

Now it's time to look more closely at the audition itself and what exactly goes on in the room.

Entering the room

Our choreographers are assessing their auditionees from the moment they enter the room. They assess attitude, professionalism and personality, as these qualities are important to the success of the rehearsal process and performance run. Stephen Mear wants to see a high level of professionalism from his auditionees:

> **Stephen Mear**: I'm very into people coming into the room and they mean business. I love that. It's very American. We English are quite apologetic sometimes. Americans aren't like that because America is so big so if you don't stand out and stand your ground, you don't get noticed. So I love people who come in a room, not arrogant, there's a fine line between arrogant and wanting to be brilliant at what you do, and you can see that, you can tell the ones who just love it and want to get this job: they're prepared, they've got the songs, they've got everything ready. There's no standing at the back chatting with their friends at the start of the stretching or the warming up.

Similarly, Bill Deamer wants to see an efficient, professional manner, partly because of the pressure on the panel to see so many performers over the days and weeks of the auditions:

> **Bill Deamer**: The golden rule is not to faff. Do not come into the room and allow nerves to make you gabble, "Well, I would have sung this, but I thought this, and I did this, but the dog ate that . . ." I sympathise but when you're seeing one actor every ten minutes, you don't want to hear that. Come in and say, "Hello! You've asked for a song: I've got this or this, what one would you like?" And then if the director says, "Well, you choose," "Ok, I'll do this one," that's it. Just say what you want to sing, and then if you sing that and we want to hear something else, then be ready with another song. Which often happens. Come in and be prepared. A tip – always have your music ready for the pianist.

All our choreographers are able to discern the level of preparation and research auditionees have put in:

> **Bill Deamer**: Do your homework and be yourself. They're my main two rules. They really are, because you can't just go in and bluff. You've got to know what you're doing. I remember doing a production of *The Boy Friend* at the Menier Chocolate Factory – it's 20s pastiche and an actor came in with a rock number!? Do your homework!

Lynne Page says the level of preparation colours the casting panel's view of the auditionee:

> **Lynne Page**: If they came in and they were singing, and they were acting, and they hadn't really prepped, you go, ok, well, you had a week to get this song together. And some people really prep, and some people don't. And those people that do, you're going to have a much more open minded and fond lens of looking at their audition because you can already see the work they put in. But

if somebody doesn't know the lyrics, or they haven't really rehearsed the sides, you can tell.

Researching the panel is important, too, and as Matthew Bourne points out, it's another aspect that can make them look more favourably on an auditionee:

Matthew Bourne: Do your research, oh definitely, about the show or the people you're auditioning for. Very wise to do that. I mean, we've all got egos, if someone mentions something that you've done that they liked, you can't help but be warm to that person, it's just human nature. But also, know what the type of show is, don't come in and do something that doesn't seem relevant at all to the production that you're auditioning for. Know the people, know their work, maybe there's things you've seen that they've done that you've liked, you think maybe that's the sort of thing they want from me. I think if you go in cold, you're not giving yourself the best advantage, really, are you.

Interestingly, when it comes to research, Matthew Bourne has noticed a shift in attitude from performers, not just for auditions but for roles and productions more widely:

Matthew Bourne: I'm a big research guy when I'm doing a show, and I want the company to be that, as well. But it's harder these days, because most people have a different view on these things. For many years, people would love all the lists of books and DVDs and things I would make them watch to develop their characters or the atmosphere of a show that we were doing. Now, it's "well that's in our own time," you know? "I'm not paid to do that," I get that a little bit now. It's never come up before, it's a different generation of people. Fair enough, they're right . . . I guess? But if you're into it and there's a film that would help you with your performance, do you really need to be paid to watch it? I don't know. But I'm old school.

The number of dancers who are seen for a show can be very high. In the previous chapter, we saw there were around 1,000 auditionees across the re-cast for *Wicked*. Bill Deamer gave a similar number for the dancers alone, in *42nd Street*:

Bill Deamer: For *42nd Street*, last year [2023], we saw approximately 900 dancers. And for that show, we were looking for twenty: ten boys and ten girls.

As dancers are likely to be assessed in groups, I wanted to know how many auditionees our choreographers would see at one time:

Stephen Mear: I try not to have any more than twenty-five. That's the most I would do because otherwise you can't see the wood for the trees, if you're not careful.

Bill Deamer: Depending on the size of studio, I normally see, at the most, thirty at once. Because you've got to give everyone a chance. it's important that you see everyone clearly and give them the chance to show what they can do. Once a routine is learnt I normally see people in groups of four.

Auditionees need some strategies to stand out in a group of twenty-five to thirty. Matthew Bourne says there's a balance between making sure they're seen but not crowding out anyone else, and that it's the panel's responsibility to observe their auditionees:

Matthew Bourne: Don't be at the back all the time but also don't just be at the front all the time. Make sure you're seen, try and keep moving around a bit. I think, hopefully, integrity shines through. It's not always their job to be seen in a room of a lot of people, we have to make sure we see them, and we have to divide them up and put them into smaller groups. That's why numbers are used. I know it's a horrible thing to have a number on but you can't possibly get all the names in that short space of time, and that is how we get to be able to see people properly and note those people properly.

In group auditions, there is also the chance to observe how auditionees interact with each other on a social-professional level. In the previous chapter, Stuart Burt made a point of noticing this, but Lynne Page says that, for her, that's something that comes later:

Lynne Page: I would love to say that I'm catching them but I'll probably be absolutely focused on what's being presented in front of me. I'll be literally single-minded and sharp-focused on what's being delivered. Possibly I might catch a kind conversation but I think that might be the casting director's more holistic way of looking at it. My process would be much further down the line to research whether a person's genuinely a positive person for the role.

Matthew Bourne is aware of how auditionees conduct themselves in his calls and gave several examples of behaviour he looks out for:

Matthew Bourne: How they are with each other, how generous they are with each other. If there's a little bit of a partnering thing to be done, how gentlemanly the men are with the women. How they speak to each other. Anyone who makes the audition about their audition rather than a shared experience with their partner, I think those sorts of things are red flags for me. Sometimes people who ask too many questions just for the sake of asking a question, just to be noticed, we can see through that. But a good question, a well-placed question that makes sense, is also a good thing to do.

Auditioning principals can be different, with solo auditions more likely. However, the standards are still rigorously upheld:

Bill Deamer: When we auditioned for *42nd Street* last year [2023], we were looking for our Peggy Sawyer, the leading lady. Nicole-Lily Baisden came in the room and after the first dance round the creative team all agreed that she looked perfect for the role. She sang, and she read, and everyone was happy. "However," I said, "if she's going to play Peggy Sawyer, she's got to be even better." So, I took her back into the rehearsal room and I worked with her for an afternoon on all the different styles of choreography in the show and at the end of the day I just shook her hand and said, "Welcome to the show: you're Peggy Sawyer." And she had certainly earnt it!

I was also interested to know how much of a routine an auditionee would need to learn in the room to be successful. Stephen Mear was more interested in the drive his auditionees show:

Stephen Mear: When people are just hungry to do your work or to do that show, it's so wonderful to see.

Shaun Aquilina: And if you've got a very passionate performer, what's the minimum amount of the routine you want to see learnt in the audition?

Stephen Mear: 40 per cent. I wouldn't accept any lower than that.

Shaun Aquilina: So that's being able to do 40 per cent of what you've set them?

Stephen Mear: Yeah. Because I know that I could get the rest out of them in a rehearsal room.

Stephen Mear prioritised his value of passion over that of technical ability, because the rehearsal period allows for that. Bill Deamer was more wary of the pressures of the rehearsal period and set his percentage a little higher:

Bill Deamer: I would expect 50, 60 per cent, really. The reason being that, a lot of the time now, rehearsals can be short, and if you've got a short rehearsal period you've got to know that they can pick it up quick, otherwise you're in trouble. I've just finished *Hello, Dolly!* and we had eight weeks rehearsal but when you've got the usual three, four weeks and you're on, then you've got to know that they can pick it up.

Matthew Bourne made the point that how effectively a dancer learns material isn't necessarily a reliable indicator of how good they are for the show:

Matthew Bourne: Some people are very quick at picking up material, doesn't mean they're the best people, it just means they're quick. Some people will take a day or two, or they'll come in the next day and they'll have mastered it, and they're as good as anyone else. So you have to bear that in mind a bit and I think Stephen's probably very aware of that, having done so many shows now, where you see how people develop but all end up in a place where you're happy. So I think that's very true, that what you can see in an audition – if people are relaxed enough to be themselves which is quite hard, admittedly – is that passion, not just for the art form, but the wanting to express something.

Lynne Page wanted a broader indication of technical ability and is interested in discovering hidden abilities in her auditionees:

Lynne Page: I will really push their skill set and see what variety of dance they've got in there. And that's always interesting to me, if they're multidisciplined, if you get somebody that may have had musical theatre training but could be a bit more left of centre and a bit more avantgarde, so you push them in different directions that they might not be expecting. I'll always have an idea of what I need for the musical and then just really try and get as much out of the performers in the auditions.

And when it comes to fast learners, the matter again comes back to technique but also personality and the potential for a positive working relationship:

Lynne Page: I would just want to know that they've got enough technique to be able to get around work that might be tricky and fast. So basically, they need to have enough technique. But I would be looking for just somebody I could work with. Obviously, if they couldn't pick up the steps and we needed people that could really do it, then that's a different thing. But for me, it's more gut, it's people that really stand out and if I really like them, and I know that they'll get there – I can tell that they'll get there – then that's important to me.

Once an auditionee is performing, panel members usually have a way of noting their audition and assessing where to place them. We'll see in the next chapter how Musical Director Gareth Valentine marks his auditionees with an A, B, C, D rating system, but here, Bill Deamer explained how he works. It's interesting to note how much attention he is paying to each auditionee as they go through the process:

Bill Deamer: I have a grid system: 1, 2, 3. 1 is excellent, no problem. 2 is yes. 3 is well, maybe if they're a great singer and actor. I always do that, because you don't want to throw out some of your best singers and actors who are not quite up to the dance at that point, but you think could get away with it choreographically. So then – this always happens at an audition – we dance them, and I see them in fours, right? And I have their CVs in front of me. And I don't just go straight into the dance – "Right, you four, please wait." I then double check through the CVs again, then I think to myself, "Yeah, well, she's not the best dancer . . . Oh wow! She sung with the Glyndebourne opera! Right, okay." And then I'll signal the dancers to begin. And so, you weigh it up: "Well, absolutely, she's got through, and she's brilliant at that, and, oh my, she's been at the National, she's a great actress." It's not easy. I'm working just as hard as they are, just pulling it together, seeing what's possible.

As well as dancer-led pieces, our choreographers all create movement and choreography for actor-led musicals. It's a particular specialism of Lynne Page, and when we discussed this, she began by telling me how it changes her audition process:

Lynne Page: Everything starts with the script so you will be very much aware whether it's more of an actor-led musical. And if it is that, then I would be looking for people that can move in an interesting way, not necessarily something that is highly skilled, but a way that they can do storytelling through movement, and that I could build something from that. So it would probably be a variety of tasks in that I might ask them to do an emotion through movement.

One of those tasks is improvisation. For Lynne Page, improvisation is the beginning of her work of creating movement that fits the actor. But it can be tough in an audition:

Lynne Page: Actors and dancers always give me feedback that they hate me asking them to improvise in an audition! But I just find out so much about people through improvisation because, unless it's a very strict "5, 6, 7, 8" musical, then I'm obviously always going to want to bring out of the actor what is going to feel comfortable for them and ultimately make them look really good on stage. But that process is usually that it will inherently come from something that's unique to them and I will mould it. So, for an actor-led musical there'll be some steps so that I know they can move in unison if I need them to, and then I'll probably do a wide range of things that is often based on some sort of narrative. If it was a joyous piece, I would ask them to do some steps but then reassure them that it's not about the steps, it's about how they can inhabit those steps with joy, and if they go wrong, it's fine.

The importance of movement was also acknowledged by Bill Deamer, who showed that it can be as expressive as dance:

Bill Deamer: It's just wonderful when you're working with actors at any level and you're dancing and you suggest, "Well, why don't we just forget the step, and just all take a little walk in a style." And just to walk in a style, with people who can really do it: magic happens, before you go near the pirouettes and the tap routines. It's an openness, an expressiveness, it's an understanding of the period that you're working in. It's experience.

One of the key factors in the audition room is the auditionee's ability to take direction. We'll see it come up for all the different creatives. For Stephen Mear, it's a matter of discipline and detail:

Stephen Mear: I choreograph little things in off-rhythms and the simplest things that can just throw you, and I see who's got the discipline to keep their eye on the assistant that's teaching it, to get it how they're doing it, and the ones who want to do it their way. There's a lot want to do it their way.

Shaun Aquilina: So that discipline is important to you?

Stephen Mear: Yeah, very. I'm big on discipline. I really am.

Bill Deamer has tested how his auditionees take re-direction by changing the whole style of a number:

Bill Deamer: I've done a jazz routine and then turned it into a tap routine for the recall. Then you've really got to know what you're doing, absolutely. But by that, I mean you've got to know what your music is. Bringing people back for a recall and you ask, "Do you remember the routine we did last week?" And they all say, "Oh yes, of course," and they do it. All good. You then explain that "now we're going to use the same music but this time with tap choreography." And then the whole room changes. Seeing how they cope with change. Can they see the creative's vision? So, if I bring them back for a recall and do the same routine, it's good to see how they've remembered the original routine and how accurate they dance it and then how they cope with changing it to a different style. And that's part of acting: listening and picking it up. And keeping it fresh.

For Matthew Bourne, taking direction and re-direction in an audition is really about whether a performer can embody the creative vision of the panel. That ability is essential to a collaborative process and may explain why all our creatives place such importance on taking direction in an audition:

Matthew Bourne: I think it's key. To do it once, then get some notes from the director and/or the musical director, and then to apply those notes in the moment, is really, really telling and really promising and hopeful for further development. You can't get everything in an audition but you think, ah! they got that note! They took that note, they understood what you were saying, that's good, that means they'll take more, and they like to get notes, and they understand what it is you're trying to go for. You can't expect people to come in and know what you want. They have a take on a number, they've come in with it, it may be completely against what you've been thinking, but if you can give them a little steer towards what you want, and they do that, then I think those people tend to win through.

And Matthew Bourne added that taking re-direction shouldn't be underestimated by performers, as sometimes it is crucial to their success:

Matthew Bourne: Often that one little note is the thing that's going to get them the job, if they really deliver that one thing. It's not just "oh, wouldn't it be nice if it was this," "oh, yeah, maybe," – it's the key to the audition. Often when someone's left, it's very regularly said that "well, they really got that note that you gave them, that was very promising." They tend to go into the tick pile straight away. I think that's a very big thing in auditions.

Taking direction develops into a larger way of working, that of collaboration. This was also key for all our choreographers. Stephen Mear says his process has developed so that now he looks for dancers who can collaborate by bringing their own creativity to the rehearsal process:

Stephen Mear: When I started, I was very "This is what I want: I want to do these steps, and this step, and I want this pattern . . ." and then I worked with Matthew Bourne, who works very different to that. He lets them create stuff in the room, whereas for me, years ago I would have said, "That's not choreography because you're not teaching," but that's total rubbish, because what he is, is a genius. So now I let people bring something to the table. If they can do tricks I'll add that in, I'll do it on the other side, if they want to do it on the other leg, I'm very open. But at first, I was too robotic with the way I was choreographing. But that's through learning from loads of people, brilliant people.

However, there is a balance, and larger groups need stricter leadership:

Stephen Mear: When you've got forty tap dancers in a room, you can't be doing that. For those big numbers, I do patterns and I do set a lot of that before I go in the room. The freer ones, I'll let people do their own tricks and lifts, what they feel happy doing, to make my stuff look better.

Collaboration goes across the audition panel, too. Matthew Bourne says he will rely on other creatives for an overall view on how an auditionee might fit into a production:

Matthew Bourne: You're very much having to listen to the needs of everyone involved in the production. It could be a director or co-director, or particularly the musical director and the music side of things, that's not something I'm an expert in. I've got views on musical abilities in people, and what they do when they sing, and how they sing, but I've got no technical ability or experience or knowledge, so I would very strongly listen to the musical director, I think, and their view on whether this person fits into the production in a way that's useful.

Another aspect of performance that becomes a deciding factor in dance auditions is musicality. Bill Deamer was particularly insistent on this, as we saw above, placing it among his principal values. It's something he's been passionate about since his training:

Bill Deamer: I was fortunate to learn a lot of my tap technique in America, and there you are encouraged not to use counts, but listen to the music. This way the orchestration becomes so much part of the choreography. I have an associate, and I have two assistants, and when we go into a studio to create a number, I break it down into counts and then orchestral sections. It's the old saying, "we dance to music, not counts." That sounds gauche but it's true. You listen to the music and where the strings are going and where the brass is going, and you can feel it, and then it all comes together. But you dance to the music . . . the times I've said it at an audition: listen to what's being played, listen to where it comes in the music. And there are people that do get it, even when it's just a piano arrangement.

I asked Bill what he sees in an audition that tells him a dancer is connected to the music. He says it's clear from the music's introduction:

Bill Deamer: I always set quite a difficult pickup into the music to start. So there's an introduction on the piano, and you can really tell when you watch a dancer in that intro, you can feel the ones who really get it because they light up! They take the music and they use that intro to take them into the scene and immediately I'm interested. You can see the ones that, from the word go, get the feel of it. It's fascinating.

Shaun Aquilina: It sounds like taking an in-breath for singing: you know whether they're going to make a good sound from the quality of the in-breath.

Bill Deamer: It's exactly the same. Absolutely.

Finally, we addressed something that all auditionees have to deal with: nerves. Matthew Bourne says it's difficult to watch, and panels try to support auditionees, especially in the UK:

Matthew Bourne: It's horrible when you see someone shaking or going very red. You can almost see it developing while they're there, or the desperation in the eyes when they can't remember the words or something. And you just do your best to try and make people feel better. And I must say, having seen auditions in America and here, I think most directors here are really lovely about the way they treat people. They allow them another chance to start again. Most directors I've worked with here allow people to do everything they've brought in, from beginning to end. They don't cut into what people are doing unless there is a problem of some sort. So I think people are very generous. And even if they weren't that good on that day, maybe even send them some notes and invite them in again. But sometimes, it's an inevitable thing, and getting over nerves is something you have to fight in this business, isn't it. And also, the whole sense of rejection and the fear of rejection, and have an attitude for yourself towards that.

At times, having a professional relationship with someone on the panel can heighten an auditionee's nerves, rather than relax them. Stephen Mear has seen that when auditionees put in too much effort for him:

Stephen Mear: I've known people that I've worked with before and had them come in, to audition for something else, and I've gone, "They're so nervous!" I'm like, Wow! And they say sometimes it's hard, they know I've got them in so they want to do a good audition for me, and the amount of times they screw up is quite interesting because they're just trying to be good because I've got them in. And it's hard to get seen for so many things nowadays.

So strategies to deal with nerves might be needed. Bill Deamer acknowledges it's difficult but suggests using the nerves and being prepared are best for an auditionee:

Bill Deamer: You must channel that energy – it's easy for me to say – channel that energy, go in, and be yourself. The panel want you to be good, we want you in the show, so go in and be good. That's easier said than done, and with the hundreds and hundreds of people that are all auditioning, it's tough! But the only way you really do it is by doing your homework, having your songs ready, being warm and fit when you get in the room, because without that you won't get through, you can't bluff.

As well as the auditionee controlling their nerves, the panel has its role in setting the tone of the auditions. Our choreographers acknowledged that they can, and should, improve the experience for auditionees. For Stephen Mear, that's something he learned from one of Britain's leading directors:

Stephen Mear: *Anything Goes* at the National, Trevor Nunn's last show that he did there was one of my early ones, and that was probably one of the best experiences in my whole theatre career. I learned from him how to be generous to people that came to audition and give them time. He would never let anybody in the room unless he'd read their CV: one, because he says most of them have done *Les Mis*, and he said, "I can't know everybody", but he said he loved to know so he could say, "Oh you've done *Les Mis*," he was so generous, he has so much respect for people coming in for auditions. He taught me how to care about people in an audition. He will go above and beyond if it means getting the best out of everybody in an audition, making them feel comfortable.

Matthew Bourne feels a similar responsibility:

Matthew Bourne: It's our job as auditioners to make sure we do see everyone, because they've given up their time, they've come in, they're prepared, they've travelled, often at their own expense. There's a side to it where we have a responsibility as well to give them a good audition, and to make sure they feel they've been seen, and to make sure they feel good about the fact they've come and given their time for nothing. I think probably too much is talked about it the other way around but I think we have a responsibility as well.

There are also times when an audition process can go on too long, frustrating both the auditionees and the panel. Stephen Mear put it succinctly:

Stephen Mear: By the third audition you should really know, and if you don't then you need to get your act together.

Casting a new show and re-casting an ongoing show

Our choreographers agree with the casting directors that the audition process changes, depending on whether they are working on a new show, a re-cast or a new production of an existing show. Stephen Mear says that, on a new show, the absence of clear direction can make it difficult to know whom to cast, and the situation is much easier if there has been a workshop stage:

Stephen Mear: A new show is a lot harder, especially if you're not directing, you're choreographing, because you're not sure what the director is going for as well as you. But we did do four years of workshops [for *The Witches* at the National Theatre], and I joined late, so by the time I got to auditions, I could go, Oh, I know what she [director Lyndsey Turner] wants, I know what she's looking for. *Betty Blue Eyes* was hard because I wasn't sure how far we were going, because we didn't do a lot of workshops, we only did a couple. But I was surrounded by Richard Eyre and Anthony Drewe and George Stiles, and we're old friends so they were easy to talk to about everything.

Bill Deamer says ongoing shows can be a matter of checking in, unless it's a substantial cast change, and then the process almost begins again:

Bill Deamer: An ongoing show, you let the associates, and the assistants, look after it. I always go in regularly and see my work to make sure it's okay, but you have to trust your associates and those people who are employed to look after the show. That's their job, that's what they do and that's great. If it's a complete cast change after a year, I recall when we did the recast of *Follies*, we revisited a lot of the show and some of it was re-directed and choreographed in a different way, that's the way the director and his creative team worked on this production. It was an intricate and amazing process. Whereas sometimes you can recast a show and keep it relatively the same. But one must always consider the actors taking over and what they can bring to the production. I'm always happy to work with a new cast and whilst keeping the choreography clean you go for a completely new chemistry, which is normally what happens. Keep a show tight and keep it going.

Matthew Bourne agrees that, at least with principals coming into a long-running show, it's important to allow some changes and creativity. He encourages this to give the leads ownership of their performance:

Matthew Bourne: I think leading performers, even in a revival, you want to give them the sense that they've brought something of themselves to it, and that we are open to some change in it, to make them feel like it's theirs. I remember that experience people had of *A Chorus Line*, when the original production was revived in London, where they were taught it almost gesture by gesture, where to pause in a line, and even the scenes were choreographed completely, and everyone felt very limited in what they could do and didn't enjoy that, I don't think. I think performers want to feel that they can make it their own and be creative within it. And I think you give more leeway to leading performers in that sense, and use what it is they have. Like all the various Fagins I've had over the years, when you've got Rowan Atkinson, you want to use what he can do, his crazy, eccentric movement. You want to say play with that and change it, let him do what do what he can do! And then someone else comes along and they are not such a great mover so you have to find some things that work for them. So it keeps it alive, as well.

Whichever type of production, there's scope for auditionees to show their creativity and surprise the panel. This can spark new creative ideas:

Bill Deamer: Often someone can audition who's totally different to what you had in mind, and they dance, and you say, "Actually they're great, we can go down that road! Yes! Let's try that!"

Being open to that level of surprise and new ideas from an auditionee is something Stephen Mear actively brings into the room:

Stephen Mear: Sometimes as a director you think, oh I know who'd be great at this part, and then somebody comes in and bamboozles you completely. You go, "Oh my God, he's brilliant!" or "She's brilliant!" So, you can get your mind changed so much. I'm always open to my mind being changed. I think that's a big thing for me: always prepare yourself to be knocked a bit to the side with people that come in and audition for you, especially people you don't know.

Casting a new production can also shift what type of performer our choreographers look for. A new production means new choreography, and having creative dancers in the rehearsal room makes the process much easier, as Matthew Bourne describes:

Matthew Bourne: I think in an original cast, you are looking for that. In an original cast of a new production, in those shows, I was definitely looking for people that I could trust to help create movement, help solve problems, who had some experience of that or who were just very good young talents who I knew would give a lot. I am much more conscious now, when I'm doing a recasting of an old production, or a revival, that you actually have the template to know what they need to do to be in it. Like *Poppins*, you need to be very versatile because there's tap in it, there's some balletic movement in it, there's the gestural movement, it's quite a mix of different styles. So you know what you're looking for and you can try them out with each of those ideas. So that gets a little easier. But a new production, you want creative people around you, I'd say, who can help you create that and solve it.

After the auditions

After the auditions, the panel begins to deliberate on who to cast. Again, the practical requirements of a production are a significant factor, and all our choreographers discussed one of the most significant in today's industry: the need for any potential ensemble member to also be able to cover a role.

Matthew Bourne: What I find is very important is the covering, the understudying situation, which often dictates who you take and who you don't take. Especially as I think, over the years, as casts have got smaller maybe, people have to multitask in a big way. So it's a kind of shared responsibility. Of course, if you're the choreographer, you'd love the best dancers you can get: not always the case, you need someone who sings well, can cover something, can play a small role, so it doesn't come down to just the one thing.

The need to cover means the creative team are often turning down performers they want:

Stephen Mear: We all have to take somebody out, it always happens, even when I'm directing it, somebody I love I'll go, "Oh, they're not gonna fit in because they can't understudy," because casts are made smaller now, so that happens to us all.

Bill Deamer says he finds it difficult when a dancer is perfect for their ensemble track but is still passed over because of the cover situation:

Bill Deamer: It does happen that some of your favourite dancers can fall by the wayside because they're not going to work out understudying a role. People have to understudy and that's hard going. It can become frustrating because sometimes casting is dictated by who a performer has to understudy. A creative team will always work through to find the very best combination and work for what is best for the show.

The casting jigsaw is so complicated that Lynne Page wants to reassure auditionees that who gets the job becomes about considerations much bigger than any one performer:

Lynne Page: When it comes to the final selection, where you put the photographs on the wall, it's never going to be about their ability, it's always about the blend, the matrix of the different personalities. And it's so complicated that sometimes I wish we could make a little video for performers and go, hey guys, here's what happens, and it is not about your skill so never walk away thinking that, it's not about your talents.

The decision-making process can go on for a long time, and Lynne Page puts the cover situation most starkly: without them, there is no show:

Lynne Page: Sometimes you have to leave it because it's just too confusing and then you have to come back again. And then, of course, there's the whole other thing of you'll find the perfect cast but you've got nobody that can cover anybody. So you haven't got a show if you get the best cast but they don't work as covers, so the cover and the swing situation is just beyond complicated.

In the first chapter, the casting directors described the trade-offs and compromises that different creatives make at this stage. For Bill Deamer, there's a balance between getting what he needs and ensuring other creatives are well-served:

Bill Deamer: You have to work with your director and creative team. It's a long and detailed process to find the right balance of who to cast. Once we have found good dancers who can act, they then must meet the musical director to find vocal ranges. It's only then that the team can put the jigsaw together. We must be sure that we have good all-round understudies if someone was to go off, but you've also still got to have the impact of a big ensemble company.

However, the effort put into auditions by the panel can pay off at this stage:

Bill Deamer: I'm at every audition, even the non-dance ones, because somewhere along the line they're going to come into the room and work with me. And because I direct as well, when you sit with the director and producers to do the main casting, I'm up to speed with the rest of the creative team, I know exactly what's working. I know everyone that's being talked about, everyone's on the same page. And that's important.

Stephen Mear focuses on what's best for the show overall and the seamless movement of the whole production. He says it's all about collaboration:

Stephen Mear: Oh god, yeah, collaboration is the biggest word. If you haven't got collaboration, it's so much hard work. You feel like you're just fighting for your dance, which I don't do anymore, I'm too old for that. I want the show to be good. I want everything to be good, not just "ooh, let's do my numbers brilliantly", that doesn't mean anything. You should never look at a show and know where the director's left and the choreographer's took over. I remember working with Stro, Susan Stroman, and she said, "As soon as that baton goes up, it's yours," well, it doesn't work like that really. She's genius but it doesn't work like that, you should blend in from one to the other.

And there is the same sense of ensuring all departments are served, even when our choreographers move into the role of director:

Stephen Mear: You have more of a say. You don't have to fight against everybody and at the end of the day, you have the last say, when you're directing, which is very nice. But I'm never a one-man band, I always trust my creative team. Like my musical director, I would never want him to feel shortchanged of not having the full amount of voices, I'm quite adamant he gets what he wants, as well.

The casting process can be a long one. Bill Deamer says one of his shows took more than a year because of the importance of getting performers with the right abilities:

Bill Deamer: *Follies* at the National Theatre took a year and two months to cast. And, before we started, director Dominic Cooke gave me a clear vision of how he saw the show. We both agreed the way we saw the seven leading ladies and that they all had to be able to dance – they were Follies girls! It's not just about them doing their big solo number and then disappearing. It took a year and two months for us to completely cast all the younger counterparts of the company and we then had what we called a "tap boot camp", to teach some of the intricate choreography before the main rehearsal period, and by the time we opened the show, all those ladies could dance!

Even if a performer ends up being cut from the final cast, they can still have greatly improved their prospects. Stephen Mear often keeps performers in mind for other productions:

Stephen Mear: There's times I've kept people on a list because I thought, God, you're brilliant, but not right for this. You can't understudy any of the parts, you're just not right for that, but I'll keep you in mind for future projects. Which I've done a lot.

Finally, it's worth remembering that the end of casting is the beginning of the next stage of the production process, rehearsing:

Bill Deamer: When you're passionate about dance and musicals, as I am, you know there's nothing quite as magical as being in a room with all those people you've auditioned. They've gone through their paces and they're with you all the way, and you say, "Right, let's start." And that's magical.

The choreographer's discipline

I wanted to know more about our choreographers' professional values, partly because that will show what kind of performer they're looking for at an audition, and partly because these are creatives who have a wealth of experience at the forefront of the musical theatre industry. The first value that came up repeatedly is discipline. It's more present in choreography and dance than in singing or acting. Bill Deamer explained what discipline is to him:

> **Bill Deamer**: Discipline is learning your trade the right way. With passion and commitment. And that is so important. If you go into a dance class and you think, "Oh, it's just another class but I'll do it," you're not really pushing yourself. It's a discipline, but without that discipline you won't enjoy your work. That's the way it is for me. That's the way my body works because I've made it work that way. But when I'm in an audition and I've only choreographed the first sixteen bars and I see people dripping with sweat, I think, "Well, how are they going to get through a three-minute number?" You need that fitness; you've got to be on it when you get in the room. And if you don't love it passionately, maybe think of doing something else, because it's an extremely tough profession.

This made me reflect on two things: that dancers have to work harder and push themselves further than singers and actors; and that choreographers are more likely to have been through that process themselves and therefore are more passionate about it. It's unusual to find an MD who is a trained singer (there are exceptions, as we'll see in the next chapter) and only a third of UK theatre directors report having worked as an actor.[1] But choreographers have nearly all started as dancers, and that may lead to higher expectations from their auditionees:

> **Bill Deamer**: Yes, I have a talent for what I do, but I invested the time and the discipline to make my body do what I wanted it to do.

> **Shaun Aquilina**: And so you expect that of others?

> **Bill Deamer**: Yes, I do, absolutely. I think drama and dance schools work hard to create a disciplined and artistic atmosphere. As a dancer, you must push your body to the extreme, because when you do that, that's when excellence happens.

That discipline goes through auditions and into rehearsals. Stephen Mear expects a disciplined level of focus and professionalism:

> **Stephen Mear**: Being late, that's a big no-no. Being on your phone: big no-no. Being on your phone in a corner while somebody is doing a scene? Get outside and do it, if you're not needed in the room. That's so rude! And be there on time, don't be late. I think that goes to any show, really. You'd never do that to Trevor

---

[1] See Thomas Hescott and Corinne Furness, *The Director's Voice: A Study of Theatre and Director Training and Development in the UK* (London: Stage Directors UK, 2018).

Nunn, you wouldn't do it to Richard Eyre. They run a beautiful room but there's a discipline in there. I'm just trying to keep it professional. Especially nowadays because you can't say anything or upset anyone, which is fine, but then do your job, then you don't have to say anything. I'm sounding like a hard old bitch, aren't I! But I really do love working with people but I do expect a discipline in a room, that's all.

When the discipline is there, rehearsals can become exciting and fun, something Bill Deamer aims for:

Bill Deamer: I like to make people giggle in a rehearsal room. With all the pressures of rehearsing a show, it's good to keep a sense of humour. There should always be a discipline in the room but never fear. We all work together as a team, however, if there's a point when I have to say, "I've got to make the decision now guys, come on, pull it together," I've never had a problem with that. I've always had the respect of the performers, giving their all to make a production work. When you're working as a team, it's a joy. It's one of the reasons I do it. It's a joy to create with a strong creative team and cast. And that's what it's all about, collaboration, with people that are on your level and understand you.

That last remark speaks to successful auditions: performers are selected who understand and enhance the creative vision for the piece. Matthew Bourne prizes that level of collaboration and creativity:

Matthew Bourne: I'm someone who really picks up on everyone in the room. I'm not dictatorial in any sense, I like a shared experience, I like a collaborative experience in the room. The best idea might come from the person who's never done a show before or it might come from the oldest person in the room, or with the most experience. But I want to hear what people have to say, and when we're in a creative mode, I think that's really important. And then there's ownership as well, which is important, that they feel they've made something, they've been part of the creation of it.

Discipline also follows into the entire run of performances, where our choreographers continue to monitor their dancers. Giving a perfunctory performance is not tolerated:

Stephen Mear: I've only ever had a couple of people mark on stage, and they will never be seen in any of my shows again.

Bill Deamer: People do get a name, if they "walk a show." Being lazy and marking a show is simply not acceptable.

Discipline in dance, then, is a commitment to the self and the training and excellence that the self can realise, a commitment to the rehearsal process and to the performance. That level of commitment shapes a dancer, and creatives see that in an audition.

Creatives in the rehearsal room

Bill Deamer made an interesting point about where the choreographer begins compared with the other creatives: whereas the director and musical director have their material, the choreographer's does not yet exist:

> **Bill Deamer**: When you start a musical, there is a script and there is a musical score – the choreographer has nothing. So, they must take that and create what they want to do physically. So, when you get into the rehearsal room they are prepared to tell a story in dance. There are many factors to consider but you've got to know your story and what you want to say.

Matthew Bourne says that, as a consequence, there's a cultural difference between musical theatre and dance companies:

> **Matthew Bourne**: In musical theatre, you often have to create the movement and teach it; in a dance company, you can have ideas and set tasks for people, and then work with the dancers and develop the movement together. In musical theatre, you've often got people of different abilities within a company so you have to gauge the work towards that but also I think they expect to be taught the movement. So you're much more physically involved, and certainly when I started doing *Poppins* and the musicals I did around that time, *Oliver!* and *My Fair Lady* and things, I was very physically involved in creating the movement, with some valued assistants that I'd worked with before. So for *Mary Poppins*, I do remember Stephen Mear, Geoff Garrett, who was our associate on it, and I, standing in front of the mirror with the S-U-P-E-R letters in front of us and working that out really slowly, one by one, and then trying to put that together.

We've looked at the importance of music in choreography, but this last point brings up the importance of text. Creating movement and dance for musical theatre also involves an awareness of the words being spoken or sung:

> **Stephen Mear**: Doing the Sondheim gig [*Old Friends*] was probably harder to choreograph because of not treading on Sondheim's lyrics. It's mega hard. I can do numbers with forty people, that doesn't faze me one second, but Sondheim was hard because you don't want to tread on his lyrics. I got that through working with Victoria Wood. I remember her saying one day, "Stephen, you know you just trod on that joke line" and I was so angry with myself because I kind of knew I was doing it. You have to respect somebody like Sondheim, and Vic, you don't want to ruin all that brilliant stuff.

I was also aware, throughout the interview process, that there were more male creatives than female, by a ratio of three to one. I asked Lynne Page if, in her experience, that was representative of the industry.

> **Lynne Page**: Yep. Pretty much. Yep, yep.

> **Shaun Aquilina**: Does that have an effect on your work?

Lynne Page: When I first started out, I didn't really think about it. I'd sometimes look around and go, oh, I'm the only woman in this production meeting, that's interesting. And, of course, now I realise that the more female voices are in the room, and the more of a balance that you have, that it's important. And so I suppose the one thing I'll push back against is if a woman might be being cast for an aesthetic reason. It's quite rare. But I guess, my lens, my female lens, is of value within the audition process, especially if it's sometimes/often in a bit of a minority.

Finally, I wanted to know about the overall vision a choreographer-director might bring to a production. Firstly, there's the dance side, which Matthew Bourne says should permeate the performance:

Matthew Bourne: The best musical theatre choreographers are people who make everyone in the show dance. And that means you've got your great dancers, they do this bit; then some character people do a moment that people really love; and then there's the leading performers; and then there's the movers who don't really dance but you give them something to do; that mixture of skills, when everyone's together doing something, that's real skill in musical theatre choreography. We can all do a great routine with a load of great dancers, that's brilliant, but you don't always have that, and that's not always what it's about.

Then there's the direction side. For Matthew Bourne, the divisions between choreography and direction have dissolved, and these have become one element through the performance:

Matthew Bourne: I think now, because I've told so many full-length narratives in a wordless way through dance, I do see the whole production now as choreography. I don't separate those directing/choreography tasks very much at all. The staging of a show is choreography; the musicality of how you get people from one place to another is all part of choreography for me. And to the point where I wonder why there aren't more choreographer-directors like the tradition is on Broadway, because they do intermingle incredibly well when you're creating a musical performance. So in terms of different kinds of choreographers, I think I'm one who is narrative based more than anything else, and that means the dancing, the singing, the book, that whole story, the arc of the whole evening, is choreography for me.

Before directing on his own, Matthew Bourne told me how privileged he felt to have worked alongside theatre directors Trevor Nunn, Richard Eyre (who we'll hear from in Chapter 4) and Sam Mendes, in creative relationships that go back over thirty years. I wanted to know what he felt he had learned from them:

Matthew Bourne: Different things. Trevor Nunn is the only director I've worked with who completely understands the use of dancing and singing in a musical. That sounds very basic but it's true. Most directors you work with on a musical who have come from theatre say, "Oh, it's a play, really, isn't it, it's a play with music." And dancing is the first thing to get cut because it's "not relevant." It's like "we need some cuts in Act 2," "Well can we cut that dance break, it's not really adding much to the story." Trevor, I felt, understands that dance can forward the plot. He understands the use of a song in the storytelling. It's basic stuff – doesn't always happen. And that's why he's so good at it, I think. And, with me, he would lead into the number and then he would go, "Over to you," and then he'd come in and he'd have a couple of notes or something, but he would hand it over, he wasn't on your back all the time. So, I don't know whether I learned that from him but I love that about him.

Richard Eyre, I learned never to say never. I mean *Poppins* is a show full of sleight of hand and tricks and theatrical magic and everything, and I would have given up with some of the things we were trying to achieve; he always fought for them to happen and he would believe that they would happen. And I now do that. I believe, even if it seems impossible. I think that's what I learned from him: there's always a way, and we'll do it; we're going to make it happen.

Sam, what did I learn from Sam? It's a long time ago! He's a bit younger than me; we were both doing our first big musical, first time working with Cameron [Mackintosh], so we were more like equals from different worlds working together, so I think what I learned from him was collaboration. To collaborate with someone on that level, which I hadn't done before, was great, and we've remained friends, I've remained friends with all of them, actually, and I feel very privileged to work with them all.

West End versus Broadway

Our choreographers have worked extensively on Broadway, auditioning for their shows, rehearsing them and seeing them in performance. So I wanted to know what differences they felt compared to the West End. Firstly, Bill Deamer said the ability of performers is equally high:

Bill Deamer: America and Broadway have some incredible performers, and the standard of musical theatre is amazing. That standard is equally high here in London. In 2024, I choreographed *Hello, Dolly!* at The London Palladium, starring Imelda Staunton. After the very successful Broadway production with Bette Midler, it was interesting to present a new London version in a different way. Director Dominic Cooke went back to the original book, and we told the story in a different way. With an incredible company of performers, the show was a joy to create. It was a smash hit.

And Stephen Mear admits that Broadway has many exceptional performers but says that's to be expected in such a large country:

Stephen Mear: It's the size of how big America is, that's all it is. We have got the same amazing talent and amazing people as they have. We just don't have as many because of the size of the country.

Though the level of ability may be the same, there are differences in the manner of rehearsing and performing, and in auditioning:

Matthew Bourne: I've just come back from doing some auditions in New York for *Old Friends*, the Sondheim show I did, and it took a while to get used to the different attitudes there, and the different way of auditioning which would be quite off-putting here but I had to accept it as a New York thing. For example, the women will go to the bathroom before they come in, and they'll change into an outfit and put heels on, very revealing skimpy dresses and things, just to sing a song. It's very unusual for that to happen in the UK. That would be quite off-putting for me in the UK because it would feel like someone was putting on a facade. But it's very much the New York way of auditioning and I think it's just standard.

Lynne Page, who had just returned from rehearsing the London production of *Tammy Faye* on Broadway, says actors there tend to be stronger dancers than in the UK:

Lynne Page: There are more actors that have a dance training, in America, I find. I don't know whether in their drama schools they've just got a stronger dance training but you'll often find straight actors will have a very good movement vocabulary and we don't quite have that in the same way, yet.

However, the ability to play and devise is stronger in the West End:

Lynne Page: I find the creativity of English performers, in that they will improv and bring lots of stuff to the table, they have more range, I think. I think on Broadway, things have to be put on so quickly that often people are so much more like, "Where do I stand? What do I do?" And you don't feel that you can create in a way of like, "Oh, let's just discover," on Broadway, like you can in the UK. So it's a different approach.

The pressures of efficiency and competition may also account for differing attitudes to making mistakes:

Lynne Page: It takes a lot to give Broadway performers permission to make mistakes. It's super hard to get on to the West End; it's super, super hard to get on in Broadway, so there's a precision that is installed. And sometimes when I invite them to be strong and wrong, it's like "what!?" and they don't like to feel that vulnerable because they want to know that "I'm in the right place at the right time," and I'm going, "No, no, I don't care what you do, just play around for a bit," and they're like, "Sorry, what!?" So, that is quite funny.

There's a difference in styles of expression, too. Matthew Bourne finds UK performers to be more genuine and truthful and gave an example from his recent auditions for the Broadway production of *Stephen Sondheim's Old Friends*:

Matthew Bourne: They're so earnest over there. It's hard to break through, to see the real person. There's less sense of irony, wit, there's a lot of people holding their chests all the time when they talk to you, like "What do you want from me? I'm here to give you what you want,": just relax, be yourself, that's what we want really. It's quite hard. And then, [English actress] Scarlett Strallen came in, and she now lives in New York, and you can feel the difference, it's a breath of fresh air, that crazy, eccentric character that Scarly is, that's so refreshing to have her in the room. And she had a take on the numbers that was very funny and not completely controlled, and at the end of it just went, "Oh, I don't know what I did there, but hope it was okay." You just don't get that with American performers, they're very aware of how they come across.

Great auditions

When I asked our choreographers about their most memorable audition experiences, some of them recalled times when auditions had worked out much better than they had hoped. Stephen Mear remembers auditioning an actor of such high quality that he didn't expect him to take the job:

Stephen Mear: Alex Hanson, who is a brilliant actor, came in for *42nd Street*, and I thought, well, surely he won't want to do it because he's done loads of acting and plays, why would he want to do *42nd Street*? I knew he could sing because I'd done *Stephen Ward* with him, and he was fantastic! To have that calibre of an actor as Julian Marsh, leading *42nd Street*, upped all the other actors.

Bill Deamer spoke about versatility. He remembers two auditions where the performers were strong in one discipline but then blew the panel away in another:

Bill Deamer: One of the best auditions I ever saw was Sam Lips, who played Billy Lawlor in *42nd Street*. He's extraordinary because he got through the dance rounds, and it was difficult dance, and I remember saying to director Jonathan Church, "Well, I bet he can't sing," and Jonathan said, "Well, he can, he was in *Singing' in the Rain*." Well, he sang, and this beautiful tenor voice came out that was just totally true and honest. He then read the scenes, and he was the perfect triple threat, leading man.

When Dawn Hope auditioned for the role of Stella in *Follies* at the National Theatre, we'd been looking for an actress to lead the big Mirror, Mirror number. We'd been auditioning for about six months. It was getting heavy going. We couldn't find anybody who could really do it. And then Dawn came in, and this time it was the other way round: she sang, and director Dominic Cooke asked me, "Can she tap," I replied, "She can!" and that was it. I remember the first performance of that routine, it had a very long, standing ovation.

Lynne Page recounted one of the most striking audition experiences I heard about during these interviews from her production of *La Cage Aux Folles*, trying to find the Cagelles, the ensemble drag performers who work at La Cage:

Lynne Page: They needed to be huge personalities. So I created like a walkdown, like a Ru Paul drag walkdown. And I asked them to each give themselves a drag name and be fierce and fabulous, and do this walkdown. And word got out that I did this at the end of the audition. And by the time we got to the tour in the UK, I had people throwing themselves on the audition table which was just hilarious, and then in New York, I had outfits arriving, I had a guy that did his walkdown and he'd organised to get a phone call halfway through it so he answered the phone and was having a chat. And then I had a guy that did a whole costume change. And then my favourite was this one guy that asked if he could go last and I was like, yeah, sure. And so he did this walk down, and then he poured a bucket of water over himself. I was like, Oh, my God!

Shaun Aquilina: Did any of them get the job?

Lynne Page: I don't think the bucket guy got the job! And I wanted to give him the job because it was so hilarious . . . but he just wasn't right.

Lynne Page also had an example of memorable movement-based auditions, and this illustrated how successful humour can be:

Lynne Page: For *Tammy Faye* at the Almeida, there's a number where I have to create a theme park on stage so I'm like, "Well, how am I gonna do that?" So then I did an improv of going, "Ok, guys, show me what a day out at this theme park looks like." And there were just some absolute gems in that. And then you really drew into those performers that went to drama school and were used to going, "Right, we're going to do this!" And the roller coasters that were created, the rides that were created, all the different games that were created, were hilarious. I found this absolutely brilliant performer called Kelly Agbowu. She works all the time and is one of the funniest people I've ever seen do an audition. So, it's a privilege to be able to run an audition and get these people to be doing crazy things.

Shaun Aquilina: Humour seems to go a long way in auditions.

Lynne Page: Yes. Indeed. An actor with funny bones is like, obviously depending on the show, is golden. Somebody that can communicate humour, it's just absolutely fantastic.

Matthew Bourne agrees with this last point:

Matthew Bourne: Oh, yeah. It tends to be the ones who make you laugh, and they leave the room and you go, Oh, that was just entertaining for ten minutes! Rather than just oh, another audition, the same songs again. You can feel it, they walk out of the room and you don't even need to say it, you just all look at each other and go, they're brilliant, they're great. You know everyone's going to agree with you. It's not gonna be, "Oh, I didn't think so." There's a sense of group feeling about someone, and, Oh! It would be great to have them, wouldn't it be great? I think that those ones are clear and obvious.

Matthew Bourne also had a memorable example of a young actor he recently cast in his production of *Oliver!*:

Matthew Bourne: Billy Jenkins, who plays Dodger, who's just seventeen, I'd never seen him before. He hasn't really done much theatre, he's done film things. He came in totally relaxed about who he is, what he had to offer, completely original, a unique performer, constantly creative, sang "Consider Yourself", a song we all know, and made it sound like he was just making the lyrics up and, with the emphasis he put and how he acted it, you just go, "Brilliant, this guy is Dodger, he's the character." It blew me away, and I didn't care whether he had much experience or not on stage, it was just, he is the character.

We'll see this quality of making lyrics or text seem new and spontaneous come up again in Chapter 4, when our directors recall their memorable auditions.

Conclusion

When we think about Musical Theatre choreography, we can think of everything from the smallest movements such as hand gestures across a kitchen table or walking a few steps across the stage, to fully embodied ballet, tap and modern dance sequences, with tricks and turns. We can also think of the full range of performers in a cast – the movers, the characters, the dancers – but look for the dance in each of them. We can think of individuals and of the group. For all of them, there are realities to be faced, and to be successful in a musical theatre audition today, multiple skills are often needed:

Bill Deamer: It's not a question of just being a dancer: you must be a triple threat. Especially when you've got understudies to think about. So, you've got to be able to act, sing and dance, which is the world I came from, when I started.

Stephen Mear agrees that today there is pressure to be an all-round performer, something that wasn't so prevalent when he started performing professionally in the 1980s:

Stephen Mear: When I started off, there were dancers, there were singers, and there were actors: they were three categories. In *Evita*, I was a dancer, then there were the singers, and then there were your principals. So I didn't have to worry too much about the singing and the acting, but I did train in that, I did know what I wasn't good at and I worked at them really hard while I was at college because I knew I would need them in the long run. I used to use every audition as though it was a class. So I just thought, well if I go and do my best, they might just remember me for something else, which happened a lot, actually, and which happens to me as a choreographer. So you always have to remember that at the back of your head, people could be casting several other shows, and whenever you do an audition, go and do your best.

Lynne Page urged performers to improve their offering at auditions:

Lynne Page: Do everything you can to get as many skills as you can: if you're an actor-mover, and then you've trained your voice: win-win! If you specialise in one thing but you can get your other strengths up: win-win! Be open to working on the skill set that is your weakest.

But for those dancers who can deliver the required passion, heart, charisma and technique, there is exciting and rewarding work to be done. The end goal of which is occasionally the pleasure of a spectacular number but more often is narrative: dancing an emotional, embodied story on the stage and sharing it with the audience.

3 Musical directors

Sean Green is a three-time winner of Best MD at the Black British Theatre Awards. He has been the musical director of shows including Two Strangers (Carry a Cake Across New York) *(Kiln Theatre),* Brokeback Mountain *(SOHO Place),* Sylvia *(The Old Vic),* Get Up Stand Up! – The Bob Marley Musical *(Lyric Theatre West End),* Priscilla Queen of the Desert *(UK tour),* Twelfth Night *(Young Vic),* The Wedding Singer *(UK tour),* One Love *(Birmingham Rep) and* Into the Woods *(Manchester Royal Exchange), as well as Assistant MD on* The Rocky Horror Show *(European tour),* Wicked *(UK & International tours),* Cabaret *(UK tour) and* Evita *(UK & European tour). He is currently the UK musical director of the West End production of* MJ: The Musical.

Stuart Morley has been musical director on shows including We Will Rock You, Elf, Big, Only Fools and Horses, *and* Tommy. *As musical supervisor, he has overseen* We Will Rock You *(US & UK Tours, Brazil, Denmark, Romania, Germany),* Only Fools and Horses *(West End & UK Tour),* The Baker's Wife *(Menier Chocolate Factory) and* Strictly Ballroom *(UK Tour). He has also been an associate musical director for the West End productions of* Cabaret *(Lyric) and* Wicked. *Stuart completed his PhD at the Royal Academy of Music and is on the teaching faculty at the Royal Academy of Music and the Royal Conservatoire of Scotland. He is currently the musical director of the West End production of* Les Misérables.

Sarah Travis won the Tony Award for Best Orchestrations for her work on Sweeney Todd *in 2005. She also won the Drama Desk Award for Outstanding Orchestrations for the same production. Sarah has been music supervisor for numerous productions, including* Grease *(West End and UK Tour),* West Side Story *(Curve),* A Little Night Music *(Watermill),* Sister Act *(UK Tour),* Fiddler on the Roof *(UK Tour) and* Chess *(UK Tour). She is also a composer, with works including* The Lost Toys Big Adventure *(Towner Gallery Eastbourne),* The Secret Garden *(Chester),* The Marriage of Figaro *(Watermill) and* Peter Pan *(Oxford Playhouse).*

Gareth Valentine has been described by The Stage *as 'one of the West End's most sought-after musical directors'. He has worked alongside many of musical theatre's leading composers, including Stephen Sondheim, Stephen Schwartz, Lord Andrew Lloyd Webber, John Kander and Maury Yeston. Since beginning his career in 1981, he has conducted numerous West End musicals, including* 42nd Street, Kiss Me, Kate, Merrily We Roll Along, Company, Chicago *and* City of Angels, *all of which won the Olivier Award for Best Musical or Best Musical Revival. He has conducted for many of musical theatre's leading performers, including Liza Minnelli, Elaine Paige, Dame Judi Dench, Catherine Zeta-Jones, Chita Rivera, Joel Grey and Wayne Sleep. As a composer, his* REQUIEM *has been performed and recorded at Abbey Road Studios; he composed a new score for* Aladdin *at the Old Vic starring Sir Ian McKellen, and composed the ballet* Strictly Gershwin *for English National Ballet.*

Introduction

For the musical director, casting begins with the score and the production. These dictate what an MD needs from their singers, long before they meet them in the audition room. They must consider the material, its vocal ranges, the type of show, its sound, and the roles that need to be cast. Roles vary from those that are vocally heavy with big musical moments to land, to singer-actor roles, to dance ensembles that add to the backing vocals. We'll see how our four MDs consider all this when choosing whom to cast.

Underneath those circumstances which shift from show to show is a set of values that remains constant. No matter what the part or production, our MDs look for characterisation, storytelling, the theatrical part of musical theatre. We'll see that our MDs are looking for a connection to text, an intelligence, a flexible mind to take direction, as well as a musicality that informs their performance, and we'll see how they assess that in the audition room.

We start with the fundamentals: singers have to hit the notes, and they have to hit them again and again as the show runs on. So, what do our MDs make of vocal technique?

Vocal technique

Our choreographers needed to be sure of both the physical technique and the narrative, expressive ability of their auditionees, and now we'll see that our musical directors need to be convinced of the equivalent abilities in their world. Vocal technique and expression go hand in hand and Gareth Valentine says it's vital that both are there. I asked him how long it takes to know whether an auditionee has the required technique:

> **Gareth Valentine**: Oh, immediately! You can tell the minute they open their mouth. I mean within five bars or something. You may not know the register but you'll find that out pretty quickly by doing the usual tricks to find out where their voice goes up and down. But then it's so much more, isn't it, than just the voice? If you find an actor who looks the part, who has great acting chops, who has a wonderful voice, and who can move, you're quids in. But that's rare.

Vocal technique is usually assessed in a first-round audition, where the auditionees sing a song of their choosing, in person, to a panel. Sean Green can also assess an auditionee's vocal ability within a few bars. He says he takes notes on voice, technique and musicality, as well:

> **Sean Green**: Some people will have you guessing right upto the last minute but, a lot of the time, people come in and they'll start singing, and I'll be like "Oh, okay! Yes: musical!" or "Very good instrument but not totally sure of how they're using it," or "Uncertain as to how the piano fits in with what you're doing." I think those things are largely obvious.

When it comes to technique, training in a particular school, such as bel canto or Estill, seems less important than what the auditionee produces. Sarah Travis says she's not aware of specific techniques as auditionees sing:

> **Sarah Travis**: No, I think it's just the sound. If I'm really honest, I'm not a singing teacher, so obviously I'm aware of various techniques but I'm not looking for those. And often on a CV it will say where they've trained which, I suppose, is important. If someone's from ArtsEd, say, they're going to get a pretty good vocal training I'd say; if they're more from a dance college, like Bird's, they're going to be much more dance heavy than vocal heavy. I don't particularly, at an audition stage, delve into exactly what technique they've learned for the voice.

And Sarah Travis added that there are obvious physical signs that alert her to whether someone is singing well:

> **Sarah Travis**: I tend to really be: what am I getting, what am I seeing in front of me? And you can tell if someone has training, if their breathing's right, you can tell if the veins are sticking right out in their throat, you know that they're singing on their throat, or they're straining, or maybe the song is just not in their range. There's a lot of stuff you pick up in five-minute auditions.

An important part of assessing vocal technique is judging whether an auditionee can sustain the long and frequent performance schedule of a musical theatre production. Stuart Morley says it's a vital part of his work:

> **Stuart Morley**: Oh, massively, yes. And that's where the music team comes into its own in the auditions, in my experience, because the directors will drive the text and the narrative and the storytelling, and then the music department has to assess if the voice can sustain eight shows a week.

Stuart Morley went on to give an example of taking an auditionee through a rigorous vocal test to ensure he could deliver what was needed as a principal in a major production:

> **Stuart Morley**: I once asked a singer to sing the audition song a few times in a row. And I was quite clear with him, I said, "The reason I'm doing this is because I want to know you have the vocal stamina to do the show." And this is *We Will Rock You*, the last sixteen to twenty minutes of the show is all about Galileo singing "We Will Rock You", "We Are The Champions", "Bohemian Rhapsody"

in a row. And that's a big sing! In the middle of that, the B flat in "Champions" is what seems to challenge a lot of performers, more so than the C. So I said, "But equally, if it hurts, the rule is always stop," and I always say that as a caveat to any performer: don't do anything that hurts. If it's hurting, it's wrong, let's stop; if it's tiring, fine, that's your job. But if it hurts, stop.

Sarah Travis is also very aware of vocal stamina and the demands of performing in a long run. Someone who struggles to get through an audition is a concern:

Sarah Travis: I'm also looking for voices that I think are going to last a six-month, eight-month tour. And you can pick that up when you see someone, if it's quite a long audition. Our finals were fifteen minutes long and that might be singing two songs and doing two or three readings. And it's interesting, even by the end of a fifteen-minute audition, sometimes I can tell whether someone's quite tired. And I think there could be all sorts of reasons: they might not be well, they may be out of practice a bit, they may be suddenly thrown into having to do quite a lot of vocal work and they've got tired quickly; but that's always a bit of an issue for me. If I think someone's getting tired towards the end of fifteen minutes, then I have to think about that.

Often, auditionees will be concerned about hitting particular notes, especially top notes, in their performances. Stuart Morley spoke about his auditions as MD of *Les Misérables* and says there's sympathy for missing it once, but more than once starts to create doubts:

Stuart Morley: In my experience the panel is always happy to give someone a second chance if they're pretty close but don't quite make a couple of the notes, so a performer never needs to worry about cracking a note the first time, they can nearly always have a second go at it. But if they miss it twice, then you think, "Okay, I don't know if they can sustain this." If they miss it once you think, maybe that was just a moment. And you know what, live theatre is live, it doesn't have to be perfect every day; if you want it to be perfect, just watch a film.

Sarah Travis will also give more opportunities to auditionees and work with them if they have shown potential:

Sarah Travis: If they crack a note or if they've gone into a different part of their voice which doesn't suit the song, I might maybe try it a tone down, if I feel it's worth exploring to see if it's just a quick case of the song is out of their range, or to see if they maybe work on their mix. I mean it all depends on time, as well, and you think, is it worth exploring or are they just not right or it's just not in their range. So you make a lot of quick decisions.

Having time to spend with an auditionee is also something Sarah Travis wants, to get the best out of them and give them a positive audition experience.

Sarah Travis: I hate five-minute auditions, I think it's cruel. I would say first rounds at least ten or fifteen minutes, because then you're going to relax someone in that time and you hopefully get a bit better out of them and give them a better experience, as well.

Shaun Aquilina: Does that mean you're also not a fan of 16-bar cuts and 32-bar cuts?

Sarah Travis: No. Hate that. But then, probably those sorts of shows are not shows I would want to be involved in.

Alongside a general vocal ability, MDs are keenly aware of the vocal demands of a show, just as our choreographers in the previous chapter were aware of the dance and movement demands. I spoke to Sarah Travis just as she had been auditioning a new tour of *Grease*:

Sarah Travis: I supervise *Grease* so I've seen a lot of people over the last couple of weeks, casting for the tour next year. So I'm looking for a pop sound; I'm looking for good vocal health because it's a tour and it's a long tour; obviously each part, I know what the vocal range is so I know exactly what I need from a range point of view. For *Grease*, I don't really need lyrical sopranos, I need much more – I hate to say it – but belty mezzos! And strong tenors. It's just that sort of show, I need big voices and big confident singers. If I was doing a Sondheim, I'd be looking for a totally different type of voice, and a casting director, hopefully, will take that into account when they're bringing the people in that they think are right for the show.

In dance-based shows, singing is not the fundamental driver of the production, and so MDs can be more relaxed about vocal ability, as Gareth Valentine explained:

Gareth Valentine: *Chicago*, for example, is predominantly a dance show and so there's less latitude for voices. Because the thing about the creative team is that we're all fighting for the best singers, the choreographer for the best dancers, the director for the more flavoursome actors, the ones who have the right cut of jib for the role. And because it's a dance show, I tend to be more lenient on the standard of voice. And also, if there isn't really that much singing to do, or if the singing is not particularly demanding then you can be equally lenient. On the other hand, a Sondheim show, for example, *Into the Woods*, which is predominantly a singer show, seen as an actor show, you're looking for really good voices who are equal to the material and if you have a director who understands that – and not all of them do – you're onto a winner.

We returned to the example of casting *Chicago,* and Gareth Valentine gave a detailed description of how the audition process for the ensemble in a dance-led show can work:

Gareth Valentine: Because it's primarily a dance show, you're going to get what they call the cattle market. You're going to get groups of up to thirty to fifty boys and girls coming in and dancing. The boys first to go, and it's a process of elimination, and they will be honed down to ten, and then two, and of those, you're going to choose your best lot. And this goes on sometimes days, sometimes weeks. Those people who can dance will now go to the next stage which is singing. Now, if I've got SATB music, I need to know that I have all my voices equally, and so I need to know I have sopranos who can sing divisi, and altos, my tenors and basses, and so I'm always marking that right from day one. You might, at the very first dance calls, sometimes hear them one by one just to sing their best ten bars or something like that so you at least find out what the registers are. Then they're going to sing a song, and they might sing a song that's not appropriate to the show. You ask them to sing something else, and often they will. So now you've got your ensemble singers, and now they're going to be asked to read a piece. Maybe one of the girls that monologues in the "Cell Block Tango" say, because they're going to be asked to, if not play the roles, then to understudy those roles, and so therefore they have to satisfy that. And so it's a long, long process. And then it's also that the panel want people who look original in some way, who are sexy, who are different shapes and sizes, or who are all the same shape and size, there are so many variants on that. So that's the ensemble, that's how that happens.

Sarah Travis is also used to working on dance-led shows and says it can be frustrating to miss out on auditionees with strong voices:

Sarah Travis: Often, a show might do dance calls first and then they cull a lot of people who might be brilliant actors and singers, but because it's a dance-heavy show, that's the way they choose to do it. I'm not massively keen on that because I feel I've probably lost a lot of people that will be good for my department, and the same with the director, so that can cause a bit of friction in the end stages where we're fighting for people and then the dance department might say, well, we're not sure about their dance, but you think, well, you've put them through the first few rounds so now we need to all compromise a bit to find the best all-rounders.

As Gareth Valentine suggested, casting a singer-actor show is different. Sean Green MD'd a production of *Into the Woods* at Manchester's Royal Exchange Theatre. The audition process there was about seeing a particular type of performer:

Sean Green: That was an almost non-musical theatre cast, people who either don't normally do musicals, or who make interesting choices about what musicals they do do. And I think it really showed in their performances. Musical theatre has a reputation of being a certain way, being a bit frothy, sometimes – I don't necessarily subscribe to it – but I think in choosing unusual people we almost picked actors first who could really sing rather than picking musical theatre performers as such. I mean, there were a couple of mainstays who've done lots of musicals in that cast, Alex Gaumond for starters, but our Jack, for instance, David Moorst, fantastic actor, fantastic singer, but doesn't subscribe to the musical theatre landscape, I would say.

Shaun Aquilina: And when you get those people in to audition, do you make sure they've got just enough vocally and musically that you can work with them or do you expect a bit more?

Sean Green: I think it's making sure they can do the job. So we heard quite a lot of different sections of the show, just to make sure that they could hit all the necessary requirements. And they could! And I thought they brought a style to it that was what the director and musical supervisor were looking for. I don't think it was necessarily "we want to see people who don't normally do musicals," I think it was just "we want to see people who are good and who have the capacity" because I don't think everyone can do Sondheim and I think the casting director worked really hard at making sure that she brought people in who could do Sondheim.

Sometimes the show is so actor-led that the singing is left behind, as Gareth Valentine found in a Sondheim production:

Gareth Valentine: It's a show which is full of character actors which means older men and older women who are really actors, not singers at all, who sometimes have never done musicals. And you know that they're just going to have to go by sheer dint of who they are, their personality, their character acting. That's the nice way of saying they can't sing, and they can't hold the tune, but I have to help them along.

Vocal demands change with each show. Sean Green has MD'd a wide range of shows, from plays with music to musicals with commercial music and rap, and each has its own requirements:

Sean Green: It's so specific, every different show. The singing in *Brokeback Mountain* was very authentic, very country, very 1950s. *Sylvia* was a completely different situation. We had to hear people speak spoken verse like rap, as well as sing. With this show [*MJ: The Musical*], a Michael Jackson sounding voice is hugely appropriate for an MJ but it's so specific it wouldn't really be useful anywhere else. I think I'm dictated by the show and by what the music, the setting, the story, is trying to tell us.

If an auditionee does not perform in the specific sound or style of the show, MDs will sometimes work to bring that out. Sarah Travis says she is willing to change the style of the auditionee's song to fit the production:

Sarah Travis: If I'm not quite hearing what I want to hear, or if they brought the wrong song choice, which often happens in a first round, say they brought a song that isn't quite in the style we're looking for, then I will sometimes go to the piano and, if they brought a Rodgers and Hammerstein song, for example, and I'm looking for something much more pop, I might go to the piano and say, "Let's do this song – you'll never have to do it this way again – but let's do it in a pop style" and totally turn it on its head.

Gareth Valentine has less sympathy for auditionees who arrive with an inappropriate song but will still give them a chance to show something else:

Gareth Valentine: If you're doing *Kiss of the Spider Woman* and somebody brings something from *We Will Rock You*, well, I think that's that, they have what's coming to them. But, even then, I'll say, "Look, do you have anything else in your collection?"

Along with the overall sound of the show, there's also the specific sound of the characters and their performance requirements. These can vary from one character to another, as Sarah Travis experiences on *Grease*:

Sarah Travis: There's a character called Vince Fontaine, who is a showman, so he comes on and he has to work an audience. So, yes, he needs to be able to sing but actually, working an audience is probably more important than the voice, because his song "Born to Hand Jive" is not a very rangy song. And actually, if someone came in and sang it perfectly but they weren't going to set an audience alight, and then someone comes in and just fills the room with energy, and you know they're going to work an audience but maybe isn't quite as strong as the other person who's a brilliant singer, then I would definitely go for the person who can work the audience. It's so character orientated, really. Whereas, the girl who's going to come in and play Sandy needs to be able to sing "Hopelessly Devoted . . ." brilliantly. We've had various Sandys, some of them have been quite feisty Sandys and good actors; some of them are much more singers; and actually the feisty Sandys are much more interesting for me and I would imagine for the audience as well. But they do need to be able to nail those songs because they're iconic. Same with the Danny: "Sandy" is a really tough song to sing and he has a new song that is really tough, but he also carries the show pretty much.

Sean Green also finds vocal differences from role to role in *MJ: The Musical*. Some of his singers need to stay faithful to song recordings, while others are encouraged to deliver fresh interpretations:

Sean Green: Certain characters in the show are there to present the music as was: so MJ, and Middle Michael, to a certain extent, present the songs as they were presented. And when other characters like Kate/Katherine [the character of Michael's mother and her cover] sing songs, for example she sings "I'll be There" with Little Michael, she has the leeway to make it her own, add riffs, licks, etc. And I'm not an MD who says, "Do this riff, do this riff," I like to know that if we're hiring a Kate/Katherine that she has the skills to make choices on the fly in the show that are going to be good and going to land. So in that sense, if I'm looking for that character, that's a very important skill for them to have that they can display to me. Other characters, not so much, because they are slightly more bound by what has existed and fit more into a mould.

And if a show has very specific requirements, such as being able to rap in *Sylvia*, those are assessed at audition, too:

Sean Green: Yeah, we definitely heard people rap. They had to do their own choice of rap as well, so it was: you bring your own musical theatre song, you bring your own choice of rap, and you rap. And they had to do bits of the show as well. And I think a lot of performers have various different facets and a performer who can do that is great and will turn up and rock it, just like somebody turning up and doing an aria.

If there are particularly difficult vocal moments in the show, these may be heard in the audition, too. Stuart Morley says a lot of consideration goes into the show material sent out to auditionees, and he follows this with an example of what's heard from a potential Eponine in *Les Mis* auditions:

> **Stuart Morley**: For a new show or for a new production, one of the first questions that you're going to get from the casting director is "what material are we sending out?" And I hate sending people too much material to learn. I don't think it's fair. I think a person's time is precious and they've got enough to do without having to learn half the score for you. So, it's important to pick the key moments for each character and include those in the audition material. From this character, I need to see this range and I need to hear this style: which sections of the score are going to tell me that? For example, in addition to "On My Own" the Eponine set material also includes a very short section from "The Robbery". There's a part where Eponine has to sing "It's Javert!" She has to sing five bars, that's in the audition pack, that's literally it. She sings those because we need to know that they can belt that particular note (the C).

If you want to check the section, the bars are 96–100 of #10 The Robbery, in Act 1. Eponine has two E5s to navigate, but what the panel needs to hear is that the auditionee can comfortably belt the C5, on 'Javert', which is now a longer, held note.

Creating the sound of the show involves assessing a lot about a singer: their technique, range, sound, whether they can sing in the style of the show, and any specialities like riffing or being able to rap. These need to be satisfied for the panel to then engage with that key consideration in musical theatre: storytelling.

Storytelling: Narrative and character

Whatever the vocal requirements, the musical theatre singer is on stage to tell a story through song. This came out again and again in the MDs' evaluation of good singing. Sarah Travis says it's all about the singer connecting to their material:

> **Sarah Travis**: I'm there for the musicality, and the vocal, and the technique, but I'm also very much someone that is about interpretation of songs. There has to be something about connection to the material/lyric. Otherwise, what's the point? Music is there to help tell a story. And it's like text, I always think of tunes as text with just a bit more of a range of pitch. But if you can't connect to it. . . it's like if you're saying the spoken word, a piece of text, and you're just reading it verbatim, with no emotion at all, well you wouldn't accept that. So, for me, the connection is everything.

And if that doesn't happen in an audition, Sarah Travis will take the time to bring it out of the auditionee:

Sarah Travis: I try and explore. If I didn't think I was getting enough emotionally from them, I would push them on that and sometimes it might mean: right, sit down and sing the song to me. Because that's another thing: some panels like auditionees to sing straight at them, some panels like them to sing over their heads; I like people to sing to the panel because I think it's much more of a connection, but that's just a personal thing. So I might get them to sit down and tell the story and try and connect them more to the narrative of the song. If it's quite an emotional song and they're not really connecting or if there's not a lot going on behind the eyes, I'd just try and push them on that a bit more.

For Stuart Morley, that narrative ability in song comes from one place:

Stuart Morley: Text. Do they understand it? You can generally fix everything else. If the role requires money notes, you need to make sure the money notes are there. Sustainability, obviously, they have to be able to replicate it eight times a week. But the big thing is, can they tell a story? Because we're not doing a concert, where we're presenting the music, we're telling a story. It's a story told through music. So if they can't tell a story and be believable, then they're not right for the show.

In the next chapter, we'll see how Sir Richard Eyre puts wit at the top of his list of characteristics in an actor. Gareth Valentine said something very similar, which he links to the narrative and character ability of an auditionee:

Gareth Valentine: Apart from a really sound, impressive voice, the overriding thing by a long way is intelligence. It sounds like a rudimentary pre-requisite, but you'd be amazed how many people stand in front of you and sing a song, and it's clear they have no connection with the lyric at all, or with the character, or with the context in which it's sung in the show. But when it's there, there's no doubt about it. I remember talking to Sam Mendes and I said, "Do you agree with me that actors who really can put a song across in the same way that they can a scene, with the same dexterity, the same understanding, the same craft, do you agree that if there's an intelligence there, if there are really well-honed critical faculties and analytical thought, do you agree that that overcomes even the good voice, that it supersedes that vocal ability?" And he said, "Yes". And I agree to some extent. What is lovely is when you get the whole thing. Case in point: Jenna Russell, who has a really big brain, and she can move, and she has a voice I could listen to for hours, and the musicality, although she professes not to have any of those! But there's a whole list of people who tick those boxes.

Sarah Travis agrees that acting, connection, and intelligence can be more important than the quality of voice:

Sarah Travis: I can't believe I'm going to say this but I'd rather hear a song sung not quite as technically well but acted better. I'd rather it that way round, definitely. Look at Judi Dench. Judi Dench has a limited vocal range but can sing "Send in the Clowns" and break people's hearts. And I've heard that song sung beautifully but it doesn't move me.

Sean Green finds this particularly important when working on a Sondheim show:

Sean Green: You have to be able to act: act, act, act! And act through song. It's actors' music.

Shaun Aquilina: Is that connection to text?

Sean Green: Yes, definitely, connection to text. An understanding of the character. And that's not to say that people don't do that and act through song but I think there's a level of detail that you can get away without, when you're doing other things. This is going to sound terrible but you can, in a sense, fake it with other music. "I'm generally in the right emotional state, and my voice sounds beautiful so I'm giving you the story." With Sondheim, this line means this, this line means this, this part of this line means this, and this part of this line means that, and you have to be dexterous enough to be able to traverse those things quickly.

This emphasis on narrative and character over vocal ability led to a split in our MDs over the casting of lead performers. Sarah Travis put narrative and character first:

Sarah Travis: Certainly for the leads, you're looking for actors. I want – even though I'm biased to the musicality and the vocal technique and their ranges – I want people who can put a song across and who can act, otherwise they can be an amazing singer but they're not going to move an audience. It's not going to be interesting to watch. So for me it's the all-round package really.

Gareth Valentine, though, warned that there are moments in a show where the dazzling vocals of the performer have to come first:

Gareth Valentine: I do find that however good an actor might be, whatever his or her prowess is in acting, audiences are not so forgiving when the moment comes to stand and deliver. I'm talking about to really stand and sing that stuff. You can have somebody who's perhaps not as good an actor but has a fantastic voice, and they can really stand there, on that stage, and land the numbers with authority, with vocal authority, and audiences are much, much more forgiving – that's something I've discovered over the years.

Stuart Morley agrees and says it can lead to difficulties in casting:

Stuart Morley: Oh, absolutely. I'm not a fan of the term 'money notes', but it's true that some of the audience are waiting for those moments and may well have bought a ticket to hear them. So if Elphaba doesn't do the big ending of "Defying Gravity" that everyone is expecting, or she doesn't nail the end of "The Wizard And I", a lot of people are disappointed. Because some people are going to a show to hear the music, absolutely, and while the storytelling is absolutely crucial audiences sometimes get frustrated when performers can't or don't deliver what we were expecting. And that's when the casting becomes tricky, because then you end up with that difficult position where everyone wants someone because they're the most incredible storytelling actor but the music department's saying, "Yes, they're a great actor, but they won't be able to sing it eight times a week."

But how does an auditionee find their way into this narrative and character way of performing, and how does that express itself in vocal choices? I took the opportunity to speak to *Les Misérables* MD Stuart Morley to explore those characters in more depth, starting with Fantine:

> **Stuart Morley**: She's a mum. So you want someone who you can empathise with. And that doesn't mean you have to be a mum to play it, by any means, but you need someone who has that sort of caring quality. And Fantine is not particularly high. So, yeah, can they hit the notes that they need to, but much more importantly, can they break your heart? And I suppose each character has a thing, a hook, and you always need to be able to empathise with them, every character in every show, that's the same across the board. But let's say Fantine versus Eponine: Eponine is a very tough teenager – she has to be. Fantine is tough in a different way, you watch her on stage, having her life ripped away from her and then she sadly dies. Eponine has to fight to survive and Fantine has to fight for Cosette. And of course everyone is driven by love. So all of the characters have massive similarities, but they also have their own individualities they need to find.

These characteristics can help an auditionee find the appropriate vocal sound. As Stuart Morley went on to discuss, these characteristics are the very things that determine that sound:

> **Stuart Morley**: Absolutely, yeah, because all of those acting choices, all those character traits, are going to have a different vocal quality to them. So, Eponine has a fighting quality and a determination to her voice, because she has to fight for her place in the world. When we first meet adult Cosette – teenage Cosette as she actually is when she first walks on stage and sings – it's a character we've never met before. We've had grumpy, moody, dying, miserable people for an hour and ten minutes, and then suddenly, we've got a fresh, young, optimistic teenager who's discovering a new kind of love for the first time. We've not really met someone like that in *Les Mis*. So, Cosette has to sound like something different, and something fresh, and youthful.

It's the same for the two leading men in the show, who contrast in a way that reveals how they should sound:

> **Stuart Morley**: So, actually, James Powell one of our two fantastic directors, said it brilliantly: "Javert is Old Testament, fire and brimstone, order; Valjean is New Testament, forgiveness and redemption." So what does that sound like? If you said to someone, "You'll be forgiven" or "You are in trouble and will face the wrath of God", one has a warmth and a lightness, and the other one has a strictness and an attack to it. So when Javert walks in to the audition room, if you think, "Oh, yeah, I want to give you a big hug," that's probably not Javert. If someone comes in looking like they have empathy and a rawness to their character, then they're

probably more a Jean Valjean. But of course, Javert has to break your heart, through his own journey, because he believes that what he is doing is right, and that it is God's will. So you can't have some one-dimensional, angry cardboard policeman character, that's not going to work. You have to empathise with them, too, otherwise we don't really care when they take their own life towards the end of the show. And "Stars", of course, is their big song where they explain what they believe in. So Jean Valjean and Javert both have a passion and both have a drive. But one has to sound more like a righteous headteacher, and the other one has to sound more like a lost soul who can and will be redeemed.

In the first chapter, we encountered the idea of essence and mould, and that, particularly once a show is past its original cast, there is a mould to each character that auditionees have to fit. As one of the longest-running shows in the West End, I wanted to know if this was the case with *Les Misérables.* Stuart Morely says auditionees often think that, but it's not what he's found:

Stuart Morley: The longer a show runs, the more there is a preordained expectation of "they want this for *Les Mis*." And when I first joined *Les Mis* I didn't know what the expectations were. I joined, I learnt the score, I had my meetings, I had lots of chats, I did my research, and I turned up. And the big (and wonderful) surprise for me personally was that there is no template for who Jean Valjean is or for what he sounds like. And the creative team are very happy for people to bring themselves to the room and offer up fresh ideas. I don't mean change all the notes and add riffs or things like that, I mean, the score is the score, but no-one is there saying, "You cry on 3, you vibrato on beat 6 there, you've got to make sure that diphthong's there, etc.".

When an MD looks for character and narrative in an auditionee's performance, one of the ways those qualities may appear is in the vocal choices the auditionee makes in their song. Stuart Morley says if those choices remain rooted in the text, they're more likely to be convincing:

Stuart Morley: When it's lyric driven, then the vast majority of the musical choices tend to sort themselves out, in my experience. I very rarely say to a singer, "Can you belt that," "Can you do this", "Can you do that." And in *Les Mis* auditions, I very rarely said anything specifically about vocal technique to the auditionees. The notes I give to singers are often character based. "What should this sound like?" Well, what are you feeling there? And what's the setting, what's the situation? So "Bring Him Home": it's a prayer, it's nighttime. "How loud should it be?" It's a prayer, it's nighttime. Everyone's sleeping around you. Or, "shall I belt that note?" Well, how passionate do you feel about this? "Very." Ok, then maybe. So the vocal choices are always driven by the text. And I think that's the thing, when someone comes into the room and they really own the material, it's because they've embodied the text. And if they do things that work for them musically, you believe it and accept those musical choices.

Musicality

Alongside technique, character and narrative, our MDs were keen to discuss musicality. Gareth Valentine described how musicality can add so much to an auditionee's performance. I asked him where musicality begins, for him:

Gareth Valentine: Listening. And I make the distinction between hearing something and listening to something. The art of listening, even listening to conversation is very, very particular, and there are some singers, not very many in musical theatre, but certainly in the opera house, who have ears like fruit bats. So when they're listening to an orchestral or a piano accompaniment, they will listen to it before they sing a note and ask themselves what's going on there, and they'll listen to every nook and cranny of the accompaniment, because that will inform to some idea, to some degree, what the intentions of the composer were, and how they should respond to it as a singer, as the thing which goes over and with the accompaniment. And when it happens it's magical, but it's very, very rare in musical theatre.

Gareth Valentine went on to explain that singers who do have that musicality create something very special:

Gareth Valentine: If you find somebody like Robert Meadmore, or like Marin Mazzie is a very good example, who are musicians, there's a connection there which is undeniable. You think about Ella Fitzgerald, you think about Mel Tormé, in those categories of music, their musicianship was just through the roof. When Ella Fitzgerald is scatting, it's extraordinary, it's almost like a supernatural ability. That ear was incredible. I've yet to see that in musical theatre. But don't forget we're dealing mostly with actors who are playing a role and they happen to sing. And my job as an MD is to use all my armoury, everything, to support them, and to explain to them why certain things are written in a certain way, what to listen for, what not to do. And sometimes I'll make things easier for them by adapting an accompaniment, or any and all the tricks in my armoury to assist their performance.

Stuart Morley pointed out that musicality in an auditionee is important to any MD because of their future relationship in performance:

Stuart Morley: Extremely important. Because, of course, you've got to conduct them. And if you're the supervisor on the panel, you're aware someone else has got to conduct them. So if someone is rhythmically struggling, then you start to question if it's going to be a nightmare to get together with the orchestra, and that's going to reflect badly on both the performer and conductor.

It's important to remember that the MD is the only one of our creatives who will go on to have a performance relationship with the auditionee once the show is running, and this factors into their assessments during the audition stage. Sean Green also looks for a level of musicality that will lead to a secure performance:

Sean Green: Some people have wonderful voices but slightly lose control over where they're placing things, or where or how things happen in the performance. I personally prefer people who are very musical and rhythmic and have a control over the performance, a confidence to knowing that you're going to be able to place a riff or a run and end exactly where you wanted to end it, and on exactly the right note, rather than, "I'm going to do a riff, and it'll end somewhere."

Sean Green also recalled the impact of an auditionee who was particularly expressive in her musicality and created a connection with him as accompanist:

Sean Green: Somebody came in and did a song, and I was playing because my pianist had to go home and she gave me an iPad – and technology destroys me! I was changing the pages and for some reason I hit something, and the song shut. So I was in the middle of a song, playing, going, Oh, my God!, looking at her home screen going "err!" It's a song I kind of know, roughly, but not really very well, and so I managed to get it back open but I didn't know which page I was on, and I thought, well, I'll slow it down and finish the song, because I know this bit. And as I was slowing it down and getting quieter, she slowed down and got quieter, but then she led me into another chorus in the same vein, in the same quiet, taken back, introverted place, and she carried on. And so I carried on following her. And I thought at that moment, that's a real skill to have. She wasn't ready to finish and even though I was saying, "Let's finish," she was saying, "No, I want to carry on and I'm going to carry on in this vein that you've set me and improvise," and we finished together. And I was like, 'Okay, that's great, that's impressive!'

Song choice

Auditionees can agonise over what song to take to a first round. Generally, a song which is not from the show they are auditioning for is advised. Sarah Travis explains why:

Sarah Travis: I would tend to say probably don't bring a song from the show first round because if you're going to get through to the second round, we're going to give you stuff from the show. I'd rather see someone bring something they've chosen which says a bit more about who they are before we then put a character on to them for the next round.

There are exceptions, though. In *MJ: The Musical*, Sean Green says those auditioning for the title role have to sing show material because the demands are so specific:

Sean Green: One of the songs in Act One is "Stranger in Moscow", which has quite a high belt, and because of where it is in the show and the emotion, it has to be full voiced and quite passionate but still sound like Michael, so we hear that. And then he has to sing multiple songs in falsetto, so in the first round we hear a cut of "Don't Stop 'Til You Get Enough", which has a high D# in falsetto. And we also hear "They Don't Care About Us", which also has high singing and a bit more bite, a bit more venom and frustration. So, we hear those things in round one and if they can't do those things, then it's like, well, we know. MJ is a very specific, specific character and role but that's an example of the criteria they have to meet in round one before they progress.

For other roles in the show, though, first rounds are a mix of show material and own choice songs:

Sean Green: With other characters we do hear their own songs, as well, because it gives us a bit more of an insight into what they do comfortably with their voice, how they see themselves, how they present themselves, and then we will hear small sections of other songs from the show.

Although the performers in *MJ: The Musical* are triple-threat actor-singer-dancers, the specific demands of each role create a weighting towards one of those disciplines, and that informs the audition process:

Sean Green: In *MJ*, there's more emphasis on the singers sing, the dancers dance, and the actors act. And the MJs themselves have to do all of it. But the dancers we have in the show are dancing – they do all have to sing, they do have to have a voice, but they are dancing, and the singers are singing, so that's where that's weighted. And we observe that in the first round of auditions and we are working to that model.

Another question auditionees often consider is whether they can change the key of their song to better suit their voice. Stuart Morley says that in most cases, keys are chosen to suit the performer, so he fully supports picking a good key for an audition. However, once auditions move to show material, the key will probably have to remain the same, unless it's a brand-new musical:

Stuart Morley: With a new musical, in my experience, you can usually change the key if you really want a certain actor to play the role. And I've absolutely done that, I've said, "That key doesn't work for you, let's just change the key. What's your money note? Then that's what the key is." And of course, that's what happened originally, it's just that we lose track of that. "On My Own" is always in D. It's in D because that was the best key for [original Eponine] Frances Ruffelle. You only have to look at *Wicked*, you can see Stephen's original handwritten score for "Defying Gravity" is not in the same key that is in the show. But I know, having been in a room with Stephen, that he doesn't often mind what key his songs are in – as long as it suits the singer and they can tell the right story through his music. So, don't be afraid to change the key of your song for the first round, it doesn't matter what key it was ever in, no-one usually minds, in my experience. However, you shouldn't ever change the key of the set material. And if the show really wants a certain performer, they will change the key: for example, *Wicked* has alternate keys for the Wizard, and *Les Mis* has an alternate key for "Empty Chairs at Empty Tables".

As well as song choices, there are vocal choices in the performance of those songs. The choice to riff in a song can be a risky one, as Stuart Morley explains:

Stuart Morley: I don't think I've ever really met a composer who's written a riff. They often tolerate them, but I don't really know how much they really enjoy them? When I'm working on *We Will Rock You* my first comment is, usually, don't riff all over the melody – and don't try and improve what Freddie sang. You don't need to. You can absolutely make it your own. Brian [May] and Roger [Taylor] are extremely generous with letting people make it their own, they're happy for people to interpret their songs. But the audience know and love the original recordings, so we have to be faithful to the melodies and not riff them away.

Another vocal choice lies between what's written down in the music and what's performed on a cast recording. Stuart Morley says it can be difficult for auditionees to choose what to do:

Stuart Morley: In many cases, the composer is likely to have been present when the original cast recording is made, so it's usually safe to assume that what is on the recording has (to some degree) been signed off by the composer. However, I would always advise using the score as the primary reference point.

So, Stuart Morley's advice is first to adhere to the written score:

Stuart Morley: I think when you walk in a room as a performer, you should embody the language of the show and be respectful of the material that you've been given. Use that as the starting point for what you build your interpretation on. My opening speech at *We Will Rock You* rehearsals is that we start with Queen. The original Scaramouche, Hannah Jane Fox: incredible! But we don't start with Hannah. That's Hannah's version. We start with Freddie, because that's the source material.

However, if a composer is in the room, Stuart has found them to be open to new ideas from performers:

Stuart Morley: With *Fools and Horses*, I've actually co-written some of the songs so when people say to me, "Well, I want to do this," much to my amazement, I don't respond with, "Well, I wrote this," even though I know exactly what I wrote; I usually say, "Right, let me hear your ideas." Someone changed the melody once, and I actually thought it was better than what I wrote so decided to keep it.

Stuart Morley alluded to another important aspect of performance, above, which he called 'entering the language of the show'. This means understanding the musical choices in the score and therefore understanding which vocal choices are appropriate to that:

Stuart Morley: You need to get inside the head of the composer. Don't just listen to that one song that you're going to audition with. Let's say you're auditioning for *Wicked*. Listen to some of Stephen Schwartz's other shows. Look at the scores, look at a note bash, see what was written down, and then, if you are going to refer to a recording, I always say to students and to performers, listen to the original cast recording. Even if it's not quite what's on the score, the composer signed that off. For me, when I was learning *Les Mis*, I went back to the original French recording, the original Barbican recording, and then the original London cast recording.

Another issue with imitating cast recordings is the authenticity of the performance. Many of our MDs want to see genuine expression and connection in an audition. Sarah Travis says that might mean choosing material that gives an auditionee the opportunity to tell a story:

Sarah Travis: Often, I'll say bring a song that has a good narrative and also shows off your voice, then you can see whether they can connect. What I'm looking for really is connection: whether they can connect to the lyric and how far they can go with that connection. And I think for me that says quite a lot about what we're going to get out of someone.

Connecting with a text can lead to making interesting choices about the song and what it's expressing. For Gareth Valentine, this often makes for an engaging audition:

Gareth Valentine: If you think about it, what is a song? A song is a point of view. When people come in and they express a point of view, it may be incongruous, it may not be in keeping with the song, but they have a point of view, and it just jumps out, and you think, well, that's interesting! I wouldn't have done it that way but there's something going on there.

Affecting the panel and creating an impact are key to good auditions. Without that, the auditionee risks losing the panel's interest:

Sarah Travis: I have sat through a lot of auditions where, I've tried not to, but I have briefly switched off because I'm not engaged and something isn't happening there. If someone has absolutely gripped me, then that's a good audition. It happened this last week, an auditionee came in and sang a song called "Freddy, My Love", which is a song that a character called Marty sings, and I've probably heard that song hundreds of times, and she just did something really interesting with it. I told her, "Well, I've heard that song many times, but you've brought something new to that." The acting choice, I mean mainly about the acting choices. But if I'm not engaged then it normally means that they're not connected to the material, I think.

With several roles to cast, an auditionee can help the panel by signalling where they see themselves in the production. Stuart Morley says it's an important consideration:

Stuart Morley: When you're picking your own song, really think about who you see yourself as in the show. I often say to students, "Okay, this is a great audition song for this show: who do you see yourself as?" "Well, ensemble." "No. Who do you see yourself as?" You have to see yourself as a character.

Even if you think there's a distant, outside chance that you are that character, you have to walk in the room saying, "I am this." Because then the panel, who are sometimes seeing around fifty people a day for at least a week or two, certainly for the big shows – *Les Mis*, *We Will Rock You*, any of those – that's a lot of people to see. So it can be a helpful signpost for the panel. Some people walk in and you think, "Are you a Scaramouche, are you a Meat/Oz? Which one are you?" Because look-wise, they look similar. Same with Eponines and Fantines. If there's an age crossover, are you a young Fantine, are you an old Eponine? And people can signpost that with their song choice for the first round, and they can subtly signpost it with what they wear. What does a young mum wear versus what does someone who's fought all their life wear? And with *Rock You*, when someone walks in in Dr. Martens, wearing relatively all black, we go: okay, so you think you're Scaramouche, great, thank you. The panel may of course see you as a different role, but in my experience, signposts are often very helpful anyway.

Preparation

A lot of what we have discussed above – song choices, vocal choices, musicality, signposting a character – can be strengthened in an audition through preparation. Preparation was mentioned by all our MDs as an important factor:

Gareth Valentine: You have a very precious three minutes in which to show yourself off to your best advantage. You have to squeeze every bit of juice out of that three minutes. Don't have a song in the wrong key. Don't have the wrong song. Know what you're going to say to the pianist. Go in so prepared.

Sarah Travis says proper preparation allows auditionees to connect with the panel on a professional level:

Sarah Travis: You want them to have done a little bit of homework as to what the musical is about and what the part is that they're up for. Most directors will want to have a quick chat with them about what they feel the part is about or what they feel the show is about. You would hope that they've read the script, at least – obviously if it's a new piece, it's more difficult – but certainly for an existing piece. So I would look for someone who's coming in who's going to sell themselves. We want everyone who comes into a room to get the job so you're willing everyone to do the best they can but, if someone's come in – and they may not even be right for the show – but they've come in with confidence, prepared, wanting to connect and interested in the project, interested in meeting the panel, and they've nailed the song that they brought in – obviously if they're talented, that's great too – but if they've done their work and they've done their homework and they've given themselves the best chance they can, then that's a good audition for me.

Stuart Morley says some auditionees don't adequately prepare for auditions:

Stuart Morley: What do you want to see when the people walk in the room from preparation? That you know the show. When we did *Elf* auditions, we had one actor say, "I haven't watched the film because I want to create my own character." Whilst there will nearly always be room for someone to make a character their own, it's pretty likely that the majority of the audience are coming to see a show like *Elf* because they enjoyed the film. We had similar scenarios at *Only Fools and Horses*: "I've never seen an episode." Right, well, you maybe should because the audience really have! And no-one really wants a new take on Rodney, we just want Rodney, it's iconic, the script is written for that, the songs are written for that. So then you end up thinking, "Do you want the job? I don't know." Preparation is partly about demonstrating that you understand the show that you're auditioning for. And that goes with the material as well. You should be as familiar as you can be with the set material. The panel will offer help and advice, but you really need people to have done their homework in order to get the best out of their audition.

Sean Green wants to see preparation as well but says he understands that it can be difficult for auditionees:

Sean Green: I'm aware that not everyone has the chance to run a song with a pianist, and not everyone has the skills to look through a piano part that they've printed off online and go, "Okay, this makes sense." I think sometimes people go, "I want to sing this song," and they'll get the sheet music from wherever they can and the sheet music is terrible. And then they'll go, "Oh! it's not in the right key," or "Oh, this isn't the key I practised in, could you take it down a little bit?" I think not everyone has the tools on hand or even the money to go and find a pianist to run the music in advance. So I am forgiving of that.

One of the basics of music preparation is giving the pianist sheet music with a piano part. Sean Green recalls a recent auditionee who unknowingly arrived with music that contained no piano part and says it affected the quality of her audition:

Sean Green: Somebody brought in "Alfie", the Burt Bacharach song, which is full of composite chords and moving patterns, and it's Burt Bacharach so it's complicated. But they just brought in a melody line and chords, and the chords can't really spell out precisely what that song is doing. The accompanist didn't know it, and I could tell by his playing that he was kind of struggling, and she was struggling, and it wasn't matching up, and she was actually quite fresh out of drama school and I said, "Oh, by the way, this music isn't great. I think you should potentially get another one with the actual piano part. There's no piano part." And she said, "Oh, I'm so sorry." And she had no idea that what she'd got wasn't really usable. I mean, it was usable because he's a great pianist but it would have been a lot easier for her and for him if she had music that actually had a piano part on it.

Sean Green is also aware of auditionees who get sheet music from other auditionees while waiting to be seen:

Sean Green: I've done auditions in the past where it's been dancers, and somebody has come in and done a song and gone out, then the next person's come in and done the same song with the same sheet music. So they basically borrow that music from that person, go, "I'll sing that song!" bring it back in, put it on the piano, say to me "And it goes like this," and I'm like, "Oh, okay, yeah, sure," and it's literally the same battered corners, same markings.

Shaun Aquilina: Does that worry you, that level of preparation?

Sean Green: Well, I mean he did know the song so I guess it's one of the songs that maybe is in his rep but he didn't bring it that day, or he was reminded of it and thought, Well, I'll give that a go today. I mean, he didn't get the job, but not because of that particular thing, but it was just an interesting thing to note, that, oh, they're both doing the same song, and it's exactly the same sheet music, and one of them borrowed it from somebody, or they've both borrowed it from somebody else, who knows.

When someone hasn't prepared, the MDs can spot it. But Sarah Travis says it's unusual:

Sarah Travis: It is obvious when someone hasn't done their prep. I have had auditions where they've just not learnt the material, especially if you give out recall material. But it's rare. Most people want the job so it is in their interest to do the prep.

Sean Green says auditionees come up with excuses as to why they have not prepared the material:

Sean Green: The thing we get quite a lot is, "Oh, my agent told me not to prepare that bit," or "My agent didn't tell me I had to do that bit," or "That material wasn't in the breakdown." And I'm aware that the emails that get sent out from casting directors are very specific and all the material is on a Dropbox, and it's very clear about if you're going for this part, you need to learn this, this, this, this. So I'm a bit, "Oh, okay, mm-hmm, yeah, you haven't looked at it."

Another tactic from auditionees isn't about preparation as much as avoiding material that might show their limitations. But Sean Green says it doesn't work:

Sean Green: People will try and not do the thing that they feel uncomfortable with. So, for instance, when I was doing *Get Up Stand Up!*, we were looking for Peter Tosh and Bunny Wailer, and they have to sing falsetto and so we sent out bits of the score that have them singing in falsetto and the person that came in did an amazing own song, very melismatic and riffy and great, but all full voiced, and I said, "Have you learned the material?" And they're like, "Oh, I didn't get the material." So I said, "Okay . . . well, shall we do some scales? I really need to hear some falsetto." And I saw his face drop. And I was like, I know you got the material, you just didn't want to do it because you didn't want to show that side of your voice, because you feel it's weak, or whatever. And when we did it, he had very little falsetto and I was like, well, the thing I need to see is the thing you've avoided doing but I'm going to get to it one way or another.

Shaun Aquilina: So you see a bit of dodging the difficult bits?

Sean Green: Yeah, sometimes. I mean, it makes sense to try and present the thing you're good at but if the thing we're looking for is a thing you're not good at, you're not going to get the job anyway. We're not going to hire you without seeing what we need to see.

Audition material from the show sometimes needs to be learnt in a few days. Stuart Morley says that being able to engage quickly with material goes to the heart of the musical theatre industry:

Stuart Morley: We work in an industry of immediacy and ultimately that's what we've all signed up for. So always learn the material to the very best of your ability. If you only got it very recently, people understand that, of course. It's generally obvious when someone hasn't really made an effort, and of course that speaks volumes about their work ethic. From memory doesn't matter to me. Except for finals, when it absolutely does! I've had people turn up to finals with scripts and scores in their hand, having been through four or five rounds, and I've thought, "Well, do you want the job, or do you not want the job?" So know the material, be familiar with the material, do as much homework as you've had time to do, and invest in the process.

And Stuart added that another part of investing in the process is turning up, looking like you've made an effort:

Stuart Morley: We work in a presentational industry. It's not about what you wear insofar as you must dress smart-casual etc., but it's about you looking like you've made an effort in how you present yourself. Because sometimes people look like they've just rocked out of bed and that can say a lot about their work ethic. And it's really important that you present yourself well. You can often tell by how someone walks in the room, how they address the pianist and how they introduce themselves, whether they're going to be right for this. And again, I've been happily proved wrong on that a few times, but nine times out of ten you're proved right on it. Be the best version of yourself in the audition room, whatever that means for you.

Taking direction

As we've seen in the first two chapters, preparation for musical theatre auditions has to be accompanied by an openness to take direction, to changing and making different choices in the audition room. Sarah Travis says that's such an important aspect to a performer that, without it, they're unlikely to get the job:

> **Sarah Travis**: I have worked with people that have come in and auditioned really well but that's what you get, they never change. And if there's any hints that they're not going to respond to direction then that's a bit of a red flag for me, I think. And I think for most directors I work with. You really do need people that are going to respond and be willing to go on a journey.

That's why Sarah Travis, as mentioned earlier, will change a song style in an audition and see if the auditionee can respond:

> **Sarah Travis**: That tells me a lot: whether they're completely rigid to a style that is in their comfort zone or whether they can take direction, and whether they're brave enough to trust someone that's asking them to go in a totally different direction. And very quickly you know if someone has an instinct to be able to flip and sing in a different style.

Gareth Valentine also wants to see auditionees who can change what they're doing, in response to a creative's direction:

> **Gareth Valentine**: What's good is when people are malleable, when they can take notes. You'd be amazed how many people come in and sing a song, and then are given quite explicit notes by a director, or by me, even by the choreographer, sometimes the producer, and they will think about the notes, and consolidate them for a moment and then sing the number again but exactly in the same way they did it. It's like a fly in amber, there's rigidity there. But if you have a flexible mind – that's really what it amounts to – and all those diversity of ideas in your head, it's just so palpable.

The auditionee who is stuck in their way of doing something is a source of great frustration to the creative team:

> **Gareth Valentine**: It's clear if they're rigid, if they're unbending, and so the performance of the song is immutable: that's no good. Sometimes you can try a second and a third time, because they look the part. And they go up there and you go 'fuck!' because in every way they're right, apart from the fact they just don't have that little mercurial flexibility.

Sean Green is happy to see any level of change in an auditionee when they're given direction:

> **Sean Green**: I think even if they don't manage to do exactly what you ask them, the fact that they are able to do something shows you about them and their process. Because some people come in to audition, and they have learned it a certain way, and that is the only way they can do it. And you can redirect them, and they will do exactly the same thing again. And that's very difficult in a rehearsal process because what you get is what you get. People who manage to take your note and do it in addition perfectly are like gold dust. But everyone is

processing and doing lots of things, and there's nerves, and often they don't hear exactly what you say, so if they do anything that's slightly different from what they did first time around, it's almost a win. The fact that they can change it even a slight amount means that they are able to be moulded in a certain direction. And you might learn that it's going to take you a long time to mould them in a direction you want to get them to, but as long as they can start the process in front of you, that's a good thing.

Like Sarah Travis, above, Stuart Morley also takes his performers in different directions to create the sound he needs. He says it's not only vital to him; it's part of what keeps a show alive and running:

Stuart Morley: I'll often try things to try to access a certain sound and also to see if people can take direction. For example, I was working on the opening of "The Docks" at *Les Mis* and we were trying to access a certain sound. I said, "What would sailors who've just got off a boat in the 1820s in France, looking for prostitutes, actually sound like, and how do we access that? What's the vocal sound? Who are you? You're people who really want something. You smell something, you think, oh, my God, that's amazing! So try singing it like you've just caught the smell of your favourite meal in the air." And then suddenly the song lifted. I didn't know if that would work. It did on that occasion. Sometimes an idea doesn't quite work, or it doesn't access the right sound, so then I'll try a different approach. Exploring the material and playing with different ideas is an important part of the process. What you want in the audition room is to see that people are willing to try things. If someone is a closed book, "No, this is how I do it," then you can't work with them because the collaborative creativity is not going to happen and every show needs that. Even on a show that's been running thirty-nine years like *Les Mis*, there is always an air of creativity in the room. And when Claude-Michel [Schönberg] and Cameron [Mackintosh] come in, they're often looking for ways to keep the show sounding and looking fresh. And that's probably why it's stayed there for thirty-nine years, because if it was stuck in a rut maybe it would have closed a long time ago.

Taking direction can be even more important at the recall stages, where the work with the creative panel can go deeper. Sean Green remembers working in detail during auditions for *Into the Woods*:

Sean Green: A lot of the auditions were quite long. I mean for context, in *MJ*, we're seeing the MJs for about twenty to thirty minutes, and other characters for ten to fifteen minutes, and seeing quite a lot of them over the course of a day; for *Into the Woods*, I remember having thirty-to-forty-minute auditions and really going into the detail of the songs and the lines and the delivery, and asking the questions about what does this line mean, what does this line mean, and what do you think about the fact that this melody goes here. It was really detailed, fascinating actually, because a lot of the people who we were bringing in were really down to learn about it and to work. They became work sessions rather than auditions, in a sense, a lot of them.

Shaun Aquilina: What effect do you think that had on the final production?

Sean Green: It definitely had a bearing on the final production in that they were ready to come in and do that kind of work in the rehearsals as well. I think that it set a tone for what the show was going to be and that that show was detailed.

Company personality

Longer, more detailed auditions also give the panel an opportunity to assess the kind of people they may end up working with. We've seen in previous chapters how important it is to be a company member, and Sarah Travis says that's something she won't compromise on:

Sarah Travis: I'm much more aware now of whether someone is going to work well in a company, whether someone's going to be collaborative, for me that's much more important now than it probably was when I was starting out. A lot of the types of shows I do are quite ensemble based, particularly the actor-muso stuff, so it's very important that you get people who are good at collaborating, are good listeners, and are nice and pleasant to work with, that's quite a big, big part of it now. It's rare that you get someone that you think, oh, absolutely not. Sometimes you think, I'm not sure, there's something going on with that person, or there's something not quite connected there, or not sure that they're going to be a team player, you can get a sense of that, but it is rare I think.

Sarah Travis added that creating a positive, supportive company is important to her personally and professionally:

Sarah Travis: Quite frankly, I'm old enough to not want to be in a room where I'm unhappy, and I'm working with someone that doesn't want to be there or isn't wanting to collaborate, isn't wanting to be in a company, maybe has a big ego. I want to work in rooms that are happy rooms because that means happy work and best work. I've been in not very happy rooms over the years and pretty much 99 per cent of the time the end result isn't as good as it could have been. So, for me, it is a big part of it.

Sean Green agrees that happy and supportive work environments are preferable and lead to stronger productions. He says he tries to model this when working:

Sean Green: As a person I try to be kind. I have worked with musical supervisors and people who haven't necessarily always been kind, either to myself or to actors, and I don't necessarily think that the best work is created through strife or through stress or through difficulty. And that's not to say I'm not willing to call out people who aren't working hard enough but I suppose the leeway I extend to actors when they are in the audition room is something that carries on into the job itself. I think that the actors are the ones telling the story and that the MD role is a support role, in that we create the music that allows the actors to tell the story. And I don't know if MDs I've worked with in the past would feel that way or would necessarily behave that way. But I like to think that it's a support role, and that's where I see myself.

As the audition process moves to the final round, these elements of personality and working relationships come to the fore, as Sarah Travis describes:

Sarah Travis: By the time you're maybe in the last recall stage, you're probably in a twenty-minute interview. So the auditionee can ask questions about the project, there will be a dialogue, it will be a much more personal chat, because also it's do we feel we can work with them? Do we feel they're going to fit into the team and vice versa? They may not want to. They might be up for two or three things at the same time, and it might be "Well, what experience is going to be the best for me?" So, it's much more about the whole because by that stage we've heard their song, we've probably heard them read, they've probably done any other sort of disciplines, they've earned their place in the final round and it's more about how we're going to work together and maybe matching them up with other members of the company or how they're going to fit in.

Nerves

Our MDs have seen plenty of nervous auditionees. Sarah Travis says she tries to be patient and supportive:

Sarah Travis: I've had auditions where, because people are so scared, they're not giving their best but I will always try and put someone at ease. If they start a song or they forget the lyric and I know it's because of nerves, it's like, "Oh, let's start it again, breathe, just relax."

And MDs have often been through an audition process themselves. Sean Green recalls auditioning to be a keys player in a show and suffering an attack of nerves:

Sean Green: I lost the ability to speak. I was so confident because I was practising the music at home like, "Oh, my God, I can play this with my eyes closed!" I rocked up to the theatre and, for starters, I hadn't even considered there were other people going for this audition. And I don't know why I didn't think that but as soon as I arrived and there were other people there, I was thinking, "Oh, there are other people that could do this job. This isn't just my job." And then it comes, "Sean Green!" and, literally, my mouth lost all moisture. And I was so scared all of a sudden, like shaking, and I had never had that before. Because growing up, I used to do am-dram, I was a performer, so I had done auditions, and I got a little bit nervous but this was a new level of nerves I'd never had before. And when I went up into the room, I sat down in front of the Supervisor and the MD and shook their hands, started to play, and it just was not going my way, not at all. And I was like, I know I can play this. And they said, "Because you'll have some conductor responsibilities occasionally, can you just play but then also cue the singers?" And I remember being frantic! Then at the end I said, "Thank you," in a very shaky voice, and I left. And I thought, I haven't got that job, and they think I can't play the piano, which is great! So I do have a gentle respect for people coming into the room and auditioning, and I like to give them the benefit of the doubt. It's obvious when they haven't done the work and that will be reflected in my notes. But largely I do try and give people the benefit of the doubt when they walk in the room because it is a stressful, stressful situation.

Gareth Valentine says nerves are part of being human, and the best strategy for an auditionee is to absolutely focus on their material:

Gareth Valentine: Nerves is a great thing, because without nerves you're a stone, you're a shell. But you're a human being, and you will be apprehensive because a job's at stake and God knows life's hard enough as it is. But here's the thing: if you're really a good actress, good actor, a good singer, a good performer, you will have thought through the song again and again and again, and know what your intention is. When you're in the audition room, you're so into the song, into your performance, every bone of your body will become the character or will become involved in expressing the song that there's no room for nerves because you're too busy being an actor, you're too busy embodying something else. And it has worked for a lot of people like that. If you're singing a song and wondering what the team are thinking about you, "Oh he looked at me like he didn't like me," if that's all going through your head, forget it. You've got to be absolutely like a laser beam, just right inside that song or monologue or dance routine.

Gareth Valentine went on to give his own example of nerves in performance and conquering them by focusing on his material:

Gareth Valentine: When I was at the Royal Albert Hall, my first conducting job there with the RPO [Royal Philharmonic Orchestra] and it was the full 5,000 people sitting there, I remember my heart banging away. I could hear the orchestra tuning, then the lights went down, the orchestra went quiet, and two guys opened the door, and you walk on to the stage and all you hear is your feet for the first six steps. Nothing else. And then the light hits you, you hear the noise of the audience, it's fucking terrifying. But I took my bow, I turned around, I took my baton up, and immediately I did the first beat, it went away. I knew exactly what I wanted to do. It was now about the music. It couldn't be about anything else. And I think if I can get actors to do that, it's a great thing, because often auditions are ruined by nerves.

When nerves do strike, Gareth Valentine will advocate for the auditionee and get them a second chance:

Gareth Valentine: Often, I'll say to a director, I know that girl can sing better than that – because he's put a line through her name – I know she can act better than that, please can you give her another try? Ask her to do such and such. I did this with Richard Eyre, same girl came back in, nailed it, she got the job. So, people get nervous, but there was luck there, because I knew her, I knew what she could do. Some people don't have that. It's just one of those things.

Sarah Travis feels a responsibility on the part of the panel to give an auditionee the best experience they can. That can mean advocating for the auditionee and staying focused over the long hours of auditions:

> **Sarah Travis**: I've been on panels where people have been on their phones while someone's auditioning which I think is, for me, not cool at all. I've had someone nudge me and say, "Stop them singing now, they're not right," and I'm saying, "No, it's their five minutes, it's their time." So I want their time to be the best it can be. If it's a long day, I would say by half four, walking into a room is very different to walking in at 10 o'clock in the morning, and then we're probably a little bit weary, but you try to, and you want to, give everyone the fairest chance. So whether they come in at 10 or 5, it's still the same experience.

Workshops

As we've seen, not all shows begin their castings with auditions; there can be a workshop stage first. Gareth Valentine recalls that one of musical theatre's foremost composers said he would much rather have a cast first and then write the material for them:

> **Gareth Valentine**: I remember Stephen Sondheim saying something to me which is very interesting. He said that the ideal thing about a show is that you cast it and then you write it. He said nobody's ever done that. But can you imagine, you simply get a bunch of actors with a vague story and then you write the show, and that will be wonderful, and to my knowledge nobody's done that. But he said that would be some show.

Sarah Travis says she's involved in many workshops and admits that it's a chance to put a cast in place without auditioning:

> **Sarah Travis**: I do a lot of new stuff now and that's more where I want to go, actually, so I'm in a lot of workshop stages of development of new work. And even though the actors are there to work the material, you are sort of auditioning them from the workshop stage as well, and if a workshop goes well, you might want to hang on to some of those people. So by the time a new piece gets to opening, you've often almost cast it through the workshop stage, but it is a very, very different process.

Stuart Morley was very involved in the workshop stages for *Only Fools and Horses The Musical,* which went on to run for over a thousand performances in the West End. He says that, in his experience, there are two types of workshop:

Stuart Morley: You have the workshop where you're presenting at the end of it to investors, to theatre owners, to producers, etc., and then you have the workshop that's just an explorative creative process. For example, our second *Fools and Horses* workshop was closed. There was no performance at the end of it and it was just for us to work on the material and try ideas out prior to going into production.

The first workshop stage of *Only Fools and Horses* used a casting director to find performers:

Stuart Morley: We did two workshops, and we auditioned for the first one. That's not always the case, sometimes you just invite actors that you already know and trust to do a workshop, but for this one we cast it with Dave Grindrod. And I recall the second workshop, we mainly just used people from the first workshop and brought in a few extra people that we knew to supplement them. We then did a full audition process prior to the show opening in London.

And, importantly, the type of performer who's useful in the workshop stage can be different from the performer who ends up being cast:

Stuart Morley: I think it's different for a workshop than it is for a production. You nearly always want input from the actors at the workshop stage. On a new production, the original cast make it their own, of course, but with a workshop you need people who are creative and who are happy to try different things every day without resisting changes and saying, "Well, yesterday we did this." You're often changing things and trying new ideas in workshops – sometimes big, sometimes small. Some performers are very good at going, "Right, that's what it is," and then they lock it in and will deliver that every single day without fail, which is brilliant. And other performers are very good at the "well, what about if we try this? What about if we try that?" approach, and I think that's what you usually want for a workshop or for brand-new production. For me it's all about booking the right people for the right job, and also about playing to people's strengths whilst supporting any weaknesses (which we all have) as best you can. Because of the speed at which you work in a workshop setting, you also need performers who can work fast and think on their feet, and if the focus is mainly on the score then it's also helpful to have performers who read music too.

As Sarah Travis commented, it's possible to cast a new show from the workshop stages; however, Stuart Morley says that's not always the case, as performers often have other commitments:

Stuart Morley: I think we probably took maybe a third of the people from the *Only Fools and Horses* workshop into the original London cast – mainly because people weren't available, and certainly not because of their talents. A workshop commitment will often be daytimes for a few days or a couple of weeks, but a run of a show is a very different commitment, especially for performers with children, which can also be a factor in who stays from the workshop stages into the production.

New shows and re-casts

Once into the audition process for a new show, the MDs suggested they were more open to ideas and interpretations from auditionees. Sean Green described how working on a new show influences his approach:

> **Sean Green**: When you're doing a brand-new show, you only have your imagination to go from, and what the music and the script say about the characters, to influence what you're looking for. I always start with quite a practical approach: can they sing the notes that are in the score and can they do it in the style that's required of the show? And then on top of that, you look at style, presence in the room, vibes are very important, especially if you're working with someone for a long time. Lots of things come into play once the person can meet the basic requirements.

Sarah Travis says she enjoys seeing creative auditionees who come with an angle the panel haven't considered:

> **Sarah Travis**: You might be in an audition process for a new piece and you're still not really quite sure exactly what you're looking for and it might be that someone comes into the room and goes in a different direction, maybe reads it in a very different way, or talks about the piece or the character they're up for in a different way, and you think, Oh, that's interesting, and I think lots of ideas will spark off. It's a much more open playing field in a way.

And because it's a new show, there's the opportunity to adapt the music to the performer, if they have captured the panel's attention:

> **Sarah Travis**: You might have songs where you know roughly where they stand, but I've had people come in singing for stuff that is not in their range or something, but they're so brilliant, you think, well, we'll make it work, I might rewrite it or we'll transpose it, but it's worth exploring that further.

Gareth Valentine described how the process develops from being a brand-new show to re-casting, with both music and expectations becoming more fixed:

> **Gareth Valentine**: I just did a brand-new show called *Sinatra*, and it was a brand-new script, and all of the songs were existing songs from the Sinatra catalogue but they were approached in a different way because they weren't just sung as Sinatra sung them, they were sung by other characters in the show. That meant different keys and a different approach, and so when we were auditioning, we didn't have a score because the show was still being written and arranged. Now we've done the show and so, when the auditions happen, now we have material, and we have ideas because they're fully fashioned characters, we know what

they need to do, we know the expectations. Sometimes we cut songs which meant that the character now was a smaller role and therefore perhaps wouldn't be as tempting to an actor who otherwise would be wonderful but not interested. You have to think about it: do we need to get that song back because we need to make it a tastier part for a prospective actor? And again with *Chicago*, it's just a little machine, or *Wicked*, they're all on staggered contracts so the auditions never end: auditioning, auditioning, and rehearsing, and rehearsing. It's like a prolific machine that eats them up and spits them out.

One other type of show that's worth considering from the MD's point of view is the actor-musician (often known as actor-muso) show. Sarah Travis says auditions for those shows are much more involved:

Sarah Travis: They're very different events because the music is so much more. . . well, the performers are doing everything! So I have much more of a say about who is cast because it's not just about their vocal ability, it's about the whole musical soundscape.

Performers are also expected to showcase more abilities and thus get more time in the room:

Sarah Travis: The auditions tend to be a little bit longer: they'll bring a song for their vocal; they might play two instruments, in which case we hear both the instruments; and often with the instruments they bring in a piece that's really not related to the show so then I will work with them and see whether they can play in a different style; and range, if it's a trumpet, say, I would explore their range to see if they are more a Trumpet 1 or Trumpet 2 (slightly lower range) and so I might get them to play some scales. This would also show their tone/ stamina/breathing technique, etc. The music casting side of an actor-muso audition is broader than in a conventional audition.

Collaborating with the rest of the panel

Once into the audition process, our MDs discussed a strong sense of collaboration with the rest of the audition panel in making decisions on whom to take forward. Stuart Morley says it can often only be in the actual auditions that panel members begin to understand one another:

Stuart Morley: In my experience, you often only have one or two pre-production meetings before auditions, sometimes in person or maybe on Zoom. On a new production of an existing show, *The Baker's Wife*, for example [Menier Chocolate Factory, 2024, Stuart as Music Supervisor] I didn't know Gordon and Matt [director Gordon Greenberg and choreographer Matt Cole] prior to this production. We'd had a couple of planning meetings and email chats, but, really, auditions was the time when we all sat together and started putting all of the creative and practical elements together. During auditions, you often engage in in-depth character discussions and also chat about the design and overall feel of the production. And so by the time you finish the auditions you usually have a much clearer idea of your fellow creatives' vision of the production, which I find very helpful when I'm orchestrating or writing vocal arrangements as I can work hard to make it sound like how I know they want it to look and feel. In my opinion and in my experience, creative collaboration is always the key to success.

Sarah Travis finds it useful when there's an existing relationship with her other panel members as this can guide the selection process:

Sarah Travis: There are some directors I work with a lot who I have a shorthand with, and I know them really well, and I know the type of person that they will like. And there's a trust so I feel I can have more of a voice. But there are other directors who maybe I don't know so much or I'm not quite so comfortable with, that I would maybe not have quite such confidence to speak up.

Shaun Aquilina: Is it possible that there are shared values between you and those directors with whom you often collaborate, in what you're looking for in an auditionee?

Sarah Travis: Yeah. Oh yeah definitely. And we will have probably talked more about the process and about what we're looking for.

When it comes to initial decisions, the panel's discussions can be brief, with members asking each other if there's something in an auditionee that's valuable to the production:

Sarah Travis: Often you have the choreographer and the director and often producers and all sorts in the room and so it might be a quick: "Are they useful for you?", "Are they useful for you?", "Are they useful for you?" and we have a consensus about whether to recall them. It's sometimes tricky because there are a lot of voices in a room and there's only a certain amount of time. I might think someone's worth exploring, the others may not because maybe they've come through a dance audition and they're not really quite good enough dance-wise or the director doesn't think they're right. So you're sort of second guessing but if I feel someone's really worth the time to explore, then I will speak up. And it might be that if I don't think someone's worth exploring and the director does, normally I know them well enough and they'll turn and say, "Sarah, could you just check this out a bit more" and then I think, "Oh, well ok they're more interested" so then I'll do it.

Sarah Travis reflected that this way of working comes down to one thing: compromise:

Sarah Travis: I love collaborating and I think your best work comes out of collaborating, and that means you have to give, take, compromise . . . a lot of compromise, actually . . . but a good collaboration means that actually the compromise is there because the end result is the best it can be. Now, whether that's a compromise that the director wants someone who's a much better actor, and I'm a little bit concerned about the vocal, we would then talk about how we can make it work. So you would have those conversations. Compromise feels like a big word there, and that's not in a negative way.

When it comes to assessing an auditionee, our MDs have their own ways of working. Gareth Valentine gives auditionees a mark from A to D and checks the vocal register. He also writes detailed notes but takes an interesting precaution to make sure auditionees don't find out what he has written:

Gareth Valentine: The way I mark is I'll write a description of them so I can remember them because we see hundreds of people sometimes over weeks and months, so I write specific things: Welsh girl, red hair, odd shoes, or something like that, and then I'll write just words. But I'll do it in Welsh. I do it in Welsh, because sometimes they come near the table and they can read the notes. And one time at the Donmar, a girl went off, took her music off the table, and took all our notes with her in a music bag, the notes for every actor we'd seen, and so from that moment, I wrote all my notes in Welsh. And then I give them marks for voice only. So I'll put A, A minus, B, B minus, down to D, and that's a pretty good way of marking for me, it's never failed me. And then I'll put what their vocal register is, and then, because girls have three voices and boys only have one, I'll find out about the chest voice, the soprano voice, and then the medium range voice. If the score demands high singing, big money notes, then I need to find out they're there because we have to satisfy the demands of the score.

I wanted to know more about what kind of performance is rewarded with the highest of Gareth Valentine's marks. He says it doesn't happen often, but it's a combination of storytelling, voice and musicality:

Gareth Valentine: Oh, very rarely will you get A's. And then one day you'll have a whole morning of A's! But A's are very rare for me, but people say I'm a hard marker. But an A for me is somebody who comes in and sings and is prepared, who really understands what they're singing about; when they're singing, they're telling you something, "I think this . . ." and they need to show me something. And then, if there's that wonderful voice as well, and on top of that musicality, now, that's very rare.

At the other end of the scale, Gareth Valentine sees the D-rated singers as a risk to the production:

Gareth Valentine: A D would normally be if it was a dancing show and there is an expectation that you're going to get people whose first discipline is dance, but they need to sing anyway, and all you want to find out is do they have a good ear, are they going to frighten the horses if we put them in the company. And sometimes the choreographer or the director says I insist on having this person, and you have them, and they're a liability. I'm not going to be discreet about that: they are a liability. And then you have tricks like you have the sound operator give them a dummy microphone or a battery pack with a flat battery. And that's the way you get around that one. But that's a secret.

Although Sean Green does not employ a rating method, he also keeps very detailed notes covering the auditionee's vocals, song choice and musicality:

Sean Green: I generally will write a note about their vib, describing it, whether it's shallow, fast, pleasant, unpleasant, bleaty, all these type of things. And I'll write about their tone. I'll write their own song choice, some notes about that, about style, about whether it's musical, timely, etc. etc. etc. And then the show material, I'll write about what's going on there as well. So I don't tend to grade but I do tend to write information, because after the person is gone we will, as a panel – currently in *MJ*, it's myself and the associate director – we will discuss whether the person has met what we need for each other, and then they'll get a tick, or a cross, or a question mark.

Assessments of voice quality can be subjective. Gareth Valentine, who as a student trained with one of Britain's leading operatic tenors, admits he has a particular view on musical theatre voices:

Gareth Valentine: My background is the Royal College of Music, and I studied as a singer and as a pianist. And Peter Pears was my singing teacher for a year. And while I think – and I can't think of an exception to this – while I think musical theatre voices I would describe as, even the best, "impressive", to me – and it's a very subjective thing this – I wouldn't say I've met any voices in musical theatre that I would describe as "beautiful". Beautiful voices to me – and again, it's a very subjective thing – is bel canto, the purity of voice, the discipline, the musical discipline, all that for me. I don't listen to musical theatre when I'm at home, I listen to opera, I listen to oratorio, sometimes jazz! Those singers have wonderfully, wonderfully pliant voices. So you could say that Elaine Paige has an impressive voice but I wouldn't describe it as beautiful as an opera voice in the purest sense. Of course, it's all terribly subjective, isn't it?

Of course, it isn't only voice that our MDs are assessing. Punctuality, preparedness, and affability are all watched as well, as indicators of an auditionee's professionalism were they to be employed:

Sean Green: There are lots of tiny little things about auditions. For starters, just being on time for your audition is super important. We've had a fair amount of lateness, and there's always trains and all sorts of things, people are traveling from a long way, I think we had people from Scotland coming down to audition for *MJ*, so it's a lot. But the funny thing is people who are coming from Scotland are the ones who are there two, three hours early; the people who are coming from West London are the ones who arrive saying, "Oh, I'm late! TfL!" But yes, the way they enter the room, the way they carry themselves, the way their music is prepared often, the way they talk to the pianist about how they want the music done, all those little things like that are very indicative of preparation.

Sean Green's last point about an auditionee's discussion with the pianist is especially important. He says it shows how auditionees approach relationships with people they might feel are less important:

Sean Green: I watch very closely how they talk to the pianist, especially when I'm not the pianist. When we get introduced, we're not introduced as our titles. So it's not, "This is Alex, the associate director, this is Sean, the musical director." We're just introduced as "Alex and Sean." And then it's "Simon will play for you, and Lee will be reading." And I feel like if we were introduced as our titles, the way they treat the pianist might be an indication of how they treat people who aren't necessarily super in charge, because sometimes people don't treat the pianist very well. In the past, they've been just a little dismissive, and sometimes that might be nerves as well. When things go wrong, sometimes you get the odd, angry glance over that way. I've definitely seen some of that. They're all very minor but you spot them.

In the first chapter, we discussed commercial casting and putting celebrity names into productions. Gareth Valentine says that casting principal roles in that way is a very different process and not always reliable:

Gareth Valentine: When the principals come along, they're handled with kid gloves, particularly if they're celebrity names. Often you wouldn't say, "Can you sing your song?", you say, "Would you mind terribly if you'd sing the song for us? It's not that we need to hear you, of course, but we just need to figure out the key." It's all bullshit but you have to make them feel like it's not. It's a "meeting," not an audition, so as not to upset anybody. Now, you can't keep calling those people back – sometimes people are called back eleven, twelve times, for roles in *Wicked* and that kind of thing – but celebrities you can see them maybe once, then you have to make an offer or not. Some people will not, of course, audition at all, if they're big, big names. And then they come into rehearsals, and then you'll find they can't do it, as happened with Roger Moore, in *Aspects of Love*. I was his coach in 1989 on the production and it was clear he had no musical bones, he couldn't sing, and a couple of days before we went to the Prince of Wales Theatre, he left because he knew he wasn't going to do it, the press would have killed him. And so Kevin Colson stepped up and played the role.[1] So sometimes that happens.

Deciding on the cast

After the final auditions, it's time for the panel to decide whom to cast. But Stuart Morley says often it's been clear from the start:

---

[1] And was nominated for a Tony Award for the role the following year.

Stuart Morley: You usually get a pretty good feel for whether someone could be the role from their first round, or certainly from their first recall when you start exploring the show material. You then hope that they do their homework and don't talk themselves out of a job that they've nearly already got! It was a massive learning curve for me the very first time I ever sat on a panel because I didn't realise how emotionally draining it would be. The panel really invests in the auditionees in a big way and you often find yourself rooting for certain people and really hoping that they get the part. And you get to the finals, you've got three people, and you want them all to get the same job, and you know that they can't. And that's why those final casting discussions can be so hard. In my experience you never take someone through to the finals who isn't ultimately right for the show, so it then becomes about the best combination and the best overall blend.

Sean Green agrees that a panel can know very early on who's going to make it into the show:

Sean Green: With the current cast of *MJ*, there's definitely a few people who we saw and I was like, "Oh, my God! I hope they maintain this." And they did. And they're in the show, which is great.

The relationship between the MD and the creative panel goes both ways in making the final decisions. Gareth Valentine says there are some directors who defer to his opinion:

Gareth Valentine: You get somebody like Bartlett Sher, the American director, and there's much more largesse there with him and he'll ask me, "What do you think about that girl's voice?" And some directors are not interested, really, it's a courtesy, they just want to make me feel like I've had a say, but he really does want to know, because he understands the importance of voices. Particularly if you're doing something like, *My Fair Lady*[2] which has certain vocal demands, he will listen to me. And Sam Mendes. I remember I did *Company* with Sam Mendes at the Donmar and he wanted Sheila Gish to play the part of Joanne, and Sheila came in, consummate actress but couldn't sing, and Sam said, "But she can't sing a note" and I said, "No." I said, "She sounds like a corncrake. It's terrible: she's perfect for the role. She's perfect. She sings like shit. You've got to contract her now." And he did, and she won the Olivier Award for Best Supporting Performance in a Musical.

In other circumstances, the director takes charge:

Gareth Valentine: Trevor Nunn is an old friend of mine but I would describe him as a benign autocracy. He will do the auditions, with Stephen Mear and I, or whoever, and then he always does this: on the last day, when you're down to your final performers, your front runners, you have all the photographs and the bios on the table, the first, second, third choice for every role. And between the

---

[2]Gareth Valentine was the musical supervisor for Sher's production of *My Fair Lady* when it came to the UK and Ireland in 2022.

casting director, the producers, the director, me and the choreographer, there are people coming and going – I mean, if those actors were privy to that, they'd die of a heart attack because they'd see they would be right there, they've got the role, and then two seconds later, they've gone, they're in a pile on the floor, and then half an hour later, they're back again but in a different role so thank God, they're not privy to that – and so you're figuring out the tracks: who's going to be best to do this role? Who's going to understudy that role? Well, we do all this. And then what happens is that we all decide: Okay, so the offers go to this girl, this girl, that boy, that boy. And then the second offers go to this and this, and there's a kind of a breakdown of who's going to be offered what. And Trevor always does the same thing: we get to that moment, all the things are on the table, and he'll go, "Oh, shit! Is that the time? I really must go" and he'll scoot off. And then two days later, we'll get an email saying, "And this is the cast."

Once a director does take a decision to cast an auditionee, Gareth Valentine says he then does everything he can to support them:

Gareth Valentine: We did *Sweet Charity* at the Donmar. Wayne McGregor was the choreographer, Josie Rourke was the director, and I was the MD. And we had a prospective leading lady and Josie Rourke loved her. And it was clear that she was an absolutely first division actress, no question about that, but you'll know from the show that those vocal numbers are demanding. Gwen Verdon sang them originally, and you'll also know that because it was Gwen Verdon, the expectation of dance was formidable. And so we had that director who really, really wanted her and Wayne did his duty by saying, "I will do everything I can to assist her if you go with her" and I said, "I, too, will do everything I can"; because this is the thing, once the director overrules their team and says, "No, I absolutely insist we have this person" from then on whatever we think about the proficiency of that person, our job is to look after them, to support them, make sure that they can do the very best they can. I've yet to come across a situation like that where they did come up with the goods but there again she did win an Evening Standard Award for Best Musical Performance which just goes to show!

Stuart Morley believes it's right that the director has the final say because they have the overall vision for the production:

Stuart Morley: The director ultimately is the only person who sees the whole picture. We all see our own pictures and we certainly try to be considerate of our fellow creatives, but ultimately the director's overall vision is the one that the audience sees. And so I fight less, the older I get. In my younger, more stubborn days I would go, "Argh, it's all about music, everything's music, it's called a musical," all those old things that people have said, but ultimately, of course, it's the director's vision that we are collectively portraying, and the music has to serve that vision, and if that means a musical compromise, then it means a musical compromise. But what I won't ever do is compromise the performer. So if I feel strongly that a certain job is not going to serve a particular performer well, then I will be very vocal in saying that. I say, "Yes, they're brilliant. Yes, they fit your vision. But they won't be able to sustain it for eight shows a week and they'll risk hurting themselves." That's never a risk I'm prepared to take.

Sometimes, a producer can step in and control the casting. Sarah Travis experienced that when a producer blocked a casting that both she and the director wanted, and it's made her more careful about the type of show she chooses to work on:

Sarah Travis: Basically the producer pulled rank and that was the end of that. "*My* show," you know, "it's *my* show." And on a big commercial venture, I get the fact that money is a massive issue. They're putting the money up, they're putting up "the risk" and I suppose if they really feel that casting someone is going to be detrimental financially then that's their option, it's their show.

There are some commercial shows that do things differently, but Sarah Travis says they're the exception:

Sarah Travis: I went to see *Sunset Boulevard*, at The Savoy. It's a very interesting, very bold production, but what really struck me was the ensemble were all shapes and sizes, all types of diversity. And that is a commercial show but it's a very brave director, Jamie Lloyd, and I admire him greatly because it is very much about the art and his vision, but that is rare I think, and it's something that I struggle with, definitely.

Returning to producers, some listen very closely to their creative team. Gareth Valentine remembers when an entire production was hanging on his opinion of the principal casting:

Gareth Valentine: I was once going to be doing *Man of La Mancha* with producer Howard Panter and he really, really wanted a famous actor, wonderful actor. Howard said, "I really want him to do it because he's box office," and he went to the trouble of having me work with the guy and we worked again, and then they heard him sing again, and in the end Howard said, "I have to make a decision. We're going to hire the Savoy Theatre for the afternoon. We're going to hire a sound man and a pianist, and we're going to get his manager and his agent into the auditorium, and he's going to stand on the stage and sing 'The Impossible Dream' and the title song." And they're really demanding numbers, really demanding numbers. And he sung them and it was just okay. And I remember being called the next day by Howard, he said, "I'm 50–50. I'm either going to put this on as a production in the West End or not. And it depends on your answer." He said, "Do you think that he's going to be able to do this role?" And I said, "Okay, you heard what I heard. You have ears, too. Imagine that it's the opening night, you're sitting in row G, and he's standing centre stage, just him, with an orchestra, singing 'The Impossible Dream' and then he sings '. . . to reach the unreachable star', what would you think about that?" And five minutes later the whole thing was cancelled. There's the answer, because unless Jesus Christ comes down again, you know it's not going to happen. Wishful thinking doesn't do it. In the end, they have to deliver the goods.

At other times, producers can set unrealistic goals for getting a particular performer into a role:

Gareth Valentine: What I also don't like is when auditions become rehearsals and you have an actor come in again and again and again, and they send them to singing teachers because they really want them to do the part. And singing teachers cannot in the space of two weeks have somebody move ten years ahead in terms of technique. It's not going to happen. There's a kind of collective, wishful thinking from the team and particularly producers: "I really want this person because it's a box office star. We know they can't sing, we know they're not a very good actor and we can see that they can't move, but we really want them!" But they're box office and it's the age we live in. It was always like that to some extent, where you wanted box office stars and often they just couldn't meet the requirements of the show, but that seems to not matter very much to some producers.

Sean Green says that sometimes the way to resolve casting disagreements is to consider the nature of the role and its most important aspect:

Sean Green: What they do in the show matters. For instance, Kate/Katherine is there largely to be a vocal powerhouse and has a couple of scenes, but not huge amounts, so therefore, if their acting isn't totally Olivier worthy but they have a voice that sings birds down from the trees, that's where the weighting lies. Whereas with other characters they have lots of scenes, they have to carry the acting and the story of the show, and they have a couple of songs, so we as a music department say, "Well, yes, okay, we can make that work for those couple of moments they have featured singing."

Similarly, Stuart Morley finds he has to choose his priorities in the casting process:

Stuart Morley: When I'm part of the casting panel I usually do either a physical or a mental checklist of "Okay, what's important to me?" before we start the process, and to some degree that will vary a bit for each project. That list is then at the forefront of my mind during the auditions. For example, for a show where the music is the primary selling point (*We Will Rock You*, for example), if someone is an amazing actor but their pitching and intonation is consistently off then I'll be sure to voice my concerns to the rest of the panel very strongly. For me it's obviously important that the show sounds good, and it will of course ultimately reflect badly on a performer too if they get cast in a show and then receive negative reviews and comments because of their tuning. Obviously, everyone on the panel will fight their own corner and sometimes it's hard to reach a compromise, but ultimately we all want what's best for the show so these discussions are an important part of the casting process.

The collaborative nature of putting a cast together can lead to insights from others on the panel. Stuart Morley says he welcomes those and being asked to contribute:

Stuart Morley: Oh, I love it and some days I hate it, because you all have your personal favourites. But I love the collaborative nature of auditions, I think it's great. It takes a lot of brains to put a casting jigsaw together. And I also realised early on that the musical director is an integral part of that process. When I was starting out, I thought that the MD might be sat at the side saying, "Well, yes, they can sing/no, they can't sing." But in one of the first casting meetings I ever attended, I was asked straight away what my thoughts and opinions were, and I realised that my voice was important, and not only musically.

We saw in the previous chapter that one of the big complications in casting today is finding covers for all the roles. Stuart Morley agrees that's often the case, though the dancers in the original London production of *We Will Rock You* were often an exception in not having to cover:

Stuart Morley: We had forty-six in the Dominion cast, I think, and we had sixteen performers who were primarily the dance ensemble and who didn't need to cover. They were all strong singers as well as being amazing dancers, but they didn't necessarily have solo rock voices. Then we had what was essentially the singing ensemble made up from all of the covers. Additionally, we had eight swings who were amazing all-rounders. Nowadays, casts tend to be smaller, so on a show like *Only Fools and Horses*, for example, pretty much everyone's a cover. So there is no ensemble as such. *Les Mis* [a cast of thirty-six], I think everyone covers something, and even the swings on that show are essentially vocal swings who are constantly jumping in and out of all of the smaller parts. And everyone's in "At The End of the Day", apart from Javert, all of the named, lead characters, Fantine, Eponine, the Thenardiers, are all beggars and workers, which is brilliant, as it really helps make the cast feel like one big family.

Another influence on casting might be a supervisory team. This is especially the case on US shows enjoying long West End runs, like *Wicked*. Sean Green has to satisfy the team watching over *MJ: The Musical*:

Sean Green: With a show that has an American team, it's a little difficult to know what they want sometimes, and they can be very exacting and focus on things that you don't expect them to focus on and make decisions that you don't necessarily agree with. With this recast, we are without them because they are putting on the production in Germany, currently, so we're going to have to present them with a handful of choices for each part, and then allow them to make a decision. Which is unusual, I'd say. I haven't done a show like this with a big American team of global supervisors and they always have the last say. And there's lots of people: there's a writer, there's a producer, there's a global music supervisor, global associate choreographer, global associate director, and the director. So it goes to the team of them and they will all look and all decide. So in that sense this round of auditions has more pressure and less pressure at the same time. Because we're trying to present them with a group of people that they could find somebody from but also knowing that we don't get to make the final decision so the pressure's off there, but also on because we have to provide the right people for them. There's no point being frustrated with that, because that's the way it is. I think I am on a good wavelength with my music supervisor, so I think that what I like, he will like. And we worked together on the first round of auditions when we first put the show on, so I have a good idea of what he likes and what he doesn't, and what the show needs and what it doesn't.

We've seen already how decisive it is that an auditionee is right for the show. That leads to one of the frustrations of casting: when an auditionee gives a brilliant performance but does not fit any of the roles. Stuart Morley remembers that happening during auditions for *We Will Rock You*:

Stuart Morley: It was a new graduate, she came in, and she just gave the performance of her life at 10 past 10 in the morning. Often you don't like to give too much away in an audition room, because it can get people's hopes up, and you often need time to confer, but on this occasion I just looked at the director and said, "That was amazing!" And he said, "Yeah. It was." And he said to her afterwards, "Look, you are not right for this show. That was the most wonderful performance of that song I've ever seen, and you are incredible. And you're not going to get a recall. But that's not because that wasn't a brilliant audition. We just don't have a place for you."

Stuart Morley went on to talk about the dangers of casting auditionees in the wrong roles and showed he was very aware of the damage it can do:

Stuart Morley: It's really important when you're auditioning people that you give the right people the right job for them, not just for us. It's a two-way process in my mind, and I would never give someone a job if I thought it would do them an injustice or a disservice, as a performer. If you put the wrong person in the show, you can really damage their mental health and their career, and that's then on us. And so when a performer asks why they didn't get the job, sometimes the answer is that they simply weren't suited for it, or they didn't have the right range. No amount of rehearsal is going to give them notes that they're physically not able to sing. That's why it's important to explore the material fully in the auditions, to make sure they can sing it eight times a week. If you don't do that and you offer someone a job that they ultimately can't sustain then that can be very damaging to them, both physically and mentally. And that's not their fault, they accepted a job that they got offered, and of course they will because everyone wants to work. So I think there's a big responsibility when sitting on a panel to give the right person the right job.

As we've seen in previous chapters, the audition culture in the US is different. Gareth Valentine says there's a much higher level of preparation and presentation:

Gareth Valentine: When you audition in America, it's a completely different approach. In New York and in Chicago, you find that people come in and if they're up for a role they will suggest something by a jacket or the way they wear their hair, a period thing, say, or a style thing, or a character thing, a rose in the lapel, hair worn in a '40s style. And then they will come in and they'll have a very impressive book with their set of songs, which can be pop songs, opera, jazz, standard golden age stuff, everything you can think of, all in their keys, all written out by somebody, and then they'll go to the pianist and they're absolutely explicit about what it is they want the pianist to do. When I did *Love Never Dies* up there with Andrew Lloyd Webber – it didn't go to New York in the end – but [director] Jack O'Brien and [choreographer] Jerry Mitchell, we were all in the room auditioning and one of the girls came in for the leading role. And we asked her whether she would take some music away with her, to learn it and come back the following week. And she said, "No, I'll take a look at it now, if I may." And she went over to the piano and ten minutes later she sung it like she'd sung it all her life. That's very unusual.

Gareth Valentine says that US performers may be able to train and prepare to those levels simply because they can afford it:

Gareth Valentine: These performers in America get paid way, way above anything we earn here. Way above, the money is incredible money! And that means that they have expenditure. They can have their singing lessons and their dancing lessons, and their everything else because they can afford it. I remember doing *Chicago* in London and two of the girls on that show, although we just opened and it was the big hit show, they were moonlighting, doing other jobs after the show at night, working in clubs and this kind of thing to earn extra money. So I think that goes some way to explaining that particular culture.

Overall, though, standards of auditioning in the UK are high. Sarah Travis says she was very happy with the performers coming in for *Grease*:

Sarah Travis: Walking into a room, which sometimes can be ten or more people on a panel, is a very vulnerable space to walk into. But most people that came in and auditioned for *Grease* – and they're all young and some of them are still at drama school because we've cast very young in that show – I have to say I was massively impressed! They came in – and they came in smiling, most of them as well, even if they were terrified – came in with a good positive attitude. So, on the whole, yeah, I was impressed.

But there are a lot of performers in the industry, as Stuart Morley pointed out:

Stuart Morley: There are an increasing number of performers out there, which links back to being the very best version of yourself that you can be, if you want the job. Every industry works like that, it's not unique to performing arts. It's important for all of us to invest in ourselves and to try to stay ahead of the game, otherwise it's easy to fall behind and get forgotten.

If an auditionee falls short at any stage in the process, they might at least get some feedback as to why. Stuart Morley says that has improved a lot:

Stuart Morley: Now so much more of the process is computerised, it's made it much easier to give feedback to auditionees. When I started out, you had your form which was stapled to someone's headshot and CV, and each round you'd write handwritten notes on that person. So to get that information back to agents was very time consuming because it needed typing up and, practically, it often just couldn't happen. Whereas now, I'm seeing casting directors typing notes in the room. So once someone's left and the panel have a quick discussion about them, the casting director can often email feedback as soon as it's requested.

Great auditions

Our MDs have been in the room for some great auditions. Gareth Valentine remembers working with an auditionee who ended up completely embodying the character:

Gareth Valentine: It happened when I was in New York, for *Sinatra*. Matt Doyle, who had won a Tony for playing Jamie in *Company*, came in, and in the audition room was Tina Sinatra (Frank's daughter) sitting next to me, director Kathleen Marshall, writer Joe DiPietro, producer Jimmy Nederlander and all those kind of people, and Matt came in for the first audition and he was wearing the slacks that Sinatra wore and a white shirt, and he had his jacket over his shoulders. And we made it quite clear that we didn't want it to be an impersonation. What's the point? There's Elvis impersonators, Sinatra, who gives a fuck about that? But that it would be the essence of Sinatra, who was this young, goofy, skinny, little guy. And he sang a couple of songs for us exactly as he'd heard it on the album. Every nuance, every idiosyncrasy was there in the singing. Talk about musicality, it was, like, it was, fuck! And then, I spoke to him, and I said, "I want you to do it in another way. I want you to do the first part of the song 'I've Got You Under My Skin' as though you're just thinking out loud. Not the Sinatra recording, but you! And then, halfway through a particular moment. I'm going to get the pianist to play big band style and swing, and that's performance mode, the light's going to go 'bang' on you, and now you're Sinatra. Over to you." And he just . . . fuck . . . I mean, some people are blessed with divine chops. He finished the number and we . . . well, the room, we just were quiet. Nobody moved. I've never seen that before. He walked out the door and Tina Sinatra said, "That's my dad. That's my dad."

And that led to another delightful moment for the panel, when they were able to tell Matt Doyle he'd got the job:

Gareth Valentine: He was going off to do *Little Shop of Horrors* and play Seymour, off-Broadway production, and we all went to a restaurant, and Tina said, "What's the protocol for telling him?" And I said, "Well, he's going to be learning that he's got the role through his agent. We have to tell the agent, we have to do the deal." She said, "Can't we tell him now?" They said, "Well, there's nothing to stop you." So they called him and said, would you come to the such and such restaurant, on such and such street? And he came in, sat next to

Tina Sinatra, and she said, "You're going to be playing my dad." And when that happens, it's wonderful. It's wonderful. It's just . . . there's no question.

Stuart Morley has also seen performers who deliver exactly what the panel were hoping for:

Stuart Morley: I'll never forget when Ian McIntosh came into audition for *We Will Rock You*. And Ian is the sweetest man, and he's now taken over as Jean Valjean. But when he walked in and started singing, everyone in the room, everyone just looked up and you went, "Oh! That's what we were waiting for!" It's a glorious moment and there's nothing better for the panel than you being the right person for the job. You want to give people a job. You want to find people.

I wanted to know more about what made Ian McIntosh's performance so exciting. Stuart Morley says it was the whole package of voice, connection, look, and entering into the language of the show:

Stuart Morley: He just walked in and nailed it. He's got a great voice and he has great presence. He obviously loves Queen. He'd obviously done his homework. He'd sort of dressed like Galileo, but without wearing a costume and we all thought, "Great!" He's all the things that Ben [Elton], Brian [May] and Roger [Taylor] would look to see in a Galileo. And then he sang, and he sounded amazing. He had the right nods to Freddie, without trying to do a Freddie impersonation, but he also invested in the lyric. And of course, whilst these pop and rock songs are not usually written for a musical with a narrative, they all have a story to tell. They have some kind of journey and often a strong emotional connection, too. Sitting in an audition room chatting to Brian May and Roger Taylor about Queen songs, I realised that conveying emotions and the ability to tell a story is important for any song, not just songs that have been written as part of a musical theatre narrative. It's so important to be able to express your emotions through the music.

Sean Green on the UK Musical Theatre industry for Black performers and creatives

Sean Green started in the industry in 2009. He has won Best Musical Director at the Black British Theatre Awards for three years in a row, and I wanted to discuss with him how he views the landscape of British theatre for Black performers and creatives. We started with the performers:

Sean Green: I think currently it's better than it has been, much better than it has been. For actors and performers, we see a lot more opportunities for casting and storytelling than when I started. When I started it was: "Oh, there's *The Lion King* and that's the Black show." That was basically it. I remember at drama school, people were like, "Oh, I'm auditioning for *Lion King*," and that was pretty much it, there was no Black Elphaba, there was no Black Eponine, there was no Black Cosette, there was none of that. Every cast was white unless you needed a Black person to be a Black person in that show. And the Black people in those shows were few and far between.

So performance opportunities have broadened into roles that weren't open before. However, Sean believes the creative side of the industry has seen less development:

Sean Green: I think there is an appetite for the music of Black people in shows – *Dreamgirls*, *MJ*, *Tina*, *Motown* – that has grown since I first started. I would say that, in my experience, the creative teams creating those shows are not always representative of the music that's happening. I can see that there aren't many Black creatives, or there weren't many.

Sean Green says he has faced challenges reaching the position of West End MD, and it's difficult to know what was behind that:

Sean Green: About halfway through my career, I was auditioning for things that potentially should have had a Black creative on the team and I was told, "Oh, you're good but you don't have enough experience to do this job yet." And so I just kept working and eventually I think I lucked out with the right project in the Bob Marley musical that came to the West End, and now because I have a West End credit, I am eligible to do shows in the West End, I suppose. But then, there's part of me that's like MDing is MDing is MDing. If you've MD'd a regional show, a tour, a number one tour, you have MD'd a show. And I think there are things you'll learn on a number one tour that is not financed very well, and is scraping by, and you have to motivate that cast and motivate that band, and they don't know if they're getting paid week to week – you'll learn more on that than you will on a West End show with a supervisor and everything running nice and smoothly. But that's what I think now.

But it wasn't only mid-career that Sean Green faced challenges. There were challenges right at the beginning too, but he says it's difficult to be clear about what lay behind them:

Sean Green: I did a postgraduate in Musical Direction and I wanted to be an MD. And, to begin with, most of the jobs I did were keys playing jobs and I do wonder if that's because nobody was interested/ready for a Black MD to lead them? I'm not sure. I'm lucky that I can do keys playing, and that was kind of cool, and I worked through that and worked my way up. But I'm aware that people that did the course with me, or the year above, year below, did step out into more MDing roles. So: question. And I can't answer that, unfortunately, because it's different experiences.

Sean Green's success very nearly didn't happen, and there was a point in his career when he considered leaving the industry. The difficulties he encountered in progressing had no clear cause:

Sean Green: In the middle of my career, I'd done *Rocky Horror*, I'd done *Into the Woods*, as MD, and then I also did the first Bob Marley musical, which was called *One Love* at the Birmingham Rep, I had done a UK tour of *Wedding Singer*, a number one tour going all around, and a show at the Young Vic. And I would be auditioning for other shows, and the auditions would go really well, but then it might go silent for a while, or I'd get the feedback: "Oh, you're really good! We're just unsure because you haven't done anything." And I had done all sorts of things – Manchester Royal Exchange, European Tour – does this mean because I haven't got a West End credit on my CV, I haven't done anything? And I would see the audition process re-open and the show go to somebody else. And I got to a point where I was like maybe this is enough, maybe this is where I stop, actually. Because, clearly, whatever I don't have, and I don't know what that is, but I don't have it, and maybe this isn't for me. For a period I was like, is this what I want? Or I suppose the question was, this doesn't want me so therefore maybe my efforts are best placed somewhere else.

As it turned out, Sean Green continued to get work and so stayed in the industry. But I asked if, for a time, the ceiling to his progression felt confusing:

Sean Green: That's definitely what it did feel like. It did feel like there was something that I was not able to do or provide or show. That type of thing happened a couple of times for various different shows – West End, UK tour – it was various different things and the feedback was always "You're really good! Where have you been? What have you done?" And I'd be like, well, you have my CV, and I've been here. I don't work in the West End because I haven't been given the opportunity to do a West End show yet, but I am here, and I'm doing this and I'm doing that. One of the feedback I got once was, "nobody really knows who you are, so maybe you should dep[3] and do that thing." And I was like, well, ok, but also, I'm an MD, so my skill is in MDing. If I dep, I'll just turn into a dep. Nobody would be saying, "That dep can MD the show from scratch, from the beginning," that's a different skill set entirely. So it was very confusing.

A possible issue Sean Green identified is the development system for Black creatives, particularly having an experienced, usually older, creative to mentor and guide them:

Sean Green: I do wonder where my mentor was. When I started, I didn't know of any Black MDs in the era before me. I didn't have anyone to reach out to, to talk about anything, and I still don't think there is anyone. In a sense, I am now that person for other people, which is nice, and there are young MDs who I know of, who I have worked with, who perhaps see me as some sort of mentor which is nice. And I am on a young MD mentorship scheme for the third year in a row, and various MDs agree to meet up with young MDs and discuss with them facets of MDing, and sit them in, etc. so that's really nice to keep it moving forwards, because it is very important. I think there are biases, unconscious biases, and I think that if I was white, my career probably would have taken off faster than it

---

[3]Deputise: Fill in for orchestral/pit players when they are unavailable.

did. But I'm not too upset about that, because I've got to where I needed to get to, and it all happened at the right time so I'm kind of okay with it. But I do wonder about certain things along those lines.

Another issue is the development pathway. Opportunities need to build steadily so that creatives can arrive at the top jobs with substantial knowledge and experience. Sean Green says that this can be missing:

Sean Green: I think about the uptake in Black stories and wanting to have Black creatives and Black people behind the scenes, and the thing I've experienced is that they haven't been given enough time to get to the level that's needed for the show. And so people are thrust into positions that are too much for them sometimes because of a need to have Black creatives where they haven't been given the space to learn in other shows and other productions, and that's really tough. That work hasn't been there for them traditionally to get them to the place where they need to be. And that's why on one hand, I'm like, "Well, I wasn't picked earlier" but on the other, actually, if I was picked earlier, I might have been a mess of nerves. I think now I'm in a situation where I know what I'm doing, I feel comfortable in the role I'm doing. And even then, I'm a mess sometimes as well, you know, emotionally. But, yeah, it's definitely interesting.

I also asked Sean Green where future development should aim:

Sean Green: I think, much like with performers, you can have colourblind casting but you can also have casting where it doesn't matter that that person is of that ethnicity, so there's been a Black Elphaba, there's been an Asian Elphaba on Broadway. One of the joys was doing *Brokeback Mountain* last year, where I was sought out not because we need a Black person MDing this visibly, or on stage, that wasn't necessary for the storytelling; that was that the writer wanted me to do the show and so reached out. When I did *Two Strangers (Carry a Cake Across New York)* at the end of the year, that was very much that Tim [director Tim Jackson] and I had been wanting to work together for a long time and he reached out and was like, "Hey, this show's coming up, I don't know what you're doing," etc. and it just happened to fit perfectly in the gap I had at the end of the year before starting *MJ*. I think MDing shows where my ethnicity is not part of the storytelling, or the music, is where things should be going next. And so you have Asian MDs who aren't necessarily MDing Asian shows. I think that's where, hopefully, it's going next. We'll see. For *MJ*, for instance, I am on stage and there will be a desire for that. And I have been asked, "Oh, do you know any other Black MDs?" because there is that desire still. But hopefully, once those people have the necessary skills and experience, you can see an Asian or a Black MD at Les Mis waving the stick, or conducting *Wicked*. And women, too! Women MDing shows that aren't *Six*! You know? Because female MDs are fierce and amazing, and I have many friends who are female MDs.

My final question to Sean Green picked up on this and whether female MDs had discussed similar difficulties with progression in the industry:

Sean Green: Yeah, I think so. Yeah. And on top of that, there is also the slightly unrealistic time demands on an MD that make it a bit harder to do if you have a family. So it's very male skewing. If you are a woman and you have a family or a child, you can't be in rehearsals day and night, and conducting a show. It's not conducive. And I think that's why, on certain shows, job sharing is a really wonderful thing that some producers are now allowing, and certain teams are wanting to do. It's tough, I mean, I spoke to a supervisor about it and he's like, "Well, I can't see that working because one of you has to be the MD . . ." And it's like, well, no. But, hopefully, things will change in that way.

Conclusion

Looking back over what our musical directors have said about auditionees, we could compile a list of the most important qualities:

- A technique that reliably hits the notes required and supplies the vocal stamina to get through a long run of performances
- A meaningful delivery of text
- An intelligent understanding of character and its projection through singing and acting
- An original perspective on the dramatic situation that also is expressed through singing and acting
- Connection to the text, to the other characters on stage, to the audience
- A flexibility of mind to take direction
- Musicality, to keep the piece together and to inform the expressiveness of their performance
- A great colleague to be around in rehearsals, backstage and in performance

But it's important to remember that all of these points are only necessary *to the extent that they meet the needs of the role.* The level of technique needed to sing Desiree Armfeldt (who sings 'Send in the Clowns') is not the same as that needed to sing Elphaba, but maybe the level of characterisation, connection to text, and connection to an audience is. The musicality needed for *Hamilton* might be different from the musicality needed for *The Last Five Years.* Auditions are specific searches, and even excellent performers can miss out – remember Stuart Morley's story of the standout audition from a young woman who met all these criteria on her own terms but not in connection to a role in *We Will Rock You,* and so she didn't get a recall. Therefore, auditionees have to play the long game. It isn't about one audition; it's about honing your craft and artistry so that you are successful in the right-fit auditions when they come along.

4 Directors

Laurence Connor is a West End, Broadway and international director. His productions include the newly staged The Phantom of the Opera *(UK and US tours),* Miss Saigon *(West End, Broadway, worldwide), co-direction of the new version of* Les Misérables *(West End, Broadway, and UK and US tours),* School of Rock *(West End and Broadway),* Joseph and the Amazing Technicolor Dreamcoat *(London Palladium), and* Chess *(Coliseum, London). He has directed arena productions of* Jesus Christ Superstar, *the 25th Anniversary Concert of* The Phantom of the Opera *(Royal Albert Hall), and the 25th Anniversary Concert of* Les Misérables *(O2, London). He has received the What's On Stage Award and Broadway World – West End Award for Best Direction for* Miss Saigon.

Sir Richard Eyre is one of Britain's leading directors of the past sixty years, working across theatre, musical theatre, opera, film and television. His numerous productions include Guys and Dolls *(National Theatre, winner of the Olivier Award for Outstanding Achievement in a Musical, 1982),* Mary Poppins *(West End 2004 and 2019, and Broadway 2006),* Betty Blue Eyes *(Novello, 2011),* Stephen Ward *(Aldwych, 2013) and* The Pajama Game *(Chichester Festival Theatre 2013, and West End 2014). He has won three Olivier Awards for Best Director and been nominated for six BAFTAs and two Tonys. He was artistic director of the National Theatre from 1987 to 1997 and was knighted in 1997 for services to Drama.*

Rupert Goold CBE has directed theatre productions for more than twenty-five years. He was artistic director of the Almeida Theatre for more than ten years before being named artistic director of London's Old Vic. His musical theatre productions include Oliver! *(Drury Lane, 2008),* American Psycho *(Almeida 2013 and Broadway 2016),* Made in Dagenham *(Adelphi, 2014),* Spring Awakening *(Almeida, 2021),* Tammy Faye *(Almeida 2022 and Broadway 2024) and* Cold War *(2023). He directed the 2019 biographical film of Judy Garland,* Judy, *starring Renée Zellweger. He has won two Olivier Awards, two Critics' Circle Awards and two Evening Standard Awards for Best Director. He was awarded the CBE in 2017 for services to Drama.*

Petra Siniawski began her career as a dancer and West End performer. She originated the role of Cassie in the first West End production of A Chorus Line *(Drury Lane, 1976) and played Anita in* West Side Story *(Shaftesbury Theatre, 1974). She went on to choreograph shows including* Jesus Christ Superstar, Hair, Guys and Dolls, The King and I, *and The Peter Hall Company's* Twelfth Night. *Petra then moved into directing, becoming associate director for West End productions of* Kiss Me, Kate *(Victoria Palace,*

2001), Ragtime *(Piccadilly Theatre, 2003) and* The Producers *(Drury Lane, 2004). Since 2006, Petra has been associate director for the West End production of* Wicked *and associate director for its tours in the UK, Ireland, Mexico and Japan.*

Introduction

Directors are both leaders and collaborators. They create an artistic vision for the production and then look to work with creatives and performers who can share that vision, enhance it, and even inspire it to go in different directions. In this final chapter, we'll hear what our directors want from an auditionee to give them that sense of shared creativity and development.

Our directors all assess the singing and dance elements of an audition. They acknowledge the measurable parts of those disciplines, such as vocal range or dance technique, and then want to engage with narrative and psychology. We'll hear some fascinating views on what makes good singing and movement for musical theatre, including Rupert Goold's idea of singing as an act of self-revelation.

Of course, they are most involved in the acting, and here our directors all have traits that they look for most in auditionees, including bravery, wit, truthfulness and humour. There's also a need for flexibility and an openness to direction, as we've heard from our other creatives.

The audition process can be a long one, but often our directors want to invest time in their auditionees to build their working relationship and be sure of the potential for development in rehearsals. As Laurence Connor says, 'It's that relationship which you cultivate in that audition room and the performances they give that really buy into the success of the show.'

We start with our directors' approaches to the audition process, which usually come after they've been involved in the project for some time.

Early process

Laurence Connor says he's been living with the show material and the production concepts long before auditions begin. He will have worked with other creatives first, ahead of meeting his potential actors:

Laurence Connor: When you're working on any show, you're a director of many parts. So, I always liken my role to the centre hub of a wagon wheel. If, for example, you imagine that you've got all these spokes leading off into various different directions – so there's the kind of director you are when you're talking to a designer, or to a lighting designer, or the costume department – you separate yourself out, with one whole vision in mind. And with every one of those creatives that you work with, there's a different energy, there's a different focus. When you get to the actors, usually the sort of actors you want and the creation of what we're about to put together is quite far down the line because you've been on a journey building an idea for some time before you start to audition actors for the role. So you start to have some clarity as to the type of performers or the kind of production that you're going to create, ahead of time. This means the scale and the size and the intellectual property of what you're creating comes before, and then, once you've established what that's going to be, you can have the fun stuff where you start to really look for the players that are going to bring that vision to life in a completely unique way. You can't really separate those because you might start off with an idea of something quite wacky and then find performers that bring something very, very specific, and suddenly you are inspired by that and it can take you slightly off on a different tangent.

For Rupert Goold, the relationship with the casting director is very important. This shapes the musical theatre audition process into one very different from plays or films:

Rupert Goold: I suppose, in general, with musicals, you're working with musical theatre casting directors and that's a slightly different skill set to straight play or film casting directors. And there's a different sort of protocol. In my experience with musicals, you're doing more, you probably see more people. You cast the net wider. Partly because each show has different sets of skills but also I think it's just the way the industry is structured. I think there's more of an understanding with the agents and the music performers that there might be more of a process in the auditioning. And I've done some shows where I've only come on board after my associate and the casting team and musical directing team have already done the first or even second round. The danger with that, of course, is that particularly musical directors can sometimes filter out people because they just can't sing it, and you go well, actually, maybe they can offer something else. So you have to be a bit wary about that.

Seeing a wide range of auditionees, then, can be important. Rupert Goold added that working with a casting director who doesn't usually specialise in musical theatre can help with that:

Rupert Goold: I've worked a lot with people like Pippa Ailion [see Chapter 1] who do a lot of musical theatre casting. She's probably done most of the musical shows we've done. But it's interesting, I did do *Cold War* with Amy Ball, who does all our straight theatre here at the Almeida, and it was interesting having a casting director going, "Oh, apparently they sing," or you know, "It says they sing on their CV," or "Their agent says they sing," but not having had the experience of hearing them sing a lot. And, of course, that had problems in many ways but it also got people out of the woodwork who I probably wouldn't have met otherwise.

Rupert Goold also noted that musical theatre has significantly diversified its performers in recent years, much as Sean Green noted in the previous chapter. Rupert Goold says that, for a while, MT wasn't moving as quickly as straight theatre:

Rupert Goold: I think musical theatre has been a bit behind straight theatre in terms of inclusion. It's got much better but I remember when I did, *Oliver!* [in 2008], for example, I insisted that if we were doing an "Oliver" play about London now, we obviously couldn't have an all-white company, and there was a bit of grouching about that. And I think we only auditioned one non-white performer in the entire process, and that's a cast of forty or something, and we cast her and she was great. Admittedly, that was a long time ago, but I think musical theatre courses are less diverse than straight acting courses and so the talent pool was less. I think that's partly to do with the idea that it's a skill set maybe that certain schools or drama schools had literally more investment in, or maybe some innately more middle-class thing, I don't know, whatever it is, but it's massively improved, that. But even then, it was a challenge. And like I say, it's got a lot better.

Another way auditionees get into the room is through putting in good auditions in previous years. Petra Siniawski says that, on *Wicked*, they'll often earmark auditionees to see in later castings:

Petra Siniawski: We have two to three weeks of principal auditions. So obviously, they come through agents, but also maybe the previous year we saw actors we felt had future potential but weren't quite ready so we would let their agents know and say, for example, "If she works on her vocals a little bit more to strengthen the technique in her soprano range, there's a good potential, and we'd like to see her again." So they are earmarked as further "down the line," putting "DTL" on our notes. And then the casting director, Jim Arnold, [see Chapter 1] will look through our list and see if people are available at that time. We usually start auditioning around five months before the first rehearsal, because the auditions take seven weeks in all, plus we have to prepare costumes.

Wicked also brings up performers through the show, with a progression of covering roles and then playing them, through tours and in the West End. It can be a longer route than getting straight through an audition, but it benefits from development and strong working relationships:

Petra Siniawski: The beauty of *Wicked* is that we are encouraged to nurture from within. For example, one of our Glindas started her journey with the show as the second Glinda Cover on the first UK Tour in 2013. Then completing her contract left the show to explore other options. After a year, she returned as first Glinda Cover in the London production, and from there gained the role of Glinda on the UK Tour in 2017, and graduating to playing the role in London. Thus showing a gradual progression in the show. Another actor who played the major role of Elphaba on the recent UK Tour, started out as an Elphaba Standby in London, and then took over the role when the show re-opened after the Covid pandemic. She was subsequently chosen to play the role on the 2023–25 National Tour. Originally, that actor came to audition as a Morrible cover. At the time, she hadn't done much, just having graduated out of college and this was her first major West End audition. During the process, because of her strong vocal ability, she was being considered for the Vocal Swing Track. It soon became very evident she was an exceptional singer and although she'll admit she wasn't the strongest actor, was somebody who was very willing to learn and keen to go on the journey in implementing everything the creative team directed at her. We all felt she had the exciting makings of an Elphaba Standby, which she was duly offered and remained in for the next two years, proving herself most worthy of this responsibility. To start, she was a little too compliant, and rarely questioned any notes given, but once the role became hers and she was able to take ownership, she became more confident, and we were able to delve more deeply together into the emotional make-up and dramatic impulses that charge Elphaba's journey throughout the storytelling. Importantly, we were seeing the "actor" emerge and not afraid to question and bring forward her ideas, which in turn was rewarding for the creative team to see and collaborate with.

And, of course, there's workshopping, which happens before auditions and may lead to casting. Rupert Goold says it's often part of his process when directing a musical:

Rupert Goold: In general, I've done newer pieces, and even with *Spring Awakening*, we did a bit of workshopping about ideas. And often the workshopping process is part of the casting process. Zubin Varla, who played Jerry Falwell, won the Olivier [Best Actor in a Supporting Role in a Musical] for *Tammy*, was in the very first workshop. Until Michael Cerveris did it in the States, we'd never had anyone other than Zubin play that part, and you end up writing for them a bit. And maybe you don't quite know what you're looking for but that workshopping process is a way of people putting their hands up and going, "This is what it is."

Another important part of the workshop process is understanding when castings aren't right. Then the creative team is forced to go a different way:

Rupert Goold: We've had people in the very first workshop of a production who were great but made us realise we needed something else. So then you go, "Ok, so now we're going to recalibrate it. Because these people are great but not quite working out."

Workshopping and promotion within a production both offer viable routes to being cast. The main process, however, remains auditioning, so let's turn to what happens in the audition room from our directors' perspectives.

First rounds

It can be important to set the tone in an audition room, and we've heard other creatives discuss that in previous chapters. Our directors try to create positive experiences in the room, and in part, that comes from having been performers themselves and having been to many auditions:

Petra Siniawski: Absolutely. I've experienced being ignored at an audition, and the panel can either be generous or quite dismissive. So, I know as a panel for *Wicked* especially, because I've been doing it for some time, we always try and make the actors feel as comfortable as possible to help get the best out of them. The production still means a lot to many aspiring, especially young, actors. They're iconic, challenging roles.

Laurence Connor understands how overwhelming the audition experience can be:

Laurence Connor: I was an actor myself and when I used to go into auditions, I would fret and be nervous and stressed, because you know as an actor that you're capable of giving what's needed, but to prove yourself in those few minutes can be like life and death, for actors. I've always tried, therefore, to create an environment in auditions for actors to feel comfortable. I don't like sending lots and lots of material to actors because I feel it stresses them out and they've got all this stuff to learn. And I don't believe you see a lot of what they can bring by making them show you that they've been sent the music three days before and can hold the music and sing it. I think sometimes that as an exercise is purely just to say, "Okay, look, we want to make sure that it's in your vocal range."

Once he's with his auditionees, Laurence Connor prefers to go into depth on a piece, getting a sense of whether they could collaborate:

Laurence Connor: I'm more likely to just take one song and really work on that, and then I'll tend to spend a bit of time working with the actor and encouraging them to try different things, leading them in certain ways just to see how they respond. Usually, I can tell quite quickly whether the actor is somebody that I really, really want to work with. But then, of course, you sometimes have to put them through another period because when you build a cast, it isn't just about one actor, it's about a company of actors and how you think they're going to work with one another. Sometimes you want to pair actors and see how they come together and create. And that's the process. So it's interesting. So, in essence, I think you have some idea of what you're looking for, but I'm usually surprised and impressed by what somebody brings into the room, and often, if I were to start the day thinking I'm going to want this person, that can all change by the end of the day.

Richard Eyre says the audition process can be tough. It can feel personal and unfair to those auditionees who don't get the job:

Richard Eyre: I used to be an actor so I know what rejection feels like. To the person being rejected, it will always feel that justice has not been done, that the process is biased. It will always feel that way. Because you're being judged. Your person, your body, your personality, your voice, your looks, are being judged, and you're being rejected. How painful is that?

Shaun Aquilina: Is there anything that could be said to soften that?

Richard Eyre: No, no, you just say, "Sorry, not for me."

Once the auditions start, there's a lot for our directors to assess about the auditionees. Laurence Connor says he's immediately looking to understand the person in front of him:

Laurence Connor: I think in a first audition I'm much more interested in how they approach the audition. So, for example, when you walk into a room, you've got this really awkward moment where you say hi to everyone, and then you've got to walk across to the piano, sort yourself out with the pianist, and stand there. Then you've got to take a beat, and then you've got to do it. In those moments, you can tell so much about a human being because you can tell if they bring their outside issues in with them. If they're rude to the pianist who's playing for them, or a little bit short with them, or treat them like they're a prop as opposed to somebody that's going to help them, that can be very telling. You see a lot in just the air in between, I think. I pay very close attention to that because you think anyone can present themselves as amazing but it's really important that you are just who you are, right from the get-go. And I think when you see an honesty in all of that, you know what you're getting.

When they begin performing, it's down to the auditionee to do something that makes them stand out. As some of the MDs said in the previous chapter, this is often about having a unique perspective on a song, whether or not the panel agrees with that perspective. And this is also part of getting to know the auditionee as a person:

Laurence Connor: Then, from a technical point of view, usually they'll be singing a song we've heard a hundred times before, so it's how they understand what they're singing, how they approach the song that they're singing, and what song they choose which matters. Sometimes they go so left field with a song, and I love it because I just think, thank God! Everyone thinks we want to hear that song like this but you didn't, so why didn't you? I'm intrigued by you. And I think that for them, they've decided, "Well, I sing this really well, and I want to show myself in a good light so I thought, what the hell, why not?" This I respect, because I think at this point all we need to really know is who you are, how you sound, and whether we think you're going to be a good fit for our show, and we'll figure the rest out later. But at this very early stage when we're seeing hundreds of hundreds of people, you just stood out, and now I'm intrigued.

Singing

Richard Eyre and Rupert Goold both see musical theatre auditions as containing an objectively measurable element – the auditionee's ability to sing the notes and perform the choreography:

Richard Eyre: The difference between musical auditions and acting auditions is that there is a quantifiable element in musical auditions: can somebody sing, can they dance? And, you can teach somebody to dance, it's very hard to teach them to sing if they don't have a sense of pitch, so immediately you're eliminating people because you say, "Well, I'm sorry, they simply haven't got the qualifications." And it's like, it's all very well saying, "I'm a high jumper," Ok, well, can you clear two meters? "No, I can't." Well, then, I'm very sorry you're not on the team. So there's that element. So you eliminate those people and then you're in a matter of preference which is to some extent subjective.

The measurable qualities can be most apparent in singing. Rupert Goold says he can be confident of bringing out someone's acting performance, but there are times he has to accept their singing isn't up to the role:

Rupert Goold: Sometimes, that can be really absolute. You go, "I don't care, you might think they're the best actor in the world, but they literally can't hit it." And there's often technical things, the break in their range, whatever it might be. And in the casting process, you realise "Oh, God, we've heard them sing this song three times now, and it's just not ever quite gonna happen and they'll be exposed on stage." Whereas, with acting, choreography to some extent, you can hide those disciplines a bit more. You can back your ability to direct someone's performance out of them or there are other things you can do as a director to make that less significant, and you can certainly reshape choreography around someone's ability (unless it's a very dancey production) but singing is unforgiving that way.

When listening to an auditionee sing, directors can face the difficult decision of whether or not to move on. On one hand, they want to give the auditionee a good experience and respect their preparation and effort, but on the other, they want to be efficient and get on to something that's more likely to lead to a successful outcome:

Rupert Goold: One thing that's tough in a musical audition is that you know within a couple of bars if someone's voice is completely wrong for something but they're singing their song. I remember my wife auditioned, when she was really young, for *Les Mis* in one of those big cattle calls and she had "Night and Day", jazz song, that she was going to sing. And she came out, moved up the staircase, into the wing, you come out one by one, like *A Chorus Line*, and she sang the first eight bars, which are all basically on one note, and then they said, "Ok, thank you!" And of course, she didn't realise and hadn't even got to the main bit of the song, and I can never be that ruthless! I hate that hold-your-hand-up, "No, thank you, that's enough." But you do sometimes have to sit there and go, "Christ, we're in this for two minutes now, and it's never going to be right." And it's hard in a musical audition because there's always that moment when you go, "Thank you," and then they say, "Do you want to see anything else?" And, you don't want people to be pushy and going, "Please let me sing, please let me sing!" because it's kind of exhausting, but sometimes it's the right thing to do, because you might hesitate and go, "Do you know what, you said you've got another song from Sondheim, can I just hear a tiny bit of it?" And you go, "Ok, wow!" And time management in an audition is really complicated. Both as a director and as the auditionee, you want to maximise the time you have together to learn about each other, and it's not very long, often it can be like less than five minutes, so although I said I don't like stopping songs, sometimes that's the best thing to do, to go, "Look, there's no point us wasting this time here, let's look at something else, and maybe you can offer that to me."

In the MDs chapter, we discussed song choice and at what stage auditionees move from their own choice songs to material from the show. Rupert Goold sees the benefit in both, though he concludes that the show material is what reveals whether an auditionee is really right for the role:

Rupert Goold: In the casting process in general, I'll come in for the second rounds. There's always an interesting thing about whether you get people to sing the show material or their own material because there are values to both. I find MDs tend to want to hear the show material. I often find you get more personality out of their own material, although people can hide their vocal deficiencies in their own material more, obviously so long as they don't pick songs that they struggle on. My wife, who's done a lot of musical theatre, she went up for a show a few years ago. Good casting for her. She's a really good actor, really brilliant singer, but there was one note in one song that just sat on her break in a weird way, and I remember hearing the same bar of music again and again and again and again, and she could never hit this one note. She's got a great ear, and I was like, "Look, maybe it's not your role," you know? And sometimes you do need to interrogate that.

Principal auditions for *Wicked* don't hear own-choice material. They go straight to show material, with both songs and acting scenes, as the casting team need to get a measure of vocal and dramatic ability:

Petra Siniawski: The principals come in and they're requested to prepare certain scenes and certain aspects of the vocal material. Because hopefully, they're already of a certain calibre, and not raw out of college. So, they get condensed material to see whether they have the emotional impact as an actor, along with the vocal ability to hit what we all know as the money notes. Once we have selected our potential candidates for the roles, we workshop them with fuller extensions of the material. So let's say an Elphaba would be singing, "The Wizard and I", "I'm Not That Girl", and "Defying Gravity", it's those three songs she has to sing the complete versions in the finals. The acting material we do is the "Cub Scene", and "Munchkinland", which is the most emotionally charged scene the two witches have together, "what a touching display of grief", that big scene that the two witches have together. For Glinda, it's "Popular", which shows her innate humour and compassion.

Something that's difficult to assess in an audition is vocal stamina. I asked Petra Siniawski if she gets a sense that an auditionee's vocal technique can meet a full contract of shows:

Petra Siniawski: Oh, I don't know about that. The long term is a tricky one, because it's very difficult to gauge as, vocally, singers could be going through a certain period and it affects their voice. So you have no idea how long somebody can maintain a role. In our show, we do not have Alternates, we have Standbys that have to be in the theatre for every performance. Most shows in the West End have Alternates who are engaged to do one to two performances a week. Our principals do all eight, and when we have nine-show weeks, during the holiday periods, the Standbys do one designated performance. Today, vocally maintaining one's show demands discipline, technique and sustained vocal care.

Rupert Goold is also aware that the vocal state of a singer in an audition may not be representative of them more generally. It's an issue that actors in plays often don't have to face:

Rupert Goold: Unlike straight acting, the singing voice as an instrument is always changing, literally through the day! I remember when we were casting *Tammy Faye*, the first workshop casting that we did was coming out of Covid, and we did see Katie Brayben - who went on to play the role – but she came in, and she's like, "I haven't sung for nine months, like anywhere." And auditioning people coming out of Covid was really interesting because people's voices were in all sorts of different places, and their upkeep of their voices had all been very different, which was not true of the actors, the actors came back and they wanted to play, they wanted to be in the room. But the singers, with the public nature of singing, and the filling of the room, felt very different. And Katie's voice was nowhere, didn't have body at all. And it wasn't until we were struggling for casting again that we came back to her and her voice had returned and developed. And again, when we did *Tammy* the first run, Katie was pregnant, she was six months pregnant by the end of that run. And then we did some recording in the studio when she was nine months, like just about to give birth. And then we did a workshop a year after she'd had a child. And then, when we did the show recently, her child was like eighteen months, two years. And her voice was in a very different place in all those iterations. Like literally, if you're nine months pregnant, your diaphragm is in a different place. I will say she sounded particularly amazing in the second trimester of her pregnancy. But it's an organic, evolutionary, fragile thing and I think you have to be aware that, if you've auditioned somebody, it's worth seeing them again, because their voice may be in a very different place, which is less true when you're doing plays.

The lead roles in *Wicked* remain among the most vocally demanding in musical theatre, and Petra Siniawski expressed concern about the level of singing training and ability that some auditionees are presenting:

Petra Siniawski: We are often quite disappointed in the lack of apparent vocal technique. They can hit the big notes but are unable to support and sustain the more lyrical aspects of the material. They can go from three years training to singing Elphaba, and if you don't have a proper technique, you can't sustain the vocal through line. You have to know what your voice can do and how to look after it, and importantly go to your singing lessons, maintenance is key. It's a lifelong vocal development, whereas you'd be surprised how many people don't look after their voices.

The vocal demands of a song can become a distraction to an auditionee, absorbing their focus. Rupert Goold says the braver choice is to commit to the drama and narrative, especially since that might lead to some flexibility from the music department:

Rupert Goold: Most times you're going to see someone auditioning for a musical with material they've been singing at home. And again, I know this for my wife: they've been working on it, and they will know where they're vulnerable in it and where they're strong – the most obvious being like the big high belt note – and so how are they going to manage that in the room? And sometimes you want to say to them, look, you are really worried about where this song finishes and it's tensing you up all the way through that song, because you know there's a cliff face that you've got to climb up. But actually, just commit to the way in. Move me, make me laugh, whatever it is. Yeah, there's no point pretending you can get there when you can't. But if we love you, maybe we'll transpose or rewrite, or there will be musical solutions.

Our directors also discussed the importance of sound in the singing voice. For Petra Siniawski, that means finding two leads with contrasting sounds, partly because, as Stuart Morley said in the previous chapter, timbre is part of character and narrative:

Petra Siniawski: The two girls have to have a different vocal timbre. The Glinda has to be much more, as you would expect, a pure soprano. Elphaba requires a stronger contemporary sound, more rocky. One Elphaba, especially, had that quality; sometimes you're thinking, "Is she going to hit the note, then yes, she does!" And she hits it brilliantly! She had that innate rawness that made her vocally exciting as Elphaba.

For Rupert Goold, sound is about beauty of tone. He has a different view on connection to text, which our MDs prized very highly, because he will find that in rehearsal:

Rupert Goold: If I'm really honest, the thing I look for most is tone. But I guess the shows I've done, if I look at *American Psycho*, *Spring Awakening*, both Duncan [Sheik] shows, *Tammy Faye*, *Cold War*, they're all rock and pop artists in different ways – Elvis [Costello] and Elton and Duncan – so I've never really looked for more of what I call an MT sound. And in fact, all those composers almost actively don't want that, they don't want vibrato, they don't want that legit sound, they're looking for voices with personality. People like Katie Brayben and the *Spring Awakening* gang, they haven't had big voices, that big musical theatre belt, they'd be more voices that are almost like singer-songwriter sounds. So I look for a voice that really moves me emotionally, more than I look for phrasing or textual detail, because I trust that I'll be able to find that in the rehearsal process.

This leads us to an important point about performance. Acting is often seen as transformation, as the actor becoming a character. But perhaps singing is not about the actor transforming into a character, but about sharing their self. That's what Rupert Goold is looking for in his auditionees:

Rupert Goold: The act of singing is an act of self-revelation. Transformative ability less so because I think once you sing, you are in that [i.e. your self is in that sound]. I mean, I guess if you're playing like Madame Thénardier, or a very strong character, you hide a bit, but the sound of a singing voice is to hear who someone is. And we recognise that: the great thing about any voice, whether it's pop voices or opera voices or musical theatre voices, is that you know, within a phrase, that's somebody's voice. And they maybe go, "Hey, but I'm playing a 1920s Oklahoman," or "I'm playing a sci-fi Martian," or "I'm playing Victoriana," and you go, "Yes, but it's always your voice. It's always you." And so the auditioning, I think, is like looking for who the truth of somebody is rather than the transformative qualities of somebody.

Dance

When it comes to movement and dance, Richard Eyre looked to the fundamentals of rhythm. He recalled an exercise employed by an Olivier Award-winning choreographer who worked on shows including *The Rocky Horror Show*, *Pacific Overtures*, and *The Baker's Wife*:

Richard Eyre: I worked with a brilliant choreographer called David Toguri, who's Japanese Canadian, and David said, "I can teach anyone to dance if they have a sense of rhythm." And he would ask actors, "Can you dance?" And they said, "Well, not really, I don't know." And he'd say, "Could you walk across the room?" And he'd click his fingers in time and ask them to walk. And surprisingly a lot of actors couldn't walk in time. And he said, "I can never teach them if they can't walk in time" because essentially dancing is all just moving your body in time.

As with singing, Rupert Goold is looking for the person in the performer:

Rupert Goold: I see a lot of really good movers but it's really rare you find dancers who have psychology. It's not just character, it's engagement in their eyes. So when we did *American Psycho*, the only performer we took from London to the States was a woman called Holly James. It was really weird, she was an ensemble track and the producers are like, "Why are we bringing a dancer over to New York?" I said, "We are never going to find someone like this." Now, there are dancers in New York like that as well but, interestingly, Holly arrived and she's not stopped working on Broadway since, and she lives there now. So I really prize movement highly, because I feel like personality in movement is really rare.

Prizing movement highly means Rupert Goold will invest significant time in his movement auditions to ensure that he's finding performers of the right ability and expression, which resonates with Lynne Page's comment in Chapter 2 about everyone on stage providing a point of interest:

Rupert Goold: Our movement auditions that Lynne and I have done, and that I used to do with Scott Ambler before he died, have been not like "tap on the shoulder, we're just looking for certain skill sets." I believe with a movement call, you want to do a good hour with them, and you owe it to them to have fun and feel that they are stimulated in that process through the hour rather than just how high can you kick your leg. You're looking for personality, always personality. The most rigorous movement calls I've done were on *Spring Awakening*. And the set had certain challenges that would require movement of a certain level. And I guess with choreography – depends on the cast size – you can hide people, obviously, but you're slightly defined by the lowest common denominator in a smaller company like that, so you go, "There's a baseline I can't slip below because the ensemble material is not going to look good."

Acting

When assessing the auditionees' performance ability, our directors are looking at acting. Richard Eyre wants auditionees to present their ideas on the character for which they audition, and this links to the concept of the essence and the mould we've looked at throughout this book:

Richard Eyre: If the character is there, complete, that's less interesting to me. That's what rehearsals are for. If it's a new piece, nobody knows the character, they're just exploring it. If it's an old piece that's existed for years then, of course, you're interested in what they bring to the character.

Shaun Aquilina: So if someone was coming back to you to do *Mary Poppins*, for example, you'd want to see something of the essence of Burt or Mary?

Richard Eyre: Exactly, exactly.

However, a fully formed and inflexible reading of character goes too far and isn't appealing:

Richard Eyre: I mean, when you audition in the States, they come dressed as the character, and they've spent ages working on it, and sometimes they do a performance and you think, that's the performance, it's never going to change. You're going to rehearse for five weeks and preview for three weeks: they're never going to change their performance.

Petra Siniawski says their re-casting for *Wicked* is always driven by the character's essence, and that's evident in the casting:

Petra Siniawski: We go for the essence. Because, as I always say, especially to our older actors, if I lined up all the Wizards and lined up all the Morribles, they couldn't be more diverse in look, physically, height, personality, but they have that vital essence needed for the role. Morrible has to be an eccentric, a larger-than-life character, but dramatically strong because of the journey of the character.

Laurence Connor has become known for his commitment to acting in his megamusical productions, such as *Les Misérables*, *Miss Saigon*, and *The Phantom of the Opera*. He tailors his auditions to what he gets from actors:

Laurence Connor: I'm very much led by what I see. I react to what I'm watching and hearing, and run with it. In an audition, I want to give myself to the actor and I want them to feel comfortable. And no actor is the same, no actor's come from the same school of thought, no actor's come from the same drama school. It's such a mixed bag of training so therefore I think you just have to see what journey they've taken as an actor, what their process is, and work with them, and see if you like it and see if you don't, and if you rub along well, and it works, then great.

Because of his commitment to the drama and storytelling of his productions, Laurence Connor wants to see auditionees guide their performances by words and meaning, rather than music:

Laurence Connor: Musical theatre is a strange acting style. When you look at my version of *Miss Saigon*, it's very drama driven, it's very actor led. Sometimes, therefore, it becomes about stripping the music out and saying, "Can we just talk it, can we just speak it?" I know actors hate that a lot of the time, because it feels like the words don't make sense when suddenly they become lyrics, but the exercise isn't to make them feel foolish, it's to break away the musicality of it. I find with the music, it becomes a bit operatic in the sense that everyone emphasises the beat rather than emphasises the word. And you go, "I want you to strip away the music so you're not emphasising the word 'and' in that sentence, but you're figuring out what it is you want to say and how you want to say it." So when you look at *Miss Saigon*, the dramatic intention of that, and the way that the actors spoke and brought that to life – half the time you didn't even realise they were singing. It felt very organic, very real. And that is a skill actors really have to work on. But then, when you're working with shows like *School of Rock*, your focus is really on comedy, characters and fun. And so you come at it with a slightly different intention because whilst you want the moments to be real and profound, you're trying to move things along, you're thinking about the comic, rhythmic timing, among other things.

Creating fully developed characters is also very important. This was evident when casting the role of Raoul in *The Phantom of the Opera*, where Laurence Connor wanted an actor with a 'strong core':

Laurence Connor: What I mean by that really is that there's a sense of purpose in what their character brings to the story. I think, sometimes as actors you hope to play one of the lead roles, but often when you don't get those roles, your thinking might be that some of those other roles are lesser or not as vital to the story, and that just isn't true. Every character has to have a core and a strength of purpose and a truth in how they deliver that role. It's as though we're a camera right now, and as a camera, the lens is pointing on this story and we're focusing over here, but it could just as well shift and make the story all about you, and we might write a musical about this character. Think of it like this – when I'm sitting on a train, it's my life and the camera's on my story, but that doesn't mean that everybody on that train doesn't have a story, or that everyone on that train isn't a real person, with real issues, with real things in their life. And I think that's the point: it's understanding exactly who you are in the story and bringing it 100 per cent, so your character is as valuable as whoever the lead character is. So with Raoul, it always felt like the *Phantom* story had been a love story between the Phantom and Christine, and I really believe that the story should be a love triangle of a complicated nature. And in order to do that, Raoul had to step up and be deserving of that, be the person that, as an audience, you're thinking, "Well, it's obvious she should be with him." He's her suitor, and he's handsome, incredibly funny, but isn't weak, and wants to fight, wants to push back. So that was the thing I was looking for in that particular character. And that's what I felt we achieved when we cast the role.

Musical theatre has plenty of comedy, too. Laurence Connor says auditionees shouldn't underestimate the effort and ability it takes to perform comedy as effectively as drama:

Laurence Connor: Even though drama is heavier and it's easier in some respects to access those emotions, comedy is so technical and so incredibly on the nose. The amount of work actors have to do to really find a joke and really polish it so that it's always funny and always great, it's hard work. And it requires the same level of attention and detail as it would to give a full force dramatic performance. The work isn't any easier. In fact, I would say it's just as hard.

And so when it comes to auditions for character roles, which often carry the comedy, Laurence Connor wants to see an actor instantly transform, bringing energy and definition to their performance, and a touch of originality that contributes to the longevity of a show:

Laurence Connor: When I'm looking for a character actor, I don't need a Thénardier to walk in smelling of booze, not wash his hair, and end up trying to pickpocket us while he's there! What I need to know is that, as actors, they're skilled enough to completely turn it around and have a go at it. Many times, I've auditioned very well-to-do actors for that role, who come in with a well-spoken accent, then they just turn on a character and are amazing! I would say the rules are: how good are you at characters? How good are you at finding the humour in places that we maybe haven't considered before? And how do you approach it? I love seeing different people's approaches. I think one of the successes of *Les Mis* is the fact we haven't literally just found the same character over and over again; we've found different actors that bring a different edge to it every time. And that's what makes the show organic.

For Richard Eyre, there's something in an actor's use of space that tells him about their quality. It may be indefinable but it's there from the moment they enter the audition room:

Richard Eyre: You can see an actor using the space in a productive way and see other actors that simply don't have that instinct. You sense it when they come in. They have a self-confidence, an assurance in themselves. It's very much like every time you see a new conductor come in to conduct an orchestra, in an orchestral rehearsal. You see the orchestra waiting there and they look at the door and the conductor walks in, goes on the podium: they've sort of made up their mind. And then the conductor, if they're sensible, doesn't say a lot of "this piece is about x, y, and z . . ." they just say, "Look, we'll go from bar 100," and then the orchestra's looking for a clear downbeat which sometimes they don't get. And you just see an orchestra say, "No, not for me."

Shaun Aquilina: Do you have a similar reaction to performers when they walk into a room, before they've even done anything?

Richard Eyre: Sometimes, sometimes.

Laurence Connor attributes an actor's use of space to one thing:

Laurence Connor: It comes down to confidence. How confident are they in their presentation? You can tell that an actor in the middle of his song is starting to think about his hands, correct? So then he thinks, "Where am I putting my hands? I'm gesturing too much. I'm going to put them in my pocket." To me that reads, "You are not thinking about this character or the song at all! You are too self-conscious of your presentation." And that's a really good example of how to switch off. So it's primarily about if they're using the space, and showing they're not scared to. If they feel they can do that, it demonstrates confidence and the understanding of how they want to portray the song. Even if they're not doing a great job, you can't help but be impressed that they are free in themselves to try things and to give it a go, make choices, even if they're the wrong ones. I admire it, and again, I think it comes back to having been an actor: knowing what it's like to be in that minute, and to know that I was probably once a trembling wreck who thought, "Oh, what am I going to do with my hands?" I recognise all of the failings, I recognise all of the things. So I would say when you see how an actor can just be present and in the space, how they can truly own it and take their three or four minutes to showcase themselves, you recognise they're really comfortable, confident and competent, in that moment.

Auditioning across the three disciplines of acting, singing and dance gives auditionees a bigger opportunity to stand out. Rupert Goold says it's not necessarily an auditionee's strongest discipline that gets them noticed:

Rupert Goold: The great thing, in most cases, about musical theatre auditions is there are more layers to them and somebody can emerge who you just hadn't had your eye on initially. Like Katie Brayben, for example, when she did *American Psycho*, I first noticed her in her movement call. Now she's a terrific actor and she's a double Olivier Award-winning singer but for some reason I hadn't really noticed her massively in those bits, but it was in her movement call I was like, "Oh, my God! this woman has got such wit and commitment to the phrase!" And then I went back over the tapes, and was like, "Oh, she can sing as well!" So sometimes one discipline will leap out.

Overall, disciplinary qualities have to meet the technical requirements of the role, but they also need to be filled with personality, with something of the individual, and with a curiosity and passion to discover more about the text and character in the coming rehearsal process. Laurence Connor finds this last point especially important:

Laurence Connor: It's a number of things. It's confidence. It's their personality. Obviously, their ability. I mean, you've got to know they can sing it and that they're gonna bring it. But it's their openness to work and how hard they want to work. I have worked with actors in circumstances where they come, they do a really excellent audition, but there's a notion of "that's how I'm going to play it, that's how I do it," and yes, that would be great if you were doing the one man show version of it but when you go into a company you need to loosen yourself up, be freer. And you're sensing them thinking, "Mmm, I'm not getting what I need to be this character". I don't believe that's how actors work, especially British actors. I think British actors are much more flexible, really work well as a company and need each other to find food to fuel themselves. So that's really what I'm looking for. I'm seeking good company members who know how to take an idea and bounce it around with other actors. It's a particular work ethic, you can tell. It's when you're seeing somebody prepared, not necessarily in the material they've been sent, but prepared to listen and take direction and work with the information you give them.

This last point echoes what Bill Deamer said in Chapter 2, that he wants to see performers take his ideas and develop them. Laurence Connor wants not just preparation of the audition material, but also a mental preparation to enter into a process with the creative team and take the lead from their ideas and develop them. Rupert Goold agrees and says it's especially important that when an auditionee has thoroughly learned their material they can still be flexible with it:

Rupert Goold: Do you want to be off book for an audition? Yes, I think ideally you do, and particularly for songs. But equally, the more you prepped it, can you change if somebody says, "Ok, now play this as though you're stuck in the basement and you're whispering to your friend because you're worried that the serial killer is going to come down the stairs, and just do the song like that?" I like giving very extreme, sometimes very counterintuitive, wilful misreading, big general notes in an audition to see if someone can make a radical rethink. If you've over prepared, that jump can be tricky. But I think it's the director's job to give a really inspiring note. And of course, often in an audition, you don't have time to do a detailed beat by beat breakdown – in this line, that's where the stress should be, and can you hold back here and diminuendo through that phrase and all the technical stuff – so often, I like giving that completely bizarre "imagine you've woken up and you realise you've turned into a mermaid and you sing this song," very different kind of note just to see what somebody's creativity is.

Laurence Connor also mentioned, above, observing how actors are with each other, needing each other's energy 'to fuel themselves'. Richard Eyre is very aware of this:

Richard Eyre: You can see it particularly in musical rehearsals. After the first audition, you're often auditioning several performers together, and you can see if someone's got a generous instinct and if they work with other people. Or, if they're very blinkered, you can see it. In the conversation you'd have with the music director and the choreographer, that would come out. Somebody would say, "Look, they're a completely wonderful dancer" and you'd say, "Yeah, yeah, I see that but are they interested in working with the other actors? Or are we essentially talking about somebody who is a soloist but who's going to be in the ensemble, and that's not going to make a good mix?"

Professionalism and personality

We've seen throughout this book that auditionees need more than their disciplinary skills: they need professionalism, a positive attitude and a likeable manner. I wanted to know what a director sees in an auditionee that tells them these traits are present:

Richard Eyre: Professionalism is a cast of mind, really: turning up on time, knowing what you're doing; and having done your homework.

For Petra Siniawski, it's about demonstrating an understanding of the production. Some auditionees have arrived with completely inappropriate material or little understanding of character:

Petra Siniawski: Initially, I like to feel they have given the audition some thought. Have they brought in the right song? We always request two appropriate, contrasting songs of their own choice. Ideally it's best not to sing a song from the show, as we are accustomed to hearing the songs as required by the show, and usually the singer will have been influenced by what they have heard on YouTube, and in some cases feel justified in riffing throughout, for example in "Defying Gravity", which is strictly not allowed in the stage production. A lot of Stephen Schwartz's material is very appropriate because he writes in a certain style and therefore ideal for us. "Astonishing" [from *Little Women*], or something similar is an excellent choice for Glinda, and "Woman" [from *The Pirate Queen*] is a popular song for Elphaba. Again, it shows they've given thought in preparing for their audition. Once we had an actor audition for the Wizard, who came in with his guitar, and requested a chair to put his foot on so he could rest his guitar on his knee! He sang his folk ballad beautifully but it had no relationship in style or content with our show let alone with the character of the Wizard!

Auditionees can also show their professionalism in what they wear, hinting at character without going into full costume:

Petra Siniawski: There was one season of auditions, when I said, "Have they got an Elphaba long black dress on a coat hanger out there?" Because they were coming in, more or less in the same style dress! But again, it showed they had thought about the character and were aware of what she wears and represents in the show.

Shaun Aquilina: So you're in favour of dressing with a suggestion of character?

Petra Siniawski: For me, it simply shows professionalism. It demonstrates they've given serious thought to their preparation and appearance in giving the right impression, and that the audition is important to the auditionee. Also it's more common in American casting.

Our directors also want to be assured that the professionalism demonstrated in auditions will continue into rehearsals and performances, and that auditionees will have a positive influence within the theatrical company. Petra Siniawski will check up on auditionees if she's unsure about them:

Petra Siniawski: Sometimes in auditions, you are aware of a noticeable, say negative, response, and if they're coming towards the finals, we check them out with past employers – something actors forget is generally carried out. If there's a niggle, we have to check that person out as you don't want a destructive element within a company, which can often turn poisonous in a long running show.

Richard Eyre engages his auditionees in an open and relaxed way to get to know them as people, not just performers. He admits to being very particular about whom he works with because of the closeness of that relationship:

Richard Eyre: I like to talk to them about their lives or where they grew up, just have them talk about themselves. It just gives me a sense of who they are. It's like meeting anybody, you get a sense of the person, which to me is as important as what the abilities of that person are.

Shaun Aquilina: Is that because you're going to be working with them very intensively and you want to know who you're taking into a rehearsal room?

Richard Eyre: Exactly. You want to know who you're going to be working with. You're going to spend an awful lot of time with these people. People say to me, you're very fussy about casting. I say, yes, I am, because I'm going to spend more time with these people than I am with my family. So yeah, I am fussy.

Rupert Goold described three approaches to getting to know this side of his auditionees. He looks at how they engage and support other auditionees; he also uses references, though he admits these can need investigating; but perhaps most interestingly, he takes note of how many performances they've missed in current or recent productions. Checking this, he says, is becoming more common because there's a growing tendency for performers to miss shows:

Rupert Goold: I think you really watch people watching, in the dance calls. You see the energy about how they watch everybody else and if they seem like they're giving energy back into the room in a positive way. And you take references, quite frankly. You take references more and more these days. It's a complicated thing that, because people get bad reputations and they're undeserved. It might be they've just clashed with one other creative team member and then some choreographer has said, "Oh, they're difficult to work with," and then that gets around, and that's really unfair on them. So you try and take more than one and be balanced. I think it also depends on the lead. If the lead sets a good example, if you can get a lead who's like a leader of the company in the right way, then people tend to follow that. And, then also in musicals, I'm afraid the other thing that's really developed is that you check how often they're on. That's become more and more of a thing. There was somebody who we auditioned for *Tammy Faye*, who I really liked, and someone said, "Oh, well, they've been off a lot." They were in a show on Broadway at the time and they'd missed eighty shows in the year prior to that. And that was the fourth most missed in that company, which means three performers in that company had missed more than eighty shows in a year. And it's become a real epidemic. And it can get into a culture of a show, like if people start taking shows off, then everybody thinks, "Oh, well, I don't feel great today, maybe I'll take mine off." And, of course you're not flogging people onto the stage, that's wrong, but you need performers to perform, particularly at the Almeida, where we don't carry understudies so like, what do you do? So, good attitude, positive in the room, supportive of each other, but also, within normal expectation, will be on stage.

A lot is assessed in the early stages of auditions, from technical abilities to acting traits such as generosity and flexibility, to professionalism and personality. Once those are weighed up, our directors, in collaboration with the rest of the panel, move the process forward.

Recalls and finals

As the auditions progress, more performers have to be cut. For Richard Eyre, this is a difficult time:

Richard Eyre: I think the most painful bit is when you're casting the ensemble, and you get to, like, the third stage of auditions and then you've got maybe twenty people in the room, and you're looking for ten. And you do various stages and then you say, "I'm sorry, x, y and z, you can go home now." That's painful for the performers. Dancers tend to be much tougher about it. And choreographers. They're much more used to that: "No [waves hand dismissively]. You can't do an entrechat. No." It's tougher than my criteria.

Shaun Aquilina: And is that a reflection of the objective, technical requirements you talked about earlier?

Richard Eyre: Absolutely. Yeah.

However, the auditionees who do get a recall can find that a source of great encouragement. Richard Eyre says he's seen auditionees come back with more belief in themselves:

Richard Eyre: Sometimes people's confidence develops from the first time, where they're not sure if they're going to be approved. The second time they're that much more confident because they know all the team approve of them.

Laurence Connor says there's a relationship that develops at the recall stages, which facilitates a more exciting way of working together. It allows him to go into depth on particular aspects of the production or role, which then informs his decision about whether to select the auditionee for the show:

Laurence Connor: Once you've whittled it down to maybe half, or however many you've whittled it down by, you start to get to know them, they're a face that's familiar to you now, you're a face that's familiar to them, and you can begin to get off the table, stand up and talk to them, and introduce yourself properly, encouraging them to play with the song and try different things. Then sometimes, if I'm working with a show like *Phantom* or *Les Mis*, where you've got a Jean Valjean or a Phantom which can have its complications in the arc of the character's journey, you definitely want to have a work session with them to take them on a journey with how you expect this physically played, or where thinking comes, or how they're going to look at the arc of age, or look at the arc of what they're going through emotionally, and that can take some time. And so I usually set aside a day of work sessions with certain actors. Like when I worked with Eva [Noblezada], on *Miss Saigon*, Eva and I spent nearly two hours just working together because she was young, she was a seventeen-year-old kid, straight out of school and was an incredible talent, but of course you're dealing with a character that has a gigantic journey. And the ability to just be able to sing it, and to put your own voice to it and find your own version of it rather than the Lea Salonga version that they've been listening to forever, requires a bit more in-depth work. Then again, sometimes you spend a lot of time with people and it just doesn't work out and then there are others that you just think, "I have to have this. We work so well together. They're amazing. They understand it. They've gone through the journey" and it's worth every minute that we spend.

Petra Siniawski was able to share some of the specific casting requirements on the acting side of *Wicked*. We started with Glinda, where there's a difference between the West End and Broadway interpretations:

Petra Siniawski: Glinda has a natural open-heartedness. There's an innate, unforced, humourous side to her, she's delightfully funny and loves being Glinda! I don't know if you've watched any of the YouTube American Glindas, their gestures are more heightened than we encourage here in the UK. We are playing to different tastes and audiences.

Shaun Aquilina: So you're going for something more real?

Petra Siniawski: Oh, yes, absolutely. That's our whole intention and [director] Joe Mantello has encouraged that. He's very much a contemporary, modern actor and director. In auditions, I often have to ask: "Who are you talking to? Then please face them." Because people often think that because Glinda arrives in a bubble, wearing a beautiful sequined, crinoline dress, a sparkling tiara and wand, it says pantomime, but it isn't! So we always say, don't play the costumes, but the emotional reality of the characters. That's why we strive to make the subtext really tell and explore with the actors what they're saying and the reasoning behind it.

It was clear from talking to Petra Siniawski that there is a dual drive for vocal and dramatic excellence in *Wicked*. And though performers need to be able to execute the show-stopping songs, the acting must be of a high standard to communicate the drama of the story and move the audience. This means finding performers for Elphaba who can bring out both her strength and her vulnerability:

Petra Siniawski: Elphaba is strong, impulsive and emotionally open, she wears her heart on her sleeve. That's why we do the Munchkinland scene, because she has to have a raw emotional journey in the scene, when Elphaba confronts Glinda with "He never loved you, he loves me!" It's Elphaba's truth, she's not trying to be bitchy to Glinda, because she sees life very much in black and white, there's no in-between, she's very straight and dramatically strong. She's a powerhouse, the driving emotional engine of the show. And in the audition process, especially when we're doing the workshops, I've got to see the actors emotionally let go. I've got to see the role's underlying vulnerability.

Shaun Aquilina: Would you say that vulnerability is the most challenging element to bring out of an actor?

Petra Siniawski: Yes. Especially the young actors. Because I think on the large majority of musical theatre courses, they're primarily concentrating on the vocals, because of the high singing demands of today's musicals. There was a time when singing the Elphaba material was a real challenge, whereas it appears less so now, because the emphasis on the training is vocally very strong; therefore, the acting has taken second place.

As the recalls go on, *Wicked* auditionees are given extra material which builds on what they've already learned in previous rounds. This means the panel can see more from the auditionees without overburdening them with material:

Petra Siniawski: With us, it's a progression of the material. First time round, you'll be given half the scene, then on the recall you'll have an extension of that scene. Like Morrible, we'll give up to a certain point in the role's opening speech. Then, if we are interested and you're recalled, we'll give the actor an extension of that scene. Exactly the same happens in the dance auditions. They learn the basic material and then if they're recalled, they learn a bit more. Then at the next recall, they learn even more, plus another dance sequence, with added monkey release work, then at the dance finals on the theatre stage, they'll also do pas de deux work. It's surprising how many dance colleges don't seem to teach double work.

Casting the ensemble can be one of the most difficult parts of the process. Not only are the ensemble tracks demanding, but it's that familiar difficulty of finding covers:

Petra Siniawski: The ensemble have the hardest job in the show. For auditions, we have a week when we solely see new talent and graduates out of college. It literally is five minutes, bring your own song. And sometimes our casting director, Jim Arnold, will ask us to look at a self-tape because obviously not everybody can come. So we have that week of discovery, new actors, maybe a couple of people that we've seen before and we're wondering how they're getting on. Always looking for both witches' covers, and for one of the ensemble who has to be able to cover both the Wizard and Dillamond, then another has to be a Fiyero cover, and can they move, as well as sing their Tenor 1 track in the show?

The *Wicked* ensemble also has one of the most specific casting specifications spoken about by our creatives: an actor who's willing to go bald for one of the ensemble tracks in the show:

Petra Siniawski: It's not a nightmare, but it's very difficult to find an actor for the ensemble who looks mature, maybe they're in their thirties, because they are required to cover both Dillamond and the Wizard, but crucially be a Tenor 1, and to be bald. We always ask through their agent before they even come into the room, if they are prepared to be bald, for a whole year?

And there are specific vocal requirements, too. As with the Eponines in *Les Mis* who have to sing a particularly difficult phrase in the audition, there is a single ensemble line in *Wicked* that's key to being cast:

Petra Siniawski: If we're interested, our musical supervisor will say, 'Oh, can you do a couple of scales for us?" And there's an ensemble line, "Like some terrible green blizzard", which is a solo line but you have to have a certain timbre to your voice and be able to sing it in high chest in a rough manner making evident you're terrified. So it can't be a nice and pure sound, it has to show that fear, and it's a shame because some people fall down on that one line. But it's very exposing, so we can't not have you sing it properly. Also exposing are the infamous three "Wickeds" sung by several of the male Ensemble in the "Opening" of the show.

As auditions reach their final stage, auditionees are expected to memorise their material. If they don't, it can leave a question over their commitment:

Petra Siniawski: Our auditions are intensive, there's no shying away from that. And the other thing that we now expect is that people are on top of their material. So we want them off-book as much as possible. They are always given time, maybe four days, to prepare the material. Sometimes, when they're not [off-book], and you're three weeks into the audition process with them, it can have a negative effect on the creatives and makes you wonder whether they really want this or not? Knowing the material shows commitment and is expected by the American creatives when we video the actors. You want to feel they really want to do this show.

Much like Sean Green's experience in Chapter 3, working with a US supervisory team on *MJ: The Musical*, *Wicked*'s casting also goes through the show's original director and MD in the United States:

Petra Siniawski: We gather together the finalists, with normally at least two, if not three, options for each role. Obviously, we have a favourite but it all depends on that year's show of talent or ability to cover the required material necessary for certain roles. Then we submit them in order of preference, with our notes and opinions on each of the actors to Joe Mantello, who is the American director and has the ultimate say and to [*Wicked* Global Musical Supervisor] Steve Oremus. Then their feedback might be in agreement with our choices, or we will be asked to look further if someone doesn't quite fit the remit, or re-film them to get the actors to adjust certain things in their presentation of the role they are up for.

One of the audition challenges with a supervisory team is that final auditions are often on video, and this affects the auditionee's performance:

Petra Siniawski: Sometimes when you film actors, they go into what I call television mode. As soon as you put a camera on them, they are inclined to underperform and, of course, we're still a theatre production. So we need their performance to be more heightened so it's evident they are able to project the character on a large stage, like ours in London.

And it remains vital that the direction is performed correctly:

Petra Siniawski: If you're in the finals and you're being rehearsed to be filmed for the American creative team, just trust and do what you're being asked to do. Because those creatives are expecting to see something specific. Just say, very fundamentally, if in the production, an actor enters stage left, don't suddenly enter stage right. I'm being very basic here, but I've been in the situation where I've coached somebody for their final audition and the actor has decided to do their own thing, and I've had the director look at me and say, "What the fuck?" Because they think that's what you've taught and you haven't! Trust we're on your side and want to show you at your best possible, and know what the original creatives want.

Taking direction

Taking direction has been a theme throughout this book, and our directors have their own perspectives on its importance. Rupert Goold believes a lot of the responsibility for taking direction lies with the creative giving it. He also says it's more important to him in particular areas:

> **Rupert Goold**: Probably more in the dialogue than the song. In my experience, it's quite rare that you find somebody just won't take direction or can't. And sometimes I think well, if they don't seem to be taking the direction, then maybe your direction is wrong; it shouldn't all be on the performer, maybe you're just not communicating it clearly enough.

Laurence Connor says actors who don't take direction leave little room for development in rehearsals. But those who do take direction, and are inspired by it, become very attractive performers to work with, so taking direction is vital for an auditionee:

> **Laurence Connor**: That's the most important thing. If somebody walks in and your instinct is "Wow! That was great! It's not really what I'm going to be wanting to do, though, so I just want to check, I want to move them . . ." and then they're completely immovable, or they don't understand, or they're not prepared to listen, you think, well what are we going to do for three weeks in a rehearsal room? This is going to be pretty tough, if you are literally just going to play that. So it's hugely important. And it's good to see them be challenged and allow those moments when you can see the penny drop with them, and they realise "I never even thought about that. Got it!" And then they're excited by the idea, they're excited to play, and then they bring it, and then they might even say, "Do you know what? I didn't nail it but I know what you want so can I do it again?" They're hungry, and that's great because you know that even if they're not able to do it in that moment, if they can understand it, and they're prepared to work at it to get it, you're more willing to give a punt to someone because you like the fact that they are hungry to work and to devour the direction so that they can be totally immersed in the show.

This type of direction gives an auditionee inspiration and creative freedom. It's different from the direction Petra Siniawski mentioned above – entering stage left or stage right – which is prescriptive and needs to be followed to allow the show to function. Rupert Goold suggests that MT performers can become more familiar with following the prescriptive type of direction than the creative kind:

> **Rupert Goold**: I don't know what the statistics are about how many of the people working in musical theatre in a given year around the country are taking over – i.e. they're going into a tour, or into a show that's come from Broadway, or a second or third re-cast – but I bet it's probably a substantial majority, and so there's a slightly more deferential way of working, like, I've got to stand over here, put me in these clothes... And so sometimes the creativity is less evident because it's not a skill set, it's not a muscle, that's being used as much as maybe people who're doing more straight theatre. I always think that these musical theatre performers are more robust, and they're more "can do", but maybe they sometimes lack a bit of creative freedom.

We've seen other creatives talk about this difference between creating new work and reproducing what's been set. Stuart Morley talked about it in connection with the workshopping process in Chapter 3. Richard Eyre says it affects the audition process; for instance, a new piece needs creative performers:

Richard Eyre: Oh, if you have a brand new piece, it's all new territory. You're much, much more open, by definition, because you're exploring, and you're looking for fellow explorers.

Shaun Aquilina: Is that an important quality for you in a performer?

Richard Eyre: Yeah, yeah. Oh, absolutely, yeah.

Whereas a re-cast or a revival has more of a defined quality, and the auditions are guided by that:

Richard Eyre: You know the piece exactly and you know the requirements of the piece so it's a much more focused process. Everyone has a track through the piece and the ensemble have got to do four, five, six different characters, and you know each track very well. So casting becomes much simpler than when you're simply looking for a variety of people with considerable abilities. So sometimes you are saying, yeah they're very good but they can't fit any of the tracks in the show.

However, Laurence Connor observed that sometimes it's the spirit of a production that needs to endure, not the particular way of doing it. Having re-staged several of the biggest musicals of the past forty years, he relies on the strength of the material and the bold choices that were made when they were first staged:

Laurence Connor: *Les Mis* is a good example because *Les Mis* is a classic show, now. Everybody knows every song, everyone knows every character, and so on. When it was created, it wasn't classic. People hadn't heard voices like Frances Ruffelle, Michael Ball and Colm Wilkinson. They were very different musical theatre styles: Colm was a rock folk singer, and Michael Ball was quite poppy, compared to now. That style has become musical theatre style but, at the time, no one was doing that, and it was groundbreaking in that way. I think understanding that the choices that were made right at the very beginning were groundbreaking and challenging and amazing and unique in their own way is a constant reminder to ourselves that if you want to keep something current, be current! Recognise what the vocal styles of the show are, look at the history of the show and how the voices of the show have changed: you might get a more soulful Eponine now, and Fantine can be a bit more folky, and things shift depending on the actors that come in. But the piece itself, the show itself, never suffers from a different vocal style because it's so solid as a book and so solid as a story. And with all these characters, the amount of combinations are endless of how different the show can be, and how organic it can remain.

Making decisions

Once the auditionees have been seen for the final time, casting decisions need to be made. Rupert Goold says it's more likely that today's casting process will involve reviewing videos of the auditions to get a better measure of one auditionee against another:

> **Rupert Goold**: The culture now is to film recalls more as well, so in the old days you used to really try and pay attention in the room – of course you do now as well – but then you also can review the tapes now and do apple to apple comparisons.

For Richard Eyre, there remains the distinction between the objective measures in singing and dance, and the subjective feeling for acting. Ultimately, it's the subjective feeling he trusts, combined with a considered approach:

> **Richard Eyre**: Auditioning is not a science. It is so much, in my area, to do with intuition and experience rather than the areas of quantifiable expertise in the singing and dancing.

> **Shaun Aquilina**: Is that intuition something you've always had or has it been honed through years of auditions?

> **Richard Eyre**: I guess it's been honed but I guess I've also always had it. And I guess I've learnt how to use it better. I don't immediately rush to conclusions, "Oh, I think that person is absolutely wonderful," I'm . . . I guess, a little more cautious.

Working on intuition can be more apparent when casting children. Richard Eyre says there's something about that process that benefits from an open, uncritical engagement:

> **Richard Eyre**: It's really interesting when you're auditioning children because, actually, it's best to switch off your rational faculties. Some children come to auditions highly prepped in a slightly objectionable fashion, you can see the ghost of their parents and teachers behind them, saying, "You've got to do this, you've got to . . ." and if you switch off your critical faculties and let them make an impression on you, it's much easier because you think oh, yes, now, why is it that I'm really drawn to that child and I'm not drawn to that child? And sometimes it's difficult to quantify. And you just have a sense that they're good.

Laurence Connor agrees and approached the children's auditions for *Joseph and the Amazing Technicolor Dreamcoat* in a similar way, remaining open to the experience and what the children brought into the room:

> **Laurence Connor**: When I came to do *Joseph*, I'd seen various productions of it, and of course I'd seen the very big production that had been at The Palladium previously, but also the productions that I'd seen that I really enjoyed were watching my children do it at school, and seeing kids with fake beards and being

uncomfortable on stage. It always used to make me laugh, and it reminded me that the show was written for children. So when I had a chance to do it, it was really about finding that balance. So then that became about auditioning children and looking for personalities and of course I had no idea what I was looking for. I just knew that I wanted those kids to be wonderful and hilarious and slightly not "professional", not necessarily stage kids, but just real kids that sometimes didn't even want to be there. To just see it for what it really is, and let the audience enjoy that for what it is. You want children to be children. I think when they become glossy and clean, they become mini adults. And actually, when you see a child on stage, yes, they've got to be able to deliver the lines but you have to spend more time as a director helping them and encouraging them to be themselves but bring those lines to life but so that they remain children and honest. Otherwise it loses its fun. It can border on being precocious and no-one wants to see that.

Rupert Goold can enter the final auditions with a specific issue he wants to see resolved. It may have been something present from the start of the process which turns out to be decisive:

Rupert Goold: I think, normally with principal finals, you're going in going, "I really like this person but this is my question mark over them: can they do this thing in the song? Can they have enough emotional depth in this bit of the scene? Can they land these jokes?" Those are pretty crude, and there are more complicated versions of that but you're recalling going, "Oh, if they can solve the one thing I'm worried about, I'm casting them." But those final recalls are really drilling into that area of weakness or doubt. And it's amazing, I'm always fascinated by them, because you go, "God! Actually, that person I really liked all through the process, that nagging worry I had about their ability to do 'this' has meant that we can't take them forward."

There might also be a combination of demands necessary to perform a role. We've seen in *Wicked* that vocal ability has to be aligned with dramatic ability to attain the impact of the witches' stories. Rupert Goold says he found a similar situation in *Tammy Faye* and was left with only one auditionee who could perform the role:

Rupert Goold: Sometimes in the casting process, you realise how important the songs are. I would say one of the hardest roles I've ever had to cast was Tammy Faye in *Tammy Faye*, because the range, musically, is huge and dynamic. Partly because the way Elton [John] works is he writes the song for himself to sing, but of course then you're moving from his voice, a male voice, to a female voice, and the MD's transposing everything as best they can. And you need a proper comedy ability with Tammy Faye as well as a leading dramatic performer. And this is with all respect to the amazing people I saw for that role, but quite frankly, Katie was pretty much the only person who literally could do it.

Katie Brayben went on to win the Olivier Award for Best Actress in a Musical for her performance as Tammy Faye and reprised the role on Broadway.

There's also the consideration of what can be attained in rehearsals and what can't. As Gareth Valentine noted in the previous chapter, vocal technique can advance relatively little in a rehearsal period. Petra Siniawski says that, though the acting and the singing for the leads in *Wicked* need to be of the highest standard, they cast based on the vocal ability in the auditions, while exploring through the workshop sessions and rehearsals to find the emotional drama:

Petra Siniawski: As long as you have somebody who is willing to trust and go on the journey with you, you can get it out of them and open up emotional depths they have never been asked to find before, and discovering what they are capable of expressing. I aim not to give the actors line readings because I want them to feel that it's their creation, it's their role, but there are moments when you are having to lead them in the right direction with the right motivation. I say, think about the subtext under that line. For example when Elphaba says, "That someone like him could actually choose someone like me." What are you saying? It's so important because basically, you're saying, I'm a freak of nature and yet he's found the beauty within me. He loves me. The actor has to bring the weight of that emotional truth to the fore, and take their time with the line. Have they any past experience to call on? Personal and collaborative exploration is essential.

Petra Siniawski recalled a particular challenge in bringing out the comedy for one of her leads:

Petra Siniawski: I've had a Glinda come to me on the first day of rehearsal and say, "I'm not funny!" Now, we knew it was going to be a journey for her, as she'd only previously played straight dramatic roles, but she sang it beautifully she very much had the Glinda look, and ticked a lot of boxes but didn't quite have the innate humour. She was the best of what we were seeing, and everybody was pleased to have her! So I assured her, "All good comedy is played honestly and straight. Trust the material because it's all there for you. Don't watch any other Glindas on YouTube, bring yourself to the role and you'll make her yours." And she ended up being a delightful Glinda and the humour happened because it happened naturally. The audience weren't laughing at her but laughing with her.

This is another case where auditions are not about a finished performance but about showing the right qualities for a journey through the rehearsal period. Rupert Goold says his decision might come down to one single quality that needs to be present if the actor is going to succeed:

Rupert Goold: Through the process, you might realise there's a non-negotiable about one part of the role. So, another part that was really hard to cast was Zula in Cold War, partly because the woman in the movie is just extraordinary, it's like Hedda Gabler in terms of its acting, but also you're singing torch songs, she's the main singer in the whole show. And I knew I wanted someone wild and a little bit feral. And Anya Chalotra, who did it, is a bit of a TV star and incredibly beautiful and a brilliant, brilliant actor, but she'd admit she's not an experienced singer, but

I was like, "The acting has to come first," and in some way we're going to get through these songs. And in fact, she did really, really well on them.

Of course, there's also the relationship with the rest of the panel to consider. We've heard many of our other creatives discuss the compromises necessary to select a cast that meets the requirements of each department. Richard Eyre agrees:

Richard Eyre: When you're auditioning, a director will always be auditioning with the musical director and the choreographer, and probably the producer. The choreographers and the music directors will have a very, very precise idea of whether they think somebody is suitable or not. Then it comes down to me expressing a preference: I prefer that person because they've got a kind of energy about them, and a kind of intelligence and a wit, and then in the end you get down to a barter process where you're saying, look, it's not the greatest voice but they give us terrific acting qualities and the dancing is great.

Rupert Goold says the bartering process may need to be led by what's important to the show overall, and the levels of acting, singing and dance it requires. But that still means great auditionees can miss out:

Rupert Goold: It's tricky because each department's fighting very hard for their thing. And you're trying to curate that. You might be going, "Look, this is not a show that's going to be led by movement," or "You may think, music department, this guy can't sing, but he's so useful elsewhere," or whatever. So, it's your job to oversee all that. And, it's always staggering in a musical because you go, "But this person whom we have absolutely loved through every round, we can't find space for them because if we cast them then we're going to be short in a certain area."

Laurence Connor agrees but says there is a positive in knowing that those auditionees might be seen for something in the future:

Laurence Connor: When you've settled on your principal line-up, you've said, "You know what, I think they, as a team, are going to really tell the story well, so I'm really happy with that." Then you have to look at the ensemble, and of course the ensemble becomes about logistics and who can cover who, who can do this, that and the other. And there would be ten casting people, for example the choreographer, myself, the casting director, musical supervisor and so on, and everyone has their agenda. So of course you say, "But they're such good actors," and "But they're such good dancers," and "We need these voices," and it becomes this negotiation with the team, because no member of the team's point is not valid. So your stance is "Well, I want great actors, but it won't be worth them acting really well if they all can't sing the notes," or, "It's got to sound great, it's got to look great" and therefore you end up bargaining with each other, and people that you are sure are going to make it into the show often don't. In this scenario, it's a case of "next time," or "I want to see them for the role," or "I really like them, I'm casting something next year, so can you make sure that they're on the list for that?"

Laurence Connor also remembers working with an ex-performer who had moved onto the creative team and his surprise at the way the casting is put together:

Laurence Connor: I have a fond memory of when I was casting *Miss Saigon* in Australia. I was working with a young dance captain who had moved onto that side of the fence for the first time. And, of course, all his friends are on this table, and he's looking at them, thinking, "Oh, great! they've all made it through," and of course, one by one, people just don't make it. And he could see why. And as an ex-performer, it made him realise, "Ah! So really, that's it. It's nothing to do with me, it's nothing to do with my talent. It's just the way it works, the way it all falls together." And in a weird way, you wanted him to call all his friends and say, "The way they cast a show – it's not us. They love us!" It's a complicated process and you only have the amount of slots that you can have. You've carefully budgeted your cast size, you've carefully worked it all out and if you could, you'd just employ everyone but then we'd be closed within a week because we couldn't afford to run the show. So it is what it is. It's a complicated process but a fun one.

As well as the relationship with other creatives, there's also the relationship with the producer. Two of our directors spoke about working with perhaps the world's leading musical theatre producer, Sir Cameron Mackintosh. Richard Eyre says he can argue passionately for an auditionee but will give way to the panel when necessary:

Richard Eyre: If you're doing auditions with Cameron Mackintosh, Cameron will get a fixed idea about someone and try to get everybody to see it his way. But generally, if Cameron said, "We have to have this person!" and you say, "Well, not for me . . ." in the end, he knows that he's got to have the approval of everybody in the room otherwise it's simply not going to work.

Laurence Connor agrees: there's a balance between insistence and acceptance from the producer:

Laurence Connor: Totally. Cameron knows his audience, 100 per cent. And actually, only a fool would not listen to Cameron Mackintosh's thoughts because he knows what he's talking about. He's been doing it way longer than I have, and he is super smart. I think there are times where he thinks he's got it completely on track where he wants it to go, but what Cameron doesn't always understand is the combination of people together, as a collective, and how they work together. Sometimes, therefore, I think you have to really dig deep and say, "No, no, no, I don't see it. It needs to be this person." Or "I don't like the way they did that scene together, I don't like the way they're working together, it's rubbing off in the wrong way." And he will totally listen. There are times when he will be quite insistent about someone, and then when you put that person in amongst other people that you are really interested in, if he sees it, he gets it. If he doesn't get it though, he will fight you, and he will usually win. But that's the way it goes. I've got to say, however, we all have the most tremendous respect for him. He's just one of the greatest producers I think the world has ever seen, and I would put him up there as probably one of the best in the world. It's very rare that you work with him and produce something that isn't good, because he demands it of you.

There's also commercial casting to consider, something all our directors are familiar with. Rupert Goold says he's had experiences where an actor has been cast without auditioning at all:

Rupert Goold: Rowan Atkinson did not audition for *Oliver!*. He came round to my kitchen and we had a cup of tea. So on Day One of rehearsals you go, "What is this gonna be like?" And you're going to build the show around that. And that's always interesting. And actually, Andrew Rannells in London and Christian Borle in New York didn't audition either [for Jim Bakker in *Tammy Faye*]. You're going on their body of work and it hasn't undone me yet.

Laurence Connor is positive, overall, about commercial casting, provided the person cast is able to act and sing the role. However, he also admits it can be overdone:

Laurence Connor: In my opinion, sometimes it's one of those things that you can get a little bored of – when you think, "Why are we going to see the show, we're going to see this person rather than the show." But there are also moments where you look at it and say, "Well, it's just brilliant." When we cast Tim Minchin, that would be commercial casting, Mel C as well, but they were superb! And I also had Chris Moyles, who was just sensational to work with. In actuality, I think when it's justified, when they really can pull something off splendidly, it can be great. Working with Sheridan Smith on *Joseph* was just joyful: an incredible actress, incredible passion, and what fun that she brings to it. And so I can lean into it and really enjoy it myself. There are certain moments where, with the scale of the show you're doing, and the amount of time you're doing it in, I can see why producers want to lean in that way, but I think, at the end of the day, what you want is for people to see your work. You want people to enjoy the show, and if bringing a star name is what's needed – as long as they really can play it – I'm not against it, at all. I am against it when it's just a ploy to sell tickets and they're not actually strong enough to play the role. That I'm not a fan of. But when they come in and surprise you, and are amazing, and do something unique – wow. A perfect example is *Sunset Boulevard*. We've just seen an incredible production, very celebrated. Nicole Scherzinger is a celebrity and just an exceptional talent and no-one can doubt that that's a truly wonderful performance. So there, you go – why not? If they can do it, let them do it.

Most valued qualities in a performer

We've heard about many qualities that our directors value when working with auditionees, such as generosity, confidence and personality, but I wanted to know if one stood out as the most important of all. For Rupert Goold, it's bravery. He wants to see performers with the courage to play and to commit to their acting choices. This was evident with the actor Matt Smith, well-known for playing Doctor Who but not an experienced singer, when he took the lead role in a musical among a cast of some of the best singers in the West End:

Rupert Goold: *American Psycho* is a really good example. We had Katie Brayben in that, we had a young Lucie Jones who went on to headline all sorts of West End shows, we had Jonathan Bailey who's in the *Wicked* movie and was in *Company*, we had Hugh Skinner who was in the second *Mamma Mia* movie, Cassie Compton who'd got down to the final 10 in *X Factor*, some really great singers, and then Matt Smith, playing Patrick Bowman, the lead role, carrying most of the songs, and Matt had never sung in his life! I did audition Matt, I said, "Look, we've got to hear you," so I went round to his house, got my iPhone out and we recorded him. And poor old Matt, he'd be singing in rehearsal and sometimes struggling with his tuning or whatever, he wasn't a musical theatre singer and he was in a room full of world class singers, but his bravery! He was like, I'm not going to care, I'm going to back myself, and I'm going to act my way through this. And you could feel them all go, "He's just a brilliant, brilliant actor" and they recognised it. Whereas sometimes, if someone doesn't do that, you can feel the good singers in the room go, "They can't do it, love. They can't do it." And you feel the atmosphere in the room is a bit weird. And so bravery, I think, is what I look for most of all, and tone and personality.

When actors lack bravery, it can scupper their audition. Rupert Goold has seen that, too, with both dance and singing:

Rupert Goold: The saddest thing I witness is really wonderful actors who could do it but who worry too much in auditions about getting it right. Actually, for me, if you're doing a choreographic phrase, let's say there's 16 bars of material, if you screw up 8 bars and get the steps wrong but really have flair and character in the 8 bars you do get right, that's much more valuable than approximately getting right all 16 but without much flavour. I think so often you see really talented people give up in choreographic auditions, and I understand it, because they're out of their comfort zone, maybe they sing and act really well but they think, Oh, I've got two left feet. And actually, that's the one thing I've always wanted to say to actors: just give it a go; you don't have to be right, you just have to be there.

And I think there's something about having to sing in front of people that is terrifying. Some people just fall apart and even experienced musical theatre performs can do that. It's incredibly exposing, vulnerable-making, because you're saying, "Okay, sing me a song," and that's maybe two, three minutes of material; in a play, you're not asking for that. And you're standing in front of people, often so many people in the room and I think people underestimate that: you have maybe two people in the music department, maybe producers, there might be a choreographic team, so it's much more intimidating than just sitting round a table for a theatre audition. So bravery is something I look for rather than transformation.

Petra Siniawski agrees. She urges auditionees to show their bravery and attempt something, because what the panel really wants to know is not whether they can do it but whether they are willing to take the risk and develop their performance through rehearsals:

> **Petra Siniawski**: Just take a risk, even if it's stupid, whatever they're asking you to do, do it, because we want to know that somebody is willing to go on that journey with us. And I don't mean in a "yes sir, three bags full, sir," way, but especially in an audition, when time is always limited, so just go for it. You'd rather see somebody immerse themselves in what is being required of them. I believe Idina Menzel got the role of Elphaba originally because there was something about her, that drive, that willingness, that hunger, which convinced the creative team. And of course the rest is history. So there's nothing better than showing commitment and enthusiasm for what you're being given.

When I asked Richard Eyre which quality he looks for most of all, he immediately answered:

> **Richard Eyre**: Wit. Wit. Intelligence, wit, quickness of thinking. Sense of humour.

> **Shaun Aquilina**: And how does that come out in an audition?

> **Richard Eyre**: How they deal with the script, and how they deal with conversation. I've never worked with a good actor who doesn't have a quick intelligence. I'm not saying they're always particularly knowledgeable or particularly articulate but if they're good as an actor, they think very quickly. And that's absolutely across the board.

I put this idea of wit to Rupert Goold and asked how it appears to him in an audition:

> **Rupert Goold**: I think in song, it's phrasing. And wit in musical theatre, I think, overlaps with musicality. Can someone rhythmically, or sometimes harmonically, bend something to their choice rather than just sing through it?

He went on to discuss the importance of wit, of quick-thinking; of making choices, and suggested that it's a mark of strong musical theatre performers that they move convincingly between speech and song:

> **Rupert Goold**: With certain kinds of repertoire, it's also can you make the movement into song feel totally organic? And that's part of the director's job to do that but can you ease into song, and then back into dialogue, and then back into song in an organic way. And I'm always struck how sometimes you might have people who have really good voices, who are really good singers, and also really good actors, but have not done much musical theatre, and who can't bring those two skill sets together. Because when they sing they make a gorgeous sound, and when they act they're really good, but actually thinking of the two things together can be challenging. So sometimes the audition might be to try and pull those things together and you can do all those exercises, where it's speaking the

lyrics and acting the lyrics as though it's a speech, but actually, it's also about how you colour your voice into song.

For Laurence Connor, wit is an indicator of quick thinking and a sense of humour, both on stage and off. He says those are invaluable in creating an effective working relationship, especially when the material is deeply emotional:

Laurence Connor: You need to know that you're going to be able to get on and work together. You're going to spend a lot of time working with people, and be in the same room together, and you want to know that you can have a giggle, especially in those very dramatic shows. In *Miss Saigon*, for example, there are moments where you have to go to very dark places and you have to have a safe room and create an environment so that the actor can really go there. But you also need to be able to crack a joke to break it, or have a moment to just go, "Ooh, that's all a bit much!" You need to know that in order to go to those places, you can be around people that feel safe and have fun doing it. So that is an important thing. And I think wit is one of those things that indicates straight away that they've got a sense of humour, they're sharp, they're fun, they think really quickly, and it's a very good marker to know that you're heading in that direction.

Petra Siniawski also agrees that intelligence can lead to a creative relationship in rehearsals. However, many of the young actors she auditions and works with are yet to develop the craft of theatrical acting that allows them to see the thoughts behind the lines or, as mentioned earlier, instincts about how to use the space:

Petra Siniawski: Maybe more experienced actors know how to do that but because we're still a young-age musical, we don't always have that same expertise. There's a rawer quality. And I mean, I have to be honest here again, sometimes I have to teach basic stagecraft. They've had three years vocational training but they don't know where upstage or downstage is! But ideally, you do look for intelligence. If somebody is thinking about things and bringing ideas to the table with you, it's a real treat to work with that collaborative input, it's a delight. But sometimes you know that person just doesn't have the experience. They haven't been in a play, they've just been in a sung-through musical. Now, yes, dramatically, you're singing through the story-telling but you're not actually doing dialogue and so timing sometimes is not ideal, or they don't quite know where the emphasis of a line needs to be, what is the through line of thought in that line. And there's another thing for me: there's a lot of finger pointing! I say, "Is that how you talk in life? Do you actually point at the person you're talking to?" There's some really bad and superficial mannerisms that go on and need to be eradicated.

Petra Siniawski added that the fundamentals of stagecraft are important because they can add so much to the narrative, as in the staging of one of Elphaba's biggest numbers. Supporting young performers to gain more experience and more stagecraft might require some adjustments in their training:

Petra Siniawski: A lot of the colleges are now under pressure, especially in the third year, to produce a lot of musicals, so everybody has a chance. So those people are learning a show, say *Ragtime*, or doing *Newsies*, or another musical, which is great, but at the same time, they're not maturing in any of those roles. They don't have enough time for discovery. As brilliant as it is for them to be exposed to so many different musicals, they're missing out some basic training. It's very evident in rehearsal, because again, I'm saying, "Who are you talking to? Why are you facing out front when you're saying that dramatic sentence or line? Why? You're talking to Glinda, or Glinda you're talking to Elphaba, why are you facing out front?" But that's not just me, that's the style of our show, to play it honest, truthful and real, as encouraged by our director, Joe Mantello. In our production, very rarely does a character face out front and only doing so when it's an important moment or statement to share, but they never break the fourth wall. So, when Elphaba starts singing the beginning of "The Wizard and I", she's kneeling, she's facing the diagonal, she's got a suitcase in front of her, as she conveys her very internal thoughts. The temptation sometimes, especially with covers, they want to show off vocally, so they'll sing at full volume, and you say no, the song is narrative, you've got to save that for the end when the dramatic climax happens. We, as an audience, need to know who this girl is. What are her inner dreams? What are her ambitions? Until now we've only seen her confronting people, and now we learn about her, what drives her, and then we're onside with her throughout her storyline. It's very beautifully constructed, very clever.

Petra Siniawski also wants to see passion from her performers. Passion was important to many of our choreographers in Chapter 2, so, as an ex-dancer and choreographer, it's understandable that Petra Siniawski values it too:

Petra Siniawski: You've got to have passion to be in our industry, be it stage management, wardrobe or wigs, whatever department, you've got to have a passion for what you do. It's not the easiest job, it's very antisocial, and you've got to have an element of craziness to you to endure some of the challenges thrown at you! Ultimately, passion drives you! It doesn't matter what your background is or position in the show, if you don't have that absolute passion then it's not the industry for you.

Be yourself

All our directors agreed on one thing – be yourself:

Rupert Goold: The weird thing about our business is, there are so many people trying to do it but actually, how many wonderful playwrights, and wonderful directors, and wonderful singers are there in a generation? I mean, yeah, quite a few but I'd say, even with a good casting director like Pippa Ailion, it's probably like one in ten. And if you have two days of casting and you get one performer, that's great. True talent is rare and what I feel with people who want to audition is accept your limitations and concentrate on your strengths. There are some things I'm not very good at directing, and I can admit that and know I direct that kind of stuff badly, so accept your limitations and concentrate on your strengths and recognise that some things you may be brought in for but unfortunately, you're probably not going to be right for, and that's fine, don't beat yourself up about that, move on. But in other things go, "Yeah, this is what I do do well, and this is how I can offer it to you. Now, it may not be exactly what you're looking for but at least let me show it, and then you can go, 'Well, maybe I didn't think I wanted it, but actually having seen it, I do want it' rather than trying to be a halfway house version of what you think you want, and I know I can't do."

Laurence Connor agrees and wants to see actors be confident in themselves rather than second-guessing the panel:

Laurence Connor: Actors don't realise how much we want them to be amazing. I think they come sometimes with a "them and us" perspective, but actually, the reality is that we're not looking for a them and us situation, we're looking for collaborators. And if we don't know you, when you walk into a room, we're just hoping that you're going to be the next Eva Noblezada, the next Ramin Karimloo, and that we find something in you. And the only way you'll ever have that is if you have the confidence to be yourself, and to be the best you can be, and show that, rather than give them what you think they want.

Petra Siniawski says it's too easy for auditionees to be influenced by great performers who have already done the role, which again takes them away from being themselves:

Petra Siniawski: I do feel for actors today, everything's on YouTube, and if you're auditioning for a role, you're going to reference YouTube. So you're going to say, "Oh, it's Kristin Chenoweth, well, she was the original, that's how I've got to play it." So you get actors coming into the audition mimicking her voice and vocals, but that's her and not you! That's how she speaks! So don't put on a voice. And I'm always having to say, "I'm sorry, I know you've prepared this, but please, speak and sing in your natural voice." Because we have to see you. We want you, not a Kristin Chenoweth substitute!

We saw in previous chapters that a strong performance from an auditionee can alter the creatives' vision of the production. Laurence Connor agrees and provided the most striking example of a performance changing his entire production concept. It's also illustrative of his directorial process, which remains responsive to inspiration from performers and the world around him:

Laurence Connor: If you've ever seen my production of *Jesus Christ Superstar*, we always knew we were going to do an arena production and we always knew it was going to be concert style, but originally, my plan was to do it very stripped bare and to have actors just walk to a microphone and sing it, and you could see the orchestra and all of that. We'd actually cast Seal to play Judas at that time and it was going to be very rock star heavy. Then, for whatever reason, Seal had to drop out, and the casting director mentioned that Tim Minchin had shown an interest in playing the role at some point. At that stage, I hadn't really known that side of Tim's work. I knew he was a terrifically funny writer, and obviously he'd written *Matilda* by then but it was quite hard to imagine him playing Judas. So, in fairness to Tim, he insisted on coming in to audition and did one of the most extraordinary auditions I think I've ever seen. He didn't do the obvious thing, he didn't walk around the piano and be relaxed about it and just show that he could sing it. He said, "Can I just do the suicide?" And I, taken aback, just said, "Ok, well, we're going for it!" He performed it like he was playing the role, and it was so powerful, so unexpected. I remember thinking at the time that he had a good voice, but was not the rock singer of Bon Jovi's ilk, or those type of names that we were kicking around. But he was and is a great actor. My concern was that in an arena, we might not be able to see that performance. So that's when I decided that I would do what I did in the O2 concert of *Les Mis* and put cameras on stage and film certain sections of it as part of the action. But this meant that the production would then have to be fully staged, fully realised, fully imagined. As it happened, I was staying at a hotel in St. Paul's during the time the Occupy movement had put all their tents up and had taken residence on the steps of St. Paul's Cathedral. I walked past just with this vision, having Tim's audition in my head, and I heard the lyric in the very first song that Judas sings, about being occupied, about being put down, and suddenly it just gelled and I realised that was how I was going to do it. That was one of the first times and probably the most absolute time that an actor came in, did something, and gave me an entirely new idea to take the production in a different direction. Much to the cost of the producers, it suddenly became a huge production and a very expensive one, but one that people still talk about today. And I think it's an amazing thing when you can be inspired by actors in that way.

Broadway

We've heard from many of our creatives how auditions differ on Broadway. Rupert Goold is shocked by the amount of material Broadway auditionees are expected to prepare:

Rupert Goold: On Broadway, I'm staggered. If you're an actor going in for a Broadway musical, it can take up most of your week, and you're not paid for it. You might meet the associate director first, and then the music team, and then you might have two or three vocal recalls with reading, and you might have lots of different sides, and then there might be one or even two movement calls booked in. You'll have many more tracks prepared, book scenes, and you might not look at any of them. You'll be expected to bring maybe two or three songs from the show, plus your book, which they would then expect maybe three different kinds of song. So it's a huge commitment. I mean, you still have to do a bit of that over here, but I think we're a bit more forgiving. And I think the expectation of being a triple threat is more hardwired into the American. Musical theatre is part of their high school culture more than it is over here, it's almost a national art form in a way that it isn't over here. So, if you cast some guy in their fifties who's playing a character role in the musical, them coming in for the tap recall, they're fine about that. There's more understanding, particularly in men, that singing and dancing is just going to be part of what you do, whereas in London it's much harder to find those guys. But I wouldn't say the standard is higher. And, in fact, I find in America, because the classical musical theatre repertoire is more performed there, actually finding the kinds of voices that I like, I found actually harder in New York. I found you get more muscle and more virtuosity, but it's also a bit more of a legit sound, in general.

There are differences on the panel's side of the table, too, notably the importance of the creative team:

Rupert Goold: The hierarchy is much stronger in New York. The directors behave like divas, as do the choreographers. Your scenes can be cut, you can't complain about that. Your new sides get put in your book in rehearsals, you're expected to be off book. The whole power dynamics are much more subservient on Broadway, so the performers tend to be more expectant of that, a little bit more passive, maybe. But then the stars are bigger, and you can be a Broadway star. I guess London's going that way now, there are those like Michael Ball, but Idina, Patti LuPone, there's so many in New York, and it's a distinct thing, and they get paid so much money now in New York as well, I mean, it's huge. They can't be bringing that really in box office, it's just the expectation. And by and large they're real pros, they know they've got to sell the show, they've got to perform the show, they're marketing. But sometimes they can be grander as well. Even more like opera.

Laurence Connor also finds Broadway auditionees are consistently accomplished across all three disciplines, but he says they can lack authenticity:

Laurence Connor: I think actors in America are very different, especially musical theatre actors. They're very polished. They're very, very good at what they do. So there's a lot of confidence that comes when they walk into a room and they bring many of the levels that you're looking for. So, for example, those triple threats when you're all arguing about voices etc. that's less of a problem in America, because there's such a strong musical theatre community with such a solid core of being able to do all three disciplines really well. I think sometimes they're a little too rehearsed. What I love about British actors is that they walk in with their umbrella and their raincoat, and sometimes they look like they've just fallen out of bed and they haven't really made that much of an effort, because they're not really there to present themselves as if they're interviewing for a bank job – they're actors. They're raw and they're artists. Whereas in America they'll come very dressed up, quaffed and clean, and sometimes that's not the character, you just want to see a real person be real. So it's harder, I think, at times to make yourself understood as to what you're looking for or what you want to see from them.

Sometimes, the way West End creatives work can be a surprise for Broadway auditionees, as we've seen in previous chapters. Laurence Connor says his relaxed manner can throw them, especially if he does more than they expect from a director:

Laurence Connor: Sometimes when I'm working with somebody and there's a line that needs to be sung and we don't have anyone to sing it, I'll just sing it, and American actors will just freak out because they don't know that you sing, they don't know that you were a performer, and they expect you to be very serious. They're used to auditioning in a different way because American directors are a little different to British directors, and it takes a while, in an audition, for you to really understand how to make the most of them as actors.

Earlier, Petra Siniawski noted the difference between American and British theatrical tastes. It's something Laurence Connor has noticed, too, with US actors tending towards a more declamatory style. In auditions, that means moving them to something more flexible and creative:

Laurence Connor: In the rehearsal room, I find sometimes the style is a little bit "face front, speak" and "as long as they can see me", whereas I think we tend to be a little more, "who are you talking to? Talk to one another, and let's be in a room rather than in a theatre." But again, their talent is incredible and there's no doubt that they come very much with an idea of how they're going to play the role. They're confident in how they're going to do that. And sometimes the challenge really is to break them away from that and let them rip up their own thoughts and start again and come up with a new idea. Those that do are the ones that you end up loving.

Great auditions

When thinking about the great auditions they'd seen, our directors often said that the truth and natural delivery of the performance made it so impactful:

Richard Eyre: In the '70s, when I was running Nottingham Playhouse, this actor who had just left RADA came in and he said, "I'm going to do a speech from *Hamlet*." And he did "Speak the speech, I pray you, as I pronounced it to you, trippingly on the tongue." And he was so real that it was as if he was reinventing the whole speech. Anyway, that actor was Tom Wilkinson. He hasn't done badly. That was an outstanding audition, it was just about intelligence and presence and charisma, and he could make it natural, and do justice to Shakespeare while at the same time appear as if he was extemporising it. Charlie Stemp is another example. When I first saw Charlie, I thought, he's just brilliant, just brilliant! And, in every department.

Shaun Aquilina: The same reasons? The wit, the energy?

Richard Eyre: Yeah, absolutely, absolutely. But Charlie is a very rare creature.

Laurence Connor recalls meeting Eva Noblezada for the first time and instantly connecting with her. Again, though, it was something about the truth in her performance that impacted him:

Laurence Connor: When I was introduced to Eva Noblezada, I was actually auditioning *Phantom* and the casting director in America had just been to this festival where kids perform and had seen Eva, and said, "She's in New York, I just thought if you've got time, let's work with her. I know you're not doing *Miss Saigon* for another year, but I think you should see her, even though you're not looking right now." I saw her and immediately thought: "That's my girl. That is my girl." Of course, I only had a video and I played it to Cameron [Mackintosh], and Cameron, because he wasn't in the room, couldn't quite get what I was getting from her. So I just said to the casting director, Tara Rubin, "Look, do not take your eye off that girl. I really want to know where she is, at all times. I think she's amazing." I then went all around the world looking for our Kim. I went to the Philippines, I went to Japan, I went all over Australia, back to New York, everywhere, looking for our Kim. Then we were doing some finals in London and we were trying to fly people back, and I said to Tara, "I need to get Eva here. I just want her in the finals for Cameron." I was doing everything trying to get her there, even offering to pay for her fight, and then she couldn't come – she didn't have a passport. So I said, "We've got to go to New York!" And we went to New York – that's also where we found Jon Jon Briones [who played the Engineer in the West End revival and again on Broadway]. Eva Noblezada came in, started to sing, and Cameron Mackintosh in that one moment, just said, "We need to stop this right now!" And I said, "Why?" And he answered simply, "Because I never thought lightning could strike twice, but it just has. We need to be filming this." And that was it. Those moments, those moments: magical.

Shaun Aquilina: Is it possible to say what she did in that performance that so affected you both?

Laurence Connor: She was so truthful. She took the direction brilliantly. The song was, "I'd Give My Life For You," and the direction I'd given to her was: you're nearly twenty but, in the past three years, you've been through more than any girl could imagine that she could go through. Carrying a child that's called bui doi, a child that is mixed race in a world that is now communist and anti-American, and you are surviving in this moment, and in one bad choice that you make, you risk the life of that child. That's the moment where you totally realise your love for that child, and that everything you need in life is for that. It's everything. And that moment of knowing how much you love something is powerful, so when you say, "I'll give my life for you", you're saying that to a two-year-old child. It is heavy. And she really took the direction. I said, strip it back, take away all of that, and when you say, "You who I cradled in my arms," I want you to think that I could have lost you. So put in your head the last line "you who I cradled in my arms . . . and

I nearly watched you die." "You who 'I did this' . . . and I nearly watched you die." It always makes you go, My God, it's heavy! She took that direction and it was so powerful. I think when Cameron saw it, he just thought, "I've never seen a girl so young be that truthful with that material." And that was it. In the first verse, he said "Stop it, it's too good." And that was it. Magic.

What's also so important for Laurence Connor, though, is that kind of working session in auditions. He says that's where the actor-director relationship starts and it's key to the success of the rehearsals and the production:

Laurence Connor: Obviously Eva Noblezada for *Miss Saigon*, Jon Jon Briones, Tim Minchin, Ramin Karimloo, David Fynn, people that I've worked with a lot, and people that I love working with, they walk in, and they just are it. And you can't help but say, "That's it. That's the role." And I think they're a part of the success of the show: it isn't just your direction, it's that relationship which you cultivate in that audition room and the performances they give that really buy into the success of the show.

For Rupert Goold, great audition memories are tied to singing and quality of voice, which leave an indelible impression:

Rupert Goold: They're always vocal. There were two of the women in *Spring Awakening*. Amara Okereke, who was in *My Fair Lady* at the Coliseum, I'd seen at a Christmas concert, and I was like, "Wow, you're great." And then I always thought, "Well, if I do *Spring Awakening*, maybe you could be great as Wendla." And I got the feedback from the agent saying she doesn't think she's right for it, it doesn't suit her voice, she's more of a classical soprano, legit sound. And I was disappointed, and I pushed back a couple weeks later, I was like, "Is she sure? Because I think she could do it." And I remember her coming in, and she said, "Look, this is not really the kind of repertoire I sing." And it was unbelievable! And then another girl called Carly-Sophia Davies, who played Ilsa in that, I couldn't speak after she sang for us first time. And Jen Damiano, who was in *Next to Normal* on Broadway, when she did *American Psycho*, again, often you're hearing a song fifty, sixty times in a week, everyone coming in "what are you gonna sing?" Oh, of course, you're going to sing this from the show! And then someone comes in and you go, "You make it sound like no-one else has for the whole week."

Sometimes, there are amazing voices that have amazing auditions but still don't get cast. Rupert Goold remembers one such audition by a young tenor who sang beautifully:

Rupert Goold: I think there's something about the whole bel canto tradition and there's something about a lyric tenor that is just transformative. And there was a boy who we didn't cast, actually, who came in. Beautiful voice, that thing about a young tenor's voice, before it's developed into the muscle with more vibrato, that has a purity of sound. I literally came back home and showed my wife and daughter this boy, [and] my daughter could not stop watching the tape. It was like crack to her. And actually, when he came to read he was a bit wooden, and we didn't cast him, but he was really special.

The emotional connection of a song goes to the heart of what musical theatre is:

Rupert Goold: Ultimately, musical theatre is an emotional art form: if it doesn't move you, no show will survive. And so you have to have that feeling of having your heart opened up when someone sings.

Shaun Aquilina: Is that more than sound? Is it interpretation, connection, those kind of qualities, too?

Rupert Goold: Yeah, it is. It is. Of course, I've seen people sing in more of a dramatic way in an audition and thought, wow, that's really thrilling. But I would say the ones probably that really stick in my mind are actually really about voice texture.

And so, for Rupert Goold, it's the singing voice that makes the musical theatre audition process so exciting and enjoyable, partly because an auditionee's ability can be a surprise:

Rupert Goold: If you're auditioning for a straight play, someone comes into a room, and from the moment they walk in through the door, you're making judgments about whether they're going to be right for the role. And of course, sometimes they read the text, and you go, "Wow! That's transformative, I never saw that in you," but you're probably seeing what you're going to get. Whereas, you just don't know with a song until the moment the first note comes out. And you go, "Oh, I did not know that was in there," or "That's completely different to what I expected," and I think that's the magic of musical theatre. Casting a musical takes a long time but it's really joyful, because you're constantly being surprised in a way that is less true with a play.

Conclusion

Directors arrive at auditions after a substantial amount of work on the project. They've engaged deeply with the score and libretto. They've conceptualised the production while retaining a flexibility of mind to alter and develop it. When they meet their auditionees, they're looking for an ability to realise that concept, and an ability and temperament to get there through rehearsals.

Rehearsing, exploring, and exchanging ideas come up again and again as important to our directors, and so the correlating traits in auditionees are important too: bravery, wit, confidence and flexibility, all make for a more exciting and effective rehearsal process. Rehearsals are so important that, rather than think of auditions as auditions to be in a show, it might be more accurate to think of them as auditions to be in a rehearsal room to be in a show.

Rehearsals have their limits, however. If an auditionee can't perform objectively measurable parts of the role, such as hitting the notes, directors must then consider whether the rehearsal process can change that. The answer is often that it can't, and the auditionee progresses no further. And we've seen that one small doubt at the beginning of the process can grow into the thing that prevents an auditionee from being cast. But there are also instances where the auditionee is so compelling that a director can shift the music, the choreography, even the whole production concept, to accommodate them. Some parts of a role are non-negotiable, others are flexible, and that can be difficult for an auditionee to gauge.

For an auditionee, the result of their audition can appear binary: yes or no. But our directors have a more nuanced view. A 'no' at one audition might lead to a call further down the line or for a different show. There's a will from our directors to employ and work with good performers.

Although the actor-director relationship is a professional one, it's also personal. As Richard Eyre remarked, the time spent together can be more than any other relationship the director has. That may be why all our directors insist that an auditionee must be themselves. It makes for better work and establishes a stronger relationship to take forward into rehearsals.

The directors' most memorable auditionees were truthful, spontaneous, and moving. That's a high standard for auditionees, but if they can meet it, and if they can present themselves openly and authentically, despite the pressure of the situation, there is the potential to begin a working relationship that will flourish through rehearsals and onto the stage.

Conclusion

Context, panel, auditionee and task

This book has been asking, 'What makes a successful musical theatre audition?' Thanks to our creatives' knowledge, experience and insight, we can now attempt to answer that.

Auditions are made up of four components: context, panel, auditionee and task. Though each component varies widely, this underlying structure remains constant. As the audition components interact and influence each other, an outcome emerges. Let's look at the components in more detail.

Context

The context of an audition includes the end casting goal and the current stage that has been reached. It's the biggest variable from one audition to another, but it defines so much of any single audition. The context might start with the show. The show is the written material to be performed: the book, music, and lyrics. That starts to define the auditionees the panel will be looking for. If it's an established show, the written material is set and must be delivered; if it's a brand-new show, there may be more malleability. Next comes the production. That's the particular way the show is being done, with its choreography, setting, staging, costumes, lighting, etc. For a new production (which could be of a new show, like *Standing at the Sky's Edge*, or an old show, like *Cabaret*), a lot of this is open, whereas a long-running production is more set (think essence and mould, from Chapter 1). The production will usually conform to the industry standard eight shows a week for an extended period, which also influences the choice of auditionee. Then comes the particular roles, whether principals, covers or ensemble. Each of these has a set of requirements, such as a weighting towards acting, singing or dance, and that's easier to know once a production is running. All of this context – show, production, role – is influencing the audition before an auditionee enters the room. Then there's the context of the current audition stage, such as first round, recall, or final, and the type of call, such as singing call, dance call or work session. They also have their own requirements (think of Stuart Burt in Chapter 1: first round singing calls are a vocal suitability check; then an auditionee comes back on show material later). And finally, there's the overview of the cast, which is about finding actors that play well off each other, finding covers for the principals, knowing which roles need to be re-cast in an ongoing production and creating a supportive company for the rehearsals and performances. All of this context significantly influences an audition, and it's often what determines whether an auditionee is "right" for the job.

Panel

The panel have been working to the context for a long time before meeting auditionees. As Laurence Connor said in the previous chapter, they've engaged with the show's script and score, with the production concept and with other creatives. When they do reach auditions, the panel balances the specific needs of the production with their values as theatre-makers. These values are consistent, and we've heard all our creatives describe what they look for: auditionees who can tell stories; embody character; deliver technically; take direction; exhibit humour, wit, passion and creativity; and are pleasant to work with. They want to engage with the auditionees as professionals and as people to form an artistic working relationship. As an auditionee, aligning yourself with these values is more likely to lead to success somewhere down the line, even if you're not right in this context.

The panel collaborate with each other to cover all the requirements in a cast, and while they know what the production needs, they remain open to creativity and inspiration. They are looking for auditionees to take into a rehearsal room first and then into a production, and they are looking to create their best theatre work.

Auditionee

The auditionee is attempting to meet the requirements of the context and the values of the panel. We saw in Chapter 1 how casting director Jim Arnold filters thousands of submissions for *Wicked* through the vocal, technical and physical requirements of the production, and all our casting directors are doing the same. In an audition, our creatives continue this assessment by setting tasks, which we'll come to, shortly.

As well as meeting the context requirements, the auditionee needs to embody and perform in a way that engages the values of the panel. Again, our creatives have been clear about their values: they want to see auditionees who dance from their core, who dance with passion, who sing with a point of view, who reveal themselves through their singing and who act with wit, humour, quick thinking, generosity and bravery. They also want creative auditionees who can change their performances as directed, personable auditionees who will be nice to work with, and professional auditionees who arrive prepared and use time effectively. These qualities could point towards a definition of what it means to be a professional musical theatre performer today.

Finally, there is the audition task. Auditionees are set tasks throughout the process, such as performing an own choice song, dance calls, chemistry reads, movement sessions, and work sessions on scenes and songs. Surrounding the task is the general interaction between the panel and auditionee. Even here, the panel is getting a sense of the auditionee's personality and assessing what they might be like as a company member. As Stuart Burt said, it's not just about the performer; it's about the person.

The tasks inform the panel about those two key questions: Does an auditionee fit the context and do they rehearse and perform in a way that embodies the panel's values? For the first question, think of moments like Sean Green, in Chapter 3, testing the falsetto range of an *MJ* auditionee. That auditionee didn't perform the task well enough to meet the show's requirements. For the second question, think of Stephen Mear wanting to see passion from his dancers, or Sarah Travis wanting connection from her singers. Sometimes both questions can be posed in one task. For example, asking for an own choice song is asking about disciplinary ability (context), but it's also asking whether an auditionee has researched the production, understood the creative vision and prepared appropriately (panel values). Think of the Wizard auditionee with his guitar and folk ballad – he gave a good answer on his ability but not so good on his understanding of *Wicked*. It's the responsibility of the auditionee to engage with the task in a manner that answers both questions.

These four components interact and influence each other, leading to decisions about who to take forward in the audition process. Only the panel can see the whole audition context and know their own values, so it's no wonder auditions can be confusing for the auditionee, leaving them wondering why a decision went a particular way. But the reasoning is there, and there are many considerations, both about the auditionee and about the wider casting process.

Panel and auditionee

The relationship between the panel and the auditionee can be fascinating. One element we haven't discussed but is a fact of the relationship is status. The auditionee has arrived to be assessed and will perform tasks, sometimes many tasks, for the panel, who are the assessors. This establishes a relationship that gives power and status to the panel. But director Rupert Goold says an auditionee has the potential to reverse it:

Rupert Goold: There's probably something interesting to be written about power. I guess the history of musical theatre is predominantly bound up with the proscenium arch. I always think the Greek or The Globe model, which is more democratised, places the performer as human, and the audience as the gods. So, you are Oedipus or Macbeth on stage and we are judging you. Whereas, in the proscenium, you place the person on stage and they are the hero, they control the room. They're literally at the centre of the frame that the room is looking at and they command that frame. And of course, if you're singing, you're singing out, and there is emotion and eroticism and power and brilliance, and you drag the room up through an aria, you can literally drag people to their feet. The performer has huge power. And most of us are in the business because they like being around performers, and they're thrilled by talent, and musical performers have talent in a more obvious way than say in straight plays. And yet weirdly, the hierarchy in musicals is that you are constantly coming in, like cattle call auditions, "you're going to do a dance call for me, you're going to come in and read these three scenes, you're going to wait half an hour and come back in and do another piece," so the power is all with the panel, often sitting behind desks, lots of them, judging you, like it's a massive cliché, of course. And there's a huge imbalance of power in the funnel of selecting people versus the massive power those people have on stage when they're delivering, much greater power than the director or the casting director or the designer. But the auditionee comes in, they have no power, they're vulnerable, they walk into the room, holding their folder, going over to the piano, they're small, we sit in judgment of them, they start singing, and we melt. We become nothing. Sometimes we stand up and applaud them when they've sung. And that happens in less than five minutes in a room together. That's an extraordinary moment of theatre. So, where is the true talent? Where is the gravity of decision making? Where is the gravity of agency in the room? And it can tip back and forth just in the space of those three minutes. They're little plays in themselves, auditions.

Auditions

Finally, a word to the auditionee. Just as our creatives bring a lifetime's work to their process, so do you. Your years of training, artistic development and personal growth all contribute to your performance in an audition. With dedication and commitment, I hope that when those two key questions are asked – what does the production need and what do the creatives want – the panel will find the answer to both is you.

Bibliography

Ackroyd, P. (2023), *The English Actor: from Medieval to Modern*, Reacktion Books Ltd.

Aquilina, S. (2022), *Musical Theatre for the Female Voice: The Sensation, Sound, and Science of Singing*, Routledge.

Bogart, A. (2001), *A Director Prepares: Seven Essays on Art and Theatre,* Routledge.

Cramer, L. (2013), *Creating Musical Theatre: Conversations with Broadway Directors and Choreography*, Bloomsbury.

Evans, R. (2014), *Auditions: The Complete Guide*, Routledge.

Hall, K. (2014), *So You Want to Sing Music Theatre*, Rowman and Littlefield.

Hemsley, T. (1998), *Singing and Imagination: A Human Approach to a Great Musical Tradition*, OUP.

Henshall, R. with Bowling, D. (2012), *So You Want To Be In Musicals?* Nick Hern Books.

Hescott, T. and Furness, C. (2018), *The Director's Voice: A Study of Theatre and Director Training and Development in the UK*, Stage Directors UK.

Kayes, G. and Fisher, J. (2002), *Successful Singing Auditions*, A&C Black.

McNamara, B. (2011), *It's the Audition, Stupid!*, Pinter and Martin.

Mitchell, K. (2008), *The Director's Craft: A Handbook for Theatre*, Routledge.

Ostwald, D. F. (2005), *Acting for Singers: Creating Believable Singing Characters*, OUP.

Rutherford, N. (2012), *Musical Theatre Auditions and Casting: A Performer's Guide Viewed from Both Sides of the Table*, Bloomsbury.

Schechner, R. (2003), *Performance Theory*, 2nd ed., Routledge Classics.

Shechner, R. (2013), *Performance Studies: An Introduction*, 3rd ed., Routledge.

Shurtleff, M. (1978), *Audition: Everything an Actor Needs to Know to Get the Part*, Bloomsbury.

Silver, F. (1985), *Auditioning for the Musical Theatre*, Penguin.

Southern, R. (1962), *The Seven Ages of the Theatre*, Faber & Faber.

Index

42nd Street   35, 47, 49, 54–7, 66–7, 85, 89

acting
  Ailion on   18–19
  Aquilina on   149, 152
  Arnold on   19
  Connor on   150–3
  Eyre on   149, 152, 154
  Goold on   152–4
  Grindrod on   19–20
  Siniawski on   149–50
Ailion, Pippa   3, 32, 42–3
  acting as audition   18–19
  auditionee's attitude and personality   26–8
  auditionees all round skill   20
  behavior of auditionees   27
  on casting process   4–5
  on creative team   9
  new shows casting process   33–4
  on preliminary stages   4–5
  pre-screens   12
  professionalism   23–4
  professional personality   21
  singing as audition   14
  West End works   36–7
Almeida Theatre   137
American Psycho   137, 147–8, 152, 169, 178
Any Dream Will Do   3, 40
Aquilina, Shaun   68, 93, 156–8, 177, 179
  on acting   149, 152
  on decision making   163
  on first rounds of audition   142
  on qualities in performer   170
  taking direction   162
Arnold, Jim   3, 27–8, 43–5, 140
  acting as audition   19
  assessing dance calls   17–18

auditionee's attitude and personality   28–9
  casting decisions   30–1
  on casting process   7–8
  on CV and headshots   9–10
  on preliminary stages   6–7
  pre-screens   12–13
  professional personality   21–2
  requirements of the show   20
  on self-tapes   11–12
  singing as audition   15–16
  on submissions for *Wicked*   5
  on training   8
Aspects of Love   123
attributes of the performer   59–61
  Bourne on   59
  Deamer on   59–61
  Mear on   59–60
  Page on   60
audition(s)   131–2, 184. *See also* first rounds of audition
  after   76–8
  auditionee   182
  context of   181–2
  great   41–4, 85–7, 131–2
  Morley on   132
  panel   182
  task   183
  Valentine on   131–2
auditionee   131, 138–40, 143, 154–5, 160, 173
  ability to sing   143, 146
  audition   182
  discipline   152
  inspiration and creative freedom   161
  most important qualities   136
  and panel   183–4
  performance ability   149
  professionalism   154
  singing training   146
  vocal technique   145

auditionee's attitude and personality
    Ailion on 26–8
    Arnold on 28–9
audition process
    Connor on 138–9
    Goold on 139–41
    Siniawski on 140–1

background checks and references
    Bourne on 64
    Deamer on 63
    Mear on 63–4
    Page on 63–4
Bailey, Jonathan 169
The Baker's Wife 119, 148
Ball, Michael 41, 162
Betty Blue Eyes 74, 137
Black creatives 133–5
    Sean Green on 132–6
    UK Musical Theatre industry for 132–6
Black performers
    Sean Green on 132–6
    UK Musical Theatre industry for 132–6
The Book of Mormon 43
Bourne, Sir Matthew 47, 66
    on attributes of the performer 59
    importance of ballet 52
    on individuality 58
    on physicality 56
    on principal values 62–3
    storytelling and choreographers 53–4
    Swan Lake 52–3
Bowles, Sally 41
Brayben, Katie 146–7, 152, 164, 169
Broadway 1, 33
    Bourne on 84, 85
    community 63
    Connor on 175–6
    Deamer on 83
    Goold on 174–5
    interpretations 157
    Mear on 84
    Page on 84
    shows 36–7, 156
    West End *vs.* 83–5
Brokeback Mountain 135
Buckley, Jessie 41
Burt, Stuart 3, 30, 43, 45
    assessing dance calls 18

    on audition slots 9
    casting decisions 30–2
    commercial casting 39
    intelligence in an actor 25
    new shows casting process 34
    on preliminary stages 6
    professionalism 24
    professional personality 22–3
    re-castings 35
    shared generosity 26
    singing as audition 14–15
    on submissions 7
    on training 8
    vocal reels, showreels and self-tapes 10–11

cast/casting
    celebrity 1, 39
    deciding on 123–31
    decisions 30–3
    new show 74–6
casting directors
    casting decisions 30–3
    CVs 4–13
    headshots 4–13
    new productions 33–41
    new shows 33–41
    overview 3–4
    preliminary stages 4–13
    professional personality 20–30
    re-casting 33–41
    reels 4–13
    submissions 4–13
casting process
    Ailion on 4–5
    Arnold on 7–8
    Deamer on 78
    Goold on 144–5, 164–5
    Grindrod on 40–1
    Morley on 127–8
    and workshopping 141
celebrity casting 1, 39
Chalotra, Anya 165
character
    narrative and 97–101
    storytelling 97–101
Chicago 3, 38, 93
choreographers
    after auditions 76–8
    assessing auditionees 65–74

background checks and
    references   63–4
  character   57–8
  creatives   81–3
  discipline   79–80
  getting casting right   48–50
  great auditions   85–7
  individuality   57–8
  other attributes of performer   59–61
  overview   48
  physicality   55–6
  principal values   61–3
  re-casting   74–6
  storytelling   53–5
  technique   50–3
  uniformity   57–8
  West End *vs.* Broadway   83–5
A Chorus Line   56, 58, 75, 137, 144
Cold War   137, 139, 147, 165
collaboration with rest of the panel   119–23
Come From Away   42
commercial casting. *See* celebrity casting
Company   124
company member   23, 27, 28, 113, 153,
    183
company personality   113–14
Connor, Laurence   137, 138, 157, 173–8
  on acting   150–3
  audition process   138–9
  on Broadway   175–6
  on decision making   163–4, 166–8
  on first rounds of audition   142, 143
  on qualities in performer   171
  taking direction   161, 162
context of audition   181–2
creatives in rehearsal room   81–3

dance
  Eyre on   148
  Goold on   148–9
  technique in   50–3
Deamer, Bill   9, 47, 49, 65, 66
  on attributes of the performer   59–61
  on casting process   78
  on individuality   57
  on performers   50, 57, 59–61
  on physicality   56
  on principal values   61–2
  on re-direction   70–1
  on right casting   49–50

storytelling and choreographers   54
  on technique   50–2
  on technique of choreographers   50–1
deciding on the cast   123–31
decision making
  Aquilina on   163
  Connor on   163–4, 166–8
  Eyre on   163, 166, 167
  Goold on   163–6, 168
  Siniawski on   165
DiPietro, Joe   131
direction
  Ailion on   21
  Morley on   112
  taking   110–13
directors
  auditions   176–9
  be yourself   172–4
  Broadway   174–6
  early process   138–60
  making decisions   162–8
  most valued qualities in performer   168–
    71
  overview   138
  taking direction   160–2
Doyle, Matt   131
Dreamgirls   133

early process
  Connor on   138–9
  Goold on   139–41
  Siniawski on   140–1
Elton, Ben   132
Eyre, Richard   137, 143, 151, 156–7,
    176–7
  on acting   149, 152, 154
  on dance   148
  on decision making   163, 166, 167
  on first rounds of audition   142
  on professionalism and
    personality   154, 155
  on qualities in performer   170
  on singing   143–4
  taking direction   162

finals   1, 13, 32, 92, 110, 124, 145,
    155–60, 164
first rounds of audition
  Aquilina on   142
  Connor on   142, 143

Eyre on   142
Siniawski on   141–2

Garland, Judy   48, 137
Get Up, Stand Up!   109
Goold, Rupert   137, 138, 143, 172–5,
      178–9, 183–4
   on acting   152–4
   audition process   139
   on Broadway   174–5
   on casting process   144–5, 164–5
   on dance   148–9
   on decision making   163–6,
      168
   on qualities in performer   169–71
   relationship with casting director   139
   on singing   144–8
   taking direction   161–2
   workshop process   141
Grease   93, 130
great auditions   41–4, 85–7, 131–2
Green, Sean   91, 139, 160
   Best Musical Director   132
   on Black creatives   132–6
   on Black performers   132–6
   on musicality   102–3
   on UK Musical Theatre industry for Black
      performers and creatives   132–6
Grindrod, David   3, 26, 32–3, 41–2, 44
   acting as audition   19–20
   assessing dance calls   16–17
   assessment of auditionees   37
   auditionee's performance   13–14
   behavior of auditionees   27
   casting decisions   31–2
   on casting process   40–1
   commercial casting   38–9
   individuality and bravery   25–6
   nerves   24–5
   new shows casting process   33
   practical perspective on auditions   24
   professional personality   21
   re-castings   35–6
   singing as audition   13–14
   on training   8–9
   TV casting   40–1
Guys and Dolls   47, 137

Hairspray   41
Hamilton   136

*How Do You Solve a Problem Like
      Maria?*   40
humour   80, 86, 138, 145, 151, 165,
      170–1, 182

individuality
   Bourne on   58
   choreographers   57–8
   Deamer on   57
   Grindrod on   25–6
   Mear on   57
Into the Woods   94, 112, 134

Jackson, Tim   135
Jesus Christ Superstar   3, 137, 173
*Joseph and the Amazing Technicolor
      Dreamcoat*   3, 137, 163

Khadime, Alexia   43
Kiss of the Spider Woman   95

La Cage Aux Folles   48, 49, 86
The Last Five Years   136
Leader of The Pack   43
Les Misérables   50, 89, 92, 97, 100, 101,
      107, 137, 157
Little Shop of Horrors   131

Mackintosh, Cameron   167
Made in Dagenham   137
Mamma Mia   3, 35–6, 40, 169
Mamma Mia: I Have a Dream   40
Manchester's Royal Exchange Theatre   94
Man of La Mancha   126
Mantello, Joe   158
Marley, Bob   133–4
Marshall, Kathleen   131
Mary Poppins   47–8, 81, 137, 149
May, Brian   132
McGregor, Wayne   125
McIntosh, Ian   132
Mear, Stephen   47–8, 65, 66
   on attributes of the performer   59–60
   on individuality   57
   on physicality   55–6
   on principal values   61
   on right casting   49–50
   storytelling and choreographers   53
   on technique of choreographers   50–1
Minchin, Tim   174

Miss Saigon 11, 137, 150, 157, 167, 171, 177–8
MJ: The Musical 96, 103, 104, 133, 160
Morley, Stuart 89, 91–2, 97–102, 104–106, 108, 110, 112, 116–19, 123–25, 127–130, 132, 136, 147, 162
   on auditions 132
   on casting process 127–8
   on musicality 102
Motown 133
Moulin Rouge 42
Moyles, Chris 168
musical directors 89–136
   Black performers and creatives 132–6
   collaborating with rest of the panel 119–23
   company personality 113–14
   deciding on the cast 123–31
   great auditions 131–2
   musicality 102–3
   narrative and character 97–101
   nerves 114–16
   new shows and re-casts 118–19
   preparation 107–10
   song choice 103–7
   storytelling 97–101
   taking direction 110–13
   UK Musical Theatre industry for Black performers and creatives 132–6
   vocal technique 90–7
   workshops 116–18
musicality 18, 72, 82, 90–1, 97–9, 102–3, 107, 121–2, 136, 170
   Green on 102–3
   Morley on 102
   Valentine on 102
Musical Theatre choreography 87
My Fair Lady 124

narrative
   character and 97–101
   and storytelling 97–101
Natasha, Pierre and the Great Comet of 1816 43
Nederlander, Jimmy 131
nerves 114–16
new productions 33–41, 74, 76, 97, 117, 119
new shows 33–41
   Ailion on 33–4
   Burt on 34

casting 74–6
   Grindrod on 33
   and re-casts 118–19
Noblezada, Eva 177–8

Oliver! 41, 47, 56, 58, 64, 81, 87, 137, 140, 168
One Love 43
ongoing productions 1, 182
ongoing show and re-casting 74–6
Only Fools and Horses The Musical 105, 116–17
Over the Rainbow 40

Pacific Overtures 148
Page, Lynne 48, 65–6
   on attributes of the performer 60
   ballet training 51–2
   dance and movement auditions 54–5
   on physicality 56
   on principal values 62
   on right casting 49–50
   storytelling and choreographers 54
The Pajama Game 137
panel
   audition 182
   and auditionee 183–4
Panter, Howard 126
The Phantom of the Opera 1, 150–1, 157
physicality
   Bourne on 56
   choreographers 55–6
   Deamer on 56
   Mear on 55–6
   Page on 56
preliminary stages
   Ailion on 4–5
   Arnold on 6–7
preparation 20, 23–4, 65
   musical directors 107–10
pre-screens
   Ailion on 12
   Arnold on 12–13
principal values
   Bourne on 62–3
   Deamer on 61–2
   Mear on 61
   Page on 62
professionalism 23–4
   Aquilina on 155

Eyre on   154, 155
   Goold on   156
   Siniawski on   154–5
professional personality
   Ailion on   21
   Arnold on   21–2
   Burt on   22–3
   casting directors   20–30
   Grindrod on   21

qualities in performer
   Aquilina on   170
   Connor on   171
   Eyre on   170
   Goold on   169–71
   Siniawski on   170–2

recalls   1, 11, 14, 22, 44, 156–60
re-casts/re-casting
   Burt on   35
   casting directors   33–41
   choreographers   74–6
   Grindrod on   35–6
   new shows and   118–19
   an ongoing show   74–6
rehearsal room, creatives in   81–3
The Rocky Horror Show   148
Rocky Horror   134
Rourke, Josie   125
Ruffelle, Frances   162

School of Rock   137, 150
self-tapes   10–12
Sinatra   131
Sinatra, Frank   131
Sinatra, Tina   131–2
singing
   Ailion on   14
   Arnold on   15–16
   Burt on   14–15
   Eyre on   143–4
   Goold on   144–8
   Grindrod on   13–14
   Siniawski on   145–7
   technique in   14–15, 17–18,
      90–7
Siniawski, Petra   137–8, 157–60, 173,
      176
   on decision making   165
   on first rounds of audition   141–2

on professionalism and
      personality   154–5
   on qualities in performer   170–2
   on singing   145–7
   taking direction   161
Skinner, Hugh   169
Smith, Matt   169
Smith, Sheridan   168
song choice   103–7
Spring Awakening   3, 42, 49, 60, 137, 141,
      147, 149, 178
Stephen Sondheim's Old Friends   84
Stephen Ward   85, 137
storytelling
   Bourne on   53–4
   choreographers   53–5
   Deamer on   54
   Mear on   53
   narrative and character   97–101
   Page on   54
"Stranger in Moscow"   103
Sunset Boulevard   126
Superstar   40
Sweet Charity   125
Sylvia   96

taking direction   1, 21, 30, 71, 110–13,
      160–2
Tammy Faye   48, 60, 84, 86, 137, 146,
      147, 156, 164, 168
task   181, 183
Taylor, Roger   132
technique in dance   50–3
technique in singing   14–15, 17–18,
      90–7
"They Don't Care About Us"   104
Tina   133
Toguri, David   148
Travis, Sarah   91
   audition process   118–19
   cast decision   126
   change a song style   111
   good auditions   106
   happy performers   130
   narrative and character   98–9
   nervous auditionees   114
   orchestrations awards   89
   panel collaboration   119–21
   personality   113–14
   preparation   107

song choice   103
    vocal technique   91–6
    workshops   116–17
Tucker, Rachel   42
TV casting   39–41
Two Strangers (Carry a Cake Across New York)   135

UK Musical Theatre industry   132–6
    for Black performers and
        creatives   132–6
    Sean Green on   132–6

Valentine, Gareth   69, 89–90, 93–95,
        98–99, 102, 106–7, 111, 115–116,
        118, 121–27, 129–31, 165
    on auditions   131–2
    on musicality   102
Valjean, Jean   132
Varla, Zubin   141
vocal technique   90–7

Webber, Andrew Lloyd   3, 40
Wedding Singer   134
West End
    Bourne on   84, 85
    vs. Broadway   83–5
    Deamer on   83
    interpretations   157
    Mear on   84
    Page on   84
West Side Story   10, 89,
        137
We Will Rock You   95, 105, 107, 128, 132,
        136
    Rock You   107
Wicked   66, 119, 123, 135, 140, 145, 146,
        149, 157–8, 164, 165
Wilkinson, Colm   162
workshopping   141
workshops   116–18, 141

Zellweger, Renée   137